Teaching to Exceed the English Language Arts Common Core State Standards

A Literacy Practices Approach for 6–12 Classrooms

Richard Beach
University of Minnesota

Amanda Haertling Thein
University of Iowa

Allen Webb
Western Michigan University

Routledge
Taylor & Francis Group

NEW YORK AND LONDON

Please visit the companion website for this book at
www.routledge.com/cw/beach

First published 2012
by Routledge
711 Third Avenue, New York, NY 10017

Simultaneously published in the UK
by Routledge
2 Park Square, Milton Park, Abingdon, Oxon OX14 4RN

Routledge is an imprint of the Taylor & Francis Group, an informa business

Library of Congress Cataloging in Publication Data
Beach, Richard.
   Teaching to exceed the English language arts common core state
standards : a literacy practices approach for 6-12 classrooms / Richard
Beach, Amanda Haertling Thein, Allen Webb.
     p. cm.
   1. Language arts (Secondary)—Curricula—United States—States.
   2. Language arts (Secondary)—Standards—United States—States.
   I. Thein, Amanda Haertling. II. Webb, Allen. III. Title.
   LB1631.B356 2012
   428.0071'273—dc23

                                                            2011036062

ISBN13: 978–0–415–80807–1 (hbk)
ISBN13: 978–0–415–80808–8 (pbk)
ISBN13: 978–0–203–14436–7 (ebk)

Typeset in Bembo
by RefineCatch Limited, Bungay, Suffolk
Printed and bound in the United States of America

SFI® Certified Sourcing
www.sfiprogram.org
SFI-00453

Printed and bound in the United States of America
by Edwards Brothers, Inc.

Contents

Preface

This book is designed to support new and master teachers as they develop outstanding English language arts curriculum and instruction. Our approach is to draw on meaningful models of teaching and learning— and the best theory and research in our profession—so that secondary English teachers can foster the success of all students as they address the challenges and possibilities of the 21st Century. In so doing, we will show how English language arts teachers can meet and exceed the Common Core State Standards that have been adopted by 44 states.

These Common Core State Standards represent the latest development in the standards movement that began in the 1980s in an attempt to hold high expectations for all students. During the past decade the uses of high stakes reading and writing testing mandated by No Child Left Behind and Race to the Top legislation has led to concerns about how standards and testing have actually limited the focus of English language arts instruction rather than raising expectations in meaningful ways.

This book takes a different approach to this often top-down standard-based curriculum and instruction approach. In writing this book, we strongly believe that having high standards is not the same thing as standardization—that assembly-line teaching that ignores the knowledge, interests, and passions of students and teachers will lower, rather than raise, expectations. We therefore believe that you need to have to consider autonomy in implementing the Common Core State Standards according to your students' own unique needs, knowledge, interests, and cultural contexts.

The framers of the Common Core State Standards recognize the importance of teachers and the necessity to meet the needs of diverse student populations. Thus the standards do not mandate curriculum or require specific works that "must be taught." The standards do not explicitly favor one instructional approach or theory over another. This means that it will be your responsibility to develop relevant curriculum and engaging instruction through translating the Common Core State Standards into practice. This book will provide you with theories and ideas to accomplish that goal.

How you implement the CCSS will depend on the instructional approach you adopt. In teaching students in the 21st Century, we believe that it is important that you go beyond traditional approaches to teaching English language arts based in the study of specific forms, narrow skills, and received knowledge. Instead, in this book we make the case for a literacy practice model for teaching language arts. This model emphasizes learning English language arts as a social and a generative activity. We know that students are most likely to be engaged when they have the responsibility to frame events, construct identities, collaborate with others, synthesize and create texts, and use 21st-Century tools in complex, multimodal ways.

The Common Core State Standards aim to create not only skilled and capable students and workers, but also citizens in a democratic society. Toward that end, English language arts students need to learn to critically engage with the limitations of status quo activities or institutions, and participate in reimagining and reshaping these activities or institutions. Rather than focus simply on critical analysis, we believe students also need to be critically engaged with the issues or problems associated with certain activities or institutions.

Students also need to be engaged with an issue or problem to acquire other literacy practices of framing events, constructing identities, collaborating with others, synthesizing and creating texts, and creating multimodal texts. They are more likely to learn these literacy practices when they are socially participating in "passionate affinity spaces" constituted by people who "organize themselves in the real world and/or via the Internet (or a virtual world) to learn something connected to a shared endeavor, interest, or passion" (Gee & Hayes, 2011, p. 69). Driven by their common interests or passions, people collaboratively share and construct new knowledge as well as assume and socialize others to adopt certain identities and levels of expertise (pp. 69–71).

As an English teacher, your job is to create these "passionate affinity spaces" that serve to engage students in using literacy practices necessary for their future success. We use the word "exceed" in our title to refer to the fact that creating these spaces involves more than having students jump through the hoops of identifying or producing formal elements of texts. Students are more likely to exceed through participation in face-to-face and virtual social spaces with authentic purposes and audiences that engage students in meaningful work. In this book, we provide a planning framework for devising these spaces, as well as multiple illustrative examples of teachers developing literacy practices teaching.

To exceed the Common Core State reading and literature standards, we describe how teachers foster critical response to texts through sharing responses in face-to-face and online discussions to which they bring their knowledge and experiences to texts. To exceed the writing standards, we describe how teachers engage students in argumentative, explanatory, and informative writing through addressing issues of concern to students for authentic purposes and audiences. To exceed the speaking/listening standards, we describe how teachers can help students develop purpose, voice, and agency. To exceed the language standards, we discuss how teachers have students investigate their uses of multiple variations of English and other languages to construct identities, engage in social interaction, and gain access to particular institutions. And, because students live in a digital world, we discuss the need to address digital/media standards that are given little attention in the Common Core State Standards.

Good teachers are constantly assessing student understanding and modifying curriculum and instruction to ensure success. This book provides methods for assessing students' work that go beyond traditional testing to capture growth in students' development in their uses of literacy practices.

Good teachers are also dedicated to their continued professional development and growth. Throughout this book and the online resources associated with it, we provide ways to reflect on what you are learning. And, through the use of virtual cases, you can engage in discussions with your peers about how to address challenges facing English language arts teachers as well as ways to grow your teaching and access the best English language arts teaching resources.

STRUCTURE OF THE BOOK: CHAPTER SUMMARIES

This book is divided into three sections. The first section, Chapters 1–4, provides an overview implementing the Common Core State Standards, English language arts curriculum models and theories, the literacy practices approach, and ways to plan instruction.

In Chapter 1, we discuss the development of the Common Core State Standards in English language arts and the effort that these standards make to address some of the limitations of previous state standards. Within this discussion we also outline some of the limitations of the Common Core, particularly their formalist/genre-based orientation. In Chapter 2, we discuss a series of different curriculum models for teaching English language arts, including those based on teaching skills, cultural content, forms/genres, processes/strategies, and literacy practices. We outline these models with the goal of helping you define your own beliefs about the viability of these different models.

In Chapter 3, we describe a literacy practice/critical engagement model in more detail, with examples of how this model can be implemented in classrooms. In Chapter 4, we discuss specific strategies for planning activities based on a literacy practices, critical engagement framework.

The second section, Chapters 5–11, focuses on methods for addressing the standards for reading, writing, digital/media, speaking/listening, and language, the major categories of the Common Core Standards. In Chapter 5, we discuss implementing the standards for teaching reading. In Chapter 6, we describe ways of interpreting different literary genres. In Chapter 7, we describe strategies for teaching critical engagement through responding to literature. In Chapter 8, we describe activities for addressing the standards for teaching writing. In Chapter 9, noting some lack of attention to media/digital literacies in the standards, we describe teaching media/digital literacies. In Chapter 10, we discuss ways of addressing the speaking/listening standards through fostering oral communication/discussions. In Chapter 11, we describe ways to implement the language standards.

The final section, Chapters 12 and 13, addresses ways to assess student work and professional development. In Chapter 12, we discuss evaluating and responding to student work through descriptive feedback and portfolio assessment. And, in our concluding chapter, we discuss ways for you to reflect on your teaching through conducting action research, as well as resources for you to continue your professional development.

Pedagogical Features

ACTIVITIES

Highlighted activities in each chapter are designed to foster further discussion of the chapter topics. These activities can be completed during class or through online discussions outside of class.

CASE STUDIES: THE *TEACHING TO EXCEED VIRTUAL SCHOOL*

Each chapter includes a case study linked to the **Teaching to Exceed Virtual School.** As an experiment in immersive learning, we have developed the *Teaching to Exceed Virtual School* that includes an intriguing series of case studies based on the teachers and approaches described in each chapter. The Virtual School is found at **LiteraryWorlds.org**, a simple, non-profit, education virtual world site specifically created to support secondary and college English teaching. In addition to the resources for our book, Literary Worlds contains a number of virtual worlds for frequently taught literary texts—material that you may want to use in your own teaching. Each of these literary worlds contains different rooms or spaces in which users interact with characters or challenges, interactions that are recorded in a chat box on the left side of your screen.

If this virtual case-studies approach is unfamiliar to you, know that it has been designed to be user-friendly and allow you to easily engage in collaborative problem-solving with other teachers or aspiring teachers as you examine and respond thoughtfully to real world English language arts teaching responsibilities. Many of the virtual cases developed for this book are based on actual teachers' work, so they are relatively authentic. The time you spend on these case studies will be well spent, allowing you to thoughtfully and collaboratively address challenges faced by class-room teachers. In the *Teaching to Exceed Virtual School*, you will find a list of the different book chapters and one case study for each chapter (Chapter 10 has two case studies). Each of these case studies addresses a particular issue discussed in each chapter having to do with challenges in teaching the topics in that chapter—summaries of each case study are included in the chapters. All include images, and many include video and sound. The technology is user-friendly, and in a short period of time you will master it.

The Virtual School provides the greatest learning when you join with several peers or colleagues and all of you experience the school's activities together, sharing ideas and responses. Set a time when two to four others can join you in logging into the school through the LiteraryWorlds.org Portal. At the Portal, each of you uses "student" as your User ID. Leave the Password blank. You are then requested to type "start." Follow the prompts to enter your name and email, and the email of your instructor, if that is relevant. A transcript of everything you and your colleagues say will be sent to you, and copied to the email you enter for your teacher. This transcript may be useful for writing papers or as instructor material for further discussion, perhaps in face-to-face class-room discussions. Given the complexities of these virtual cases, there are no "right answers." Once you enter through the Portal, you will see that a character with your name, and the name of each of your colleagues, now appears in the Literary Worlds Welcome Center.

You and your colleagues should meet in the *Teaching to Exceed Virtual School*. Once in the school, you enter different "Hallways," each of them a case study for a different chapter. The hallways connect to classrooms, and so on—each space designed for extensive discussion before moving to the next. (The "Look" button refreshes the view.) The "Hallway" provides context for the case based on the school and classroom environment. You and your colleagues engage in a discussion by responding to prompts. Toggle the "say" switch and "talk" by typing in the box on the lower left, and a transcript of your conversation scrolls on the upper left side of the screen. When you finish your discussion, your group should next go to a "Classroom" to further explore and discuss the case. Finally, you will head to a third room (and sometimes fourth room), in which you continue to address the questions related to a certain case, questions that practicing teachers are continually faced with in their day-to-day work.

At the time this manuscript goes to press, we are considering creating some pre-formatted identities that might be interesting to experiment with in role plays in the Virtual School. Stay tuned to latest developments by examining "Instructions" that you find in the *Teaching to Exceed Virtual School*. If you need further assistance in using the site, click on the "Help" button at the top of the page.

COMPANION WEBSITE

This book's Companion Website (www.routledge.com/cw/beach) with student and instructor resources leads readers to a wiki with three kinds of links: "Chapter Resources"; "Literary Worlds Site" designed to foster interactivity through participation in an online teaching planning simulation; "Classroom Teaching Resources" (unit/lesson plans, curriculum resource links, and related readings for each chapter, as well as information and resources for each of the four basic Common Core State Standards categories and each of the types of literacy practices). References to links are noted throughout the book by "@= link topic—alerting readers to go to the relevant chapter on the website, and then to "links," to locate information and resources specific to that topic.

Acknowledgments

We would like to thank a number of people for their assistance in writing this book. This book would not have been possible without the ongoing support and ideas provided by our Routledge editor, Naomi Silverman, who helped shape the focus and direction of this book. We also thank Kevin Henderson, and the copyeditor, Nikky Twyman, for their assistance in working on this book.

We also want to thank Kristin Koski for her excellent work on the *Teaching to Exceeding Virtual School*, the teachers who contributed to this site, and Western Michigan University for supporting Kristin's work. Jason Glatz, also of Western Michigan, provided significant design help with the images and charts.

PART I

Foundations and Theoretical Frameworks for English Language Arts Instruction

The Common Core State Standards for English Language Arts Instruction in Grades 6–12

Origins, Goals, Challenges

CHAPTER OVERVIEW

The 6–12 English Language Arts Common Core State Standards and High Expectations

A Literacy Practices Approach

Teaching Composition Using Online Role Play

Limitations of a Standards-Based Approach

Developing Curriculum Specific to Your Classroom

Case Study: English Department Chairs' Hallway (Understanding the Common Core State Standards)

Future Chapters: Theoretical Frameworks/Foundations of English Language Arts Instruction

---

As an English language arts teacher, your curriculum will likely be shaped by the Common Core State Standards, now adopted by most states. Over the history of instruction in our field a number of different approaches to curriculum and instruction have evolved, including approaches based on reading and writing skills; on knowledge of specific literary works, genres, or forms; on reading and writing processes or strategies; and, most recently, on mastery of literacy practices. Standards-based curriculum, an increasing part of school reform efforts since the 1980s, can be informed by a variety of approaches. English language arts teachers need to understand how to implement the Common Core State Standards (2010) in the light of the best thinking and research on the teaching of English. While drawing on the whole repertoire of approaches and theories, this book especially emphasizes a literacy practices approach—an approach we believe will make implementing the Common Core State Standards effective and meaningful.

Precisely in order to achieve outstanding intellectual and academic accomplishment, the Common Core State Standards set general goals for student learning but they do not specify *what* or *how* to teach. They do not create a common, core, required, or national curriculum of any kind. As Rebecca Sipe (2009) notes, "standards provide a definition of what is possible, but *standards are not curriculum documents*" (p. 41). Nor do they specify, describe, or set forward any general or specific teaching methods. It is teachers as "knowledgeable and engaged professionals [who] are the most important factor in the improvement of adolescent literacy" (p. 41). So it is significantly up to you as the teacher, collaborating with your colleagues and districts, to develop the curriculum and teaching approaches you will use. To do so, you need know about different curriculum frameworks so that you can formulate your own beliefs and make decisions about your curriculum and the instructional activities you want to utilize. This chapter will start you down that road.

THE 6–12 ELA COMMON CORE STATE STANDARDS AND HIGH EXPECTATIONS

The Common Core State Standards were initiated by the National Governors Association and the Council of Chief State School Officers in conjunction with Achieve, Inc., the American College Testing Program (ACT), publishing/testing companies, and 16 education associations in the Learning First Alliance. Although the standards were not created by the federal government, states adopted the standards in order to apply for funding from President Obama's "Race to the Top" educational grant initiatives in 2010. Previously, under the state-created standards sponsored by George Bush's "No Child Left Behind," governors became concerned that the different state standards and different ways that those standards were assessed made it appear that some states were doing a better educational job than others. To be fair, there was also concern that, despite the extensive effort to foster standards-based reform under No Child Left Behind, there were still many high school students who lacked the abilities and skills associated with being successful in college, a problem particularly acute in lower-income communities where people of color are overrepresented. The hope of the Common Core State Standards is that, this time, a more consistent set of goals across states will make standards-based reform more effective.

While there are problems in adopting a standards-based approach that we discuss later in this chapter, the public at large perceives standards as:

Checks on a dysfunctional system, a way of holding adults in the system accountable to the children they are educating. Without them, they feel, school personnel would be comfortable with the same mediocre results. How can we blame a large segment of the population for feeling that way . . . The external conversations about standards are a testament both to the increasing importance of public education and to the public's waning faith in that public education system. (Duncan-Andrade & Morrell, 2008, pp. 158–159)

We believe that English language arts teachers can view the adoption of the Common Core State Standards as an opportunity to generate an innovative, engaging curriculum that will enhance instruction in our discipline, raise intellectual aspirations for all students, and, to the extent possible, improve the public's regard for schools.

Learning in the 21st Century

In implementing the Common Core State Standards, it's also important that any English language arts curriculum is consistent with the demands of learning and living in the 21st Century based on a knowledge economy. The Partnership for 21st Century Skills (P21), an organization of 16 states, has proposed a curriculum framework that identifies the importance of 21st Century learning areas, including life and career skills, critical thinking, communication, collaboration, creativity, technology and information/media literacy (http://www.p21.org). For example, given the complexity of life in the 21st Century, they stress the importance of "flexibility and adaptability, initiative and self-direction, social and cross-cultural skills, productivity and accountability, and leadership and responsibility" (Partnership for 21st Century Skills, 2011). The P21 has produced a toolkit that aligns their framework with the Common Core State Standards (http://tinyurl.com/P21CommonToolKit). For example, the P21 framework encourages a focus on the themes of global awareness, financial literacy, civic literacy, health literacy, and environmental literacy. To address health literacy, the toolkit proposes the following activity of 8th grade:

After completing a literature circle unit of teen problem novels, students brainstorm a list of significant social, emotional, or health issues teens face today. Working in groups, students research one issue and create a public service announcement on a closed YouTube channel (viewable only by students in the class) to persuade their peers about one action they should take regarding this issue. Students will select and use references from literary readings (e.g., citing how a particular novel presents the issue) as well as research from nonfiction sources to illustrate major points. (p. 17)

Of course, everyone shares the goal of setting high expectations for all students consistent with the demands of life in the 21st Century. Whether your implementation of the Common Core State Standards will meet these high expectations depends on your passionate commitment to making higher standards meaningful, relevant, and attainable for the increasingly diverse students in America's public schools.

In your professional career you may encounter people advocating the integration of standards in ways that narrow or limit learning. Such an approach is not in keeping with the Common Core State Standards, nor with the pedagogy put forward in our book. As the Common Core's introduction states, these standards are designed to foster attentive and critical reading of complex literature and "the staggering amount of information available today in print and digitally" (p. 3). The standards exist to establish a "wide, deep, and thoughtful engagement" that will "build knowledge, enlarge experience, and broaden worldviews." They are meant to be the basis for "any creative and purposeful expression in language." The kind of thinking the standards are intended to foster is "essential" to national and global citizenship.

A LITERACY PRACTICES APPROACH

For teaching English language arts, we propose a literacy practices approach that will allow your students to meet and exceed the standards put forward by the Common Core initiative. This approach builds on the knowledge and experiences of your students, draws on the worlds they live in, and connects those worlds to texts, language practices, and critical issues.

Our approach also draws on the need to redesign classrooms and schools to create what we refer to in the Preface as "passionate affinity spaces" (Gee & Hayes, 2011, p. 69). These spaces are constituted by seven characteristics:

- People's shared endeavor and interest in achieving a common goal.
- A deep passion that results in strong commitment to achieve this goal.

- People's production of knowledge or products based on standards for what constitutes high quality.
- People who adopt leadership or mentoring roles to involve and assist other or new members.
- Knowledge that is distributed according to individuals' expertise and uses of language, genre, images, or digital tools mediating participation in a space.
- Continual, varied involvement by different people who adopt alternative learning trajectories in a space.
- An openness to keep learning and changing in acquiring new forms of expertise. (pp. 69–71)

Creating these spaces requires that you go beyond simply devising a set of tasks or activities and, instead, envision ways to draw upon and exploit students' knowledge, experiences, and passions in ways that help them commit to achieving shared goals. It also requires attending to the social aspects of effective collaborative learning so that students are willing to assist and mentor each other given their shared commitments.

All of this entails adopting roles of social planner, facilitator, and co-learner that differ from the traditional teacher role of conveyor of knowledge. It entails learning about and building on your students' knowledge and expertise in planning activities so that they perceive themselves as valued members of the classroom affinity space. From this perspective the ELA curriculum goes beyond covering a body of knowledge to learning the literacy practices involved in operating in and contributing to these passionate affinity spaces.

Sometimes as a new or student teacher you face the challenge of operating in spaces and curricula over which you have little control. This requires a politically delicate balancing act of adopting status quo spaces and curriculum while at the same time being willing to experiment with new ways of teaching ELA. For example, while you may be required to adopt your school's curriculum mandates tied to the Common Core State Standards, you can also develop innovative ways of teaching that curriculum by framing the construction of your classroom affinity space as itself the curriculum. You also need to recognize that you can have a significant role in determining what reading, writing, speaking, listening, and media texts are taught in your classroom; what topics, issues, themes, and ideas you will cover; and what sequence will best achieve the Common Core State Standards. You will be in the best position to justify these choices if you are able to articulate their basis in your beliefs about student learning. This book will aid you in sorting through those beliefs.

You also need to recognize that your own passionate commitment to your subject matter and methods is a primary asset in motivating your students. If your students perceive you as knowledgeable and excited about learning, then they may be more likely to be excited. This book is intended to further fuel the fire of your passion to teach English. We set forward a deep and professional knowledge of teaching and learning, and English language arts content, so that you will engage students, texts, and the real world. Yes, this book is based in solid research, sound educational theory, and best practice teaching. It emerges from more than 75 combined years that the authors have themselves been public school language arts teachers, and teachers of public school language arts teachers. It also links you with a wealth of online resources that you can draw on for planning instruction (@ = Resources on implementing the CCSS).

TEACHING COMPOSITION USING ONLINE ROLE PLAY

To illustrate what we mean by engaging students based on high expectations tied to the Common Core State Standards, we describe Liz Boeser's use of an online role-play activity to teach argumentative writing in a 12th grade college composition class (Doerr-Stevens, Beach, & Boeser, 2011). This activity illustrates one approach to addressing the standard for argumentative writing, "write arguments to support a substantive claim with clear reasons and relevant and sufficient evidence."

When she first started teaching this class, based on an inherited curriculum for teaching the five-paragraph essay form of the "college essay," Liz noted that her students were not particularly engaged in generating these essays on topics with which they had little interest and in an activity that amounted to filling in the boxes of the template for the five-paragraph essay format written primarily for the teacher. Liz therefore decided to try something different. She employed online role plays in which students wrote about issues that concerned them. She noted that many students were concerned about the issue of their school's Internet policies that blocked access to sites assumed to be inappropriate for students. These policies resulted in blocking access to many sites they needed for conducting research on topics they were studying. Liz asked students to adopt fictional pro-con roles related to advocating for different ways to address this issue. For example, some students took on the role of students who wanted to remove the blocks on sites, while others assumed the role of administrators who were concerned about students accessing pornography. She also had students analyze the quality of arguments posted in a previous class's online role play based on specific criteria related to adopting of an ethos, formulation of a position, use of supporting evidence for that position, gaining audience identification with one's positions, and the use of counterarguments. Next, students created fictional biographical profiles on a Ning social networking site defining their stances on this issue. They then voiced their positions and responded to others' positions on the Ning forum over a one-week period, exchanges that involved formulating arguments and refuting those arguments using counterarguments.

Liz also told the students that, by engaging in this activity, they would be able to use material from their writing to formulate recommendations to the school's administration for changing the Internet policies. At the completion of their online interactions, the students stepped out of their roles and, drawing on the material from their online exchanges, wrote position papers and presented their recommendations to the administration. Based on those recommendations, the administration unblocked access to sites.

This activity involved setting high expectations to engage students by:

- Recognizing the limitations of the traditional five-paragraph essay written only for the teacher.
- Basing the activity on students' specific concerns and interests related to problems with the school's Internet policies.
- Providing a specific social purpose for writing to share positions with both peers and, ultimately, the school administration.
- Engaging students in adopting fictional roles in which they could experiment with assuming positions and beliefs they may not subscribe to themselves.
- Providing students with criteria and norms constituting effective arguments.

ACTIVITY: RESPONSE TO THE ONLINE ROLE-PLAY ACTIVITY

What is your response to this activity? What kinds of expectations did Liz have about her students' ability to complete this activity? What were her assumptions about how this activity may engage her students? What might be some similar writing and/or online activities that you could devise for teaching writing?

LIMITATIONS OF A STANDARDS-BASED APPROACH

Although this book will argue that the Common Core State Standards can be interpreted in productive ways that enhance students' literacy learning, adoption of a standards-based approach has sometimes resulted in rigid, top-down approaches to instruction and assessment. It is important that you as an English language arts teacher have a clear understanding of this history so that you won't fall prey to these same traps in implementing standards and so that you can defend substantive, authentic, and high expectation approaches (@ = Limitations of the CCSS).

One problem with adopting any set of standards is the risk of "standardizing." The Common Core State Standards recognize that *standardization* is not the same thing as *holding high standards*. The needs, abilities, knowledge base, and interests of teachers and students vary from school to school, from classroom to classroom, and even within every classroom—they cannot be standardized.

Much of the resistance to top-down, bureaucratic imposition of standards has derived from teachers who value a bottom-up focus on their own unique, local school cultural contexts and particular students' needs, interests, and knowledge. Enforcing the same learning on all students, as some have mistakenly advocated on the basis of "standards," slows down the most capable students and leaves behind those already struggling, creates inappropriate limitations on what students can accomplish, and in effect, dumbs down teaching and learning. Narrow textbooks, pre-packaged or scripted curricula, mass-marketed work-sheets, and one-size-fits-all-teaching or curriculum implementation do not and will not fulfill the high expectations of the Common Core State Standards. Conceptions of English language arts that are out of date, uninformed about advances in teaching English such as, evolving literary canons, emerging literary and social science scholarship, and changing literacy demands in the digital age are not appropriate to an innovative and progressive vision of school improvement intended by these stand-ards. Informed administrators and curriculum specialists understand this and work to support teacher professional knowledge, research, decision-making, risk-taking, and freedom to experiment, grow, and improve, year after year.

Advocates for adopting a standards-based approach argue that standards enhance student achievement. However, there is also no strong evidence indicating that adopting standards will necessarily improve student achieve-ment. For instance, there is no strong correlation between National

Assessment of Education Progress (NAEP) scores and high state standards (Mathis, 2010). There is also no strong correlation between international test performance and countries with national standards (Tienken, 2008). Canada has no national standards but its students scored well in international reading tests (Mullis et al., 2006). Likewise, research suggests that standards may have negative effects on non-white students' performance and drop-out rates (Mathis, 2010).

Adopting standards may also lower rather than raise achievement for the following reasons:

Homogenization of Instruction

A standards-based approach can result in the homogenization of instruction in which teachers teach the same content using the same methods regardless of differences in their classroom contexts or students (Kohn, 2010).

Such homogenization often occurs when schools or districts adopt "teacher-proof," scripted curriculum programs or mandated textbook series that allow for little teacher development of their own curricula. For example, in her second year of teaching in an upper-middle-class suburban high school, Kyle Krol experienced the adverse effects of the homogenization of instruction. Just before she was hired, her school adopted an English language arts "model curriculum" created by her state's department of education and based on new state standards. In her district all teachers were to teach the same books, and teachers created common assessments for each text for all students at each grade level. Preparing to be a teacher, Kyle sought opportunities to study multicultural literature; in her new job, she was greatly disappointed to see very little diversity in the adopted curriculum. In Kyle's words:

Since I began teaching I've wanted to expand the curriculum, but my first year was mostly about surviving rather than looking critically at what I teach and why I was teaching it. American literature conjures up a strong multicultural image for me. I've followed Sherman Alexie's characters on the struggle to find them themselves; I've explored the New Mexican desert of Rudolfo Anaya's novels; I've traveled down Harlem streets with Hughes and experienced Hurston's southern lifestyle. I imagined, when I received my first teaching assignment of American literature, that these authors would be the ones to grace my classroom. However, the way that my English 10 colleagues read the new state standards and the common assessments required by my district made it almost impossible to fit these authors into a "dead white guy" curriculum.

I began to struggle through a year of teaching the curriculum as it was, feeling that I was doing a disservice to my students and my educational upbringing. I was required to stay on track with what other teachers in my grade level were doing, when they were testing, and how much time they were spending on units.

ACTIVITY: RESPONDING TO KYLE'S SITUATION

What do you think of Kyle's situation? What appears to be her and her colleagues' beliefs about curriculum? What are some possible reasons that they hold these beliefs? If you were in Kyle's place, what might you do?

Fragmented Curricula

Another problem with standards implementation is that it can result in a fragmented curriculum organized around addressing isolated standards as opposed to an integrated, well-balanced curriculum that builds increasingly sophisticated connections and understandings between units. For example, teachers may be told to list a specific "standard for the day" on the board and then teach just to that standard, leading to standards-based grading where teachers check off that students have "achieved" a standard. Attempting to address individual standards in isolation shifts the goal of your teaching, from fostering engaging learning that addresses the complexity of skills and ideas involved in any language arts activity, to an intellectually impoverished isolation of skills and knowledge in the name of "meeting a standard."

Overly Specific Content Standards

Another limitation of many state English language arts standards has been that they specified certain content that needed to be taught—for example, specific usage or grammar rules. This led to direct instruction of that content rather than setting benchmarks to support a deep understanding of content and meaningful instruction. Extensive research has shown that the isolated study of school grammar separated from student writing does not improve learning. Mandating specific content to be taught undermines the learning of all students, not only those who are "ahead" or "behind," but those "in the middle" as well. For high expectations standards implementation it is critical that teachers have the autonomy to match learning to needs, skills, prior knowledge, student interest, and changing contexts.

This calls for significant creativity, ongoing change, and growth in creating your own curriculum.

Teaching to the Test

Perhaps the most problematic aspect of standards-based reform—as evidenced in the mandates associated with the No Child Left Behind law—is the linking of standards to multiple-choice standardized tests that are used to label students, teachers, and/or schools as "failing" if scores do not increase over time (what is defined as "annual yearly progress"). Given these dire consequences, teachers are mistakenly encouraged to focus their instruction on "teaching to the test" by narrowing the curriculum, focusing on limited skills, reducing complex and meaningful questions, and closing students out of the critical task of constructing knowledge. These approaches must be strongly resisted by all who are determined to ask more, rather than less, of our students.

Failure to Acknowledge Cultural Diversity

Moreover, the use of assessments based on acquisition of narrowly understood knowledge or skills serves to privilege those students with access to that knowledge or cultural capital (Bourdieu, 1974) and exclude other students without that access—a failure to recognize the cultural diversity of America's student population. As Stornaiuolo, Hull, and Nelson (2009) note:

Traditional assessments of reading and writing, while widely understood to be neutral measure of children's skills, continue to reward those children who share the linguistic and cultural backgrounds of the test-makers . . . As long as assessments continue to privilege one kind of linguistic capital (Bourdieu, 1974), schools in particular and the public in general will continue to understand literacy as an autonomous and value-neutral set of basic skills. (p. 390)

Yet it is critical that the educational system and the implementation of standards support the success of students of all cultural backgrounds. This association between standards and standardized testing led to the adoption of what Joe Kincheloe (2001) describes as simplistic, "technical standards" focusing on acquiring content associated with standardized tests. For Kincheloe, in contrast to reductionistic, "technical standards," "standards of complexity" recognize the ambiguity, irrationality, and contradictions associated with learning in culturally diverse American schools. While "technical standards" attempt to standardize learning by ignoring and erasing cultural diversity and assuming the existence of an assumed "common culture" associated with white, middle-class communities, "standards of complexity" recognize that students may not meet "technical standards," not due to lack of ability or intelligence, but because they may not have access to or experience with this "common culture" or cultural capital (p. 41). Because the majority of students in schools in 2030 will be students from non-dominant cultures, it is essential that teaching and learning be relevant to students from non-dominant backgrounds.

The success of Common Core State Standards will be connected to the assessments states adopt to measure student learning. The more open-ended, less content-focused nature of these standards calls for the use of more open-ended, less content-focused performance assessments—assessments based on students' actual "show-me" demonstrations of their ability to employ literacy practices related to addressing the meaningful goals of the Common Core State Standards.

The Influence of Economic Inequities on Student Performance

Finally, we want to point out that standards-based instruction is limited in its ability to address one of the most persistent issues facing American schools—the "achievement gap" between non-dominant students and middle-class white students. Much of this "achievement gap" is related to the increasing economic inequality in America that has resulted in an increased number of children living in poverty—one in five American children are poor. This economic inequality is evident in the fact that, according to a report by the Pew Research Center (Kochhar, Fry, & Taylor, 2011), the median wealth of white U.S. households in 2009 was $113,149, compared with $6,325 for Hispanics and $5,677 for blacks—a ratio of 20:1 for blacks and 18:1 for Hispanics.

Poverty is related to low achievement in schools; there is a direct correlation between poverty and reading test scores (Riddile, 2010). Reductions in taxes have resulted in cuts in funding for schooling in low-income urban neighborhoods—areas that are also experiencing increased unemployment, substandard housing, lack of social services/healthcare, limited access to grocery stores with fresh and healthy food, etc. As a result, students in low-income families are continually coping with issues that influence school performance, including inadequate housing, parents under financial stress, lack of nutritious food and quality healthcare, and poor access to computers/libraries/tutorial resources.

For example, if a family needs to move frequently to pursue changing employment, students do not stay in the same school for long, resulting in discontinuities of teacher knowledge of students. Adopting standards-based instruction will not address these inequities. As Diane Ravitch (2010) notes:

If a district has disproportionate numbers of students who are very poor, don't speak English, are homeless, or have high needs, standards alone will not suffice to remedy their needs. Really terrific national standards may well increase the gap in performance between affluent districts and those with large numbers of low-income students. Nor will standards rectify the problems of districts that are impoverished and highly segregated. (p. 2)

Addressing these inequities requires not only increased resources for low-income schools, but also changes in the larger economic system itself related to employment, housing, minimum wages, and healthcare. These students especially need access to literacy practices related to power and agency (Janks, 2010). Moreover, teachers working in low-income schools need to recognize the significant cultural differences that students in those schools bring to their learning and find ways to implement the standards that build on their students' cultural knowledge and background. As Kincheloe (2001) notes, school culture is often alien for many students:

For students who live outside these wider cultural relationships, it becomes extremely difficult to understand why the school requires particular tasks to be performed or why certain knowledge is important. A cultural outsider may feel bewildered by the demands of the school. Growing up in the mountains of rural Tennessee, I witnessed dirt poor but savvy mountain children capable of brilliant out-of-school accomplishments fall victim to their cultural exclusion from the discourse community of schooling. (p. 49)

As the authors of this book, we want to be honest with you from the outset. Yes, the high-quality curriculum and instruction we invite you to learn from this book will help your students achieve and surpass the Common Core State Standards. Yes, the approaches that we set forward are backed by the latest research and best theories of learning. Yes, drawing on the book you can create curriculum and teaching methods appropriate for English language arts students of all social and cultural backgrounds. However, as the familiar African proverb states, "It takes a village to raise a child." In an address at Columbia Teachers College in New York on May 18, 2011, Linda Darling-Hammond (2011), distinguished professor of education at Stanford and former president of the American Educational Research Association stated:

> We live in a nation that is on the verge of forgetting its children. The United States now has a far higher poverty rate for children than any other industrialized country (25 percent, nearly double what it was thirty years ago); a more tattered safety net—more who are homeless, without healthcare and without food security; a more segregated and inequitable system of public education (a 10:1 ratio in spending across the country); a larger and more costly system of incarceration than any country in the world, including China (5 percent of the world's population and 25 percent of its inmates), one that is now directly cutting into the money we should be spending on education; a defense budget larger than that of the next twenty countries combined; and greater disparities in wealth than any other leading country (the wealthiest 1 percent of individuals control 25 percent of the resources in the country; in New York City, the wealthiest 1 percent control 46 percent of the wealth and are taxed at a lower level than in the last sixty years). Our leaders do not talk about these things. They simply say of poor children, "Let them eat tests." And while there is lots of talk of international test score comparisons, there is too little talk about what high-performing countries actually do: fund schools equitably; invest in high-quality preparation, mentoring and professional development for teachers and leaders, completely at government expense; organize a curriculum around problem-solving and critical-thinking skills; and test students rarely—and never with multiple-choice tests. (Indeed, the top-performing nations increasingly rely on school-based assessments of learning that include challenging projects, investigations and performances, much like what leading educators have created here in the many innovative New York public schools.)

Teachers and schools are important to creating opportunity in our country, but they are only a part. True democracy and equal opportunity require what Martin Luther King, Jr. called "a revolution of values," including new state and national priorities, and a profoundly different use of resources. In the current context teachers are taking the blame for conditions that are not of their making, and which they work hard every day to address.

DEVELOPING CURRICULUM SPECIFIC TO YOUR CLASSROOM

The Common Core State Standards are a relatively general set of standards that do not dictate specific content to be taught. Given the limitations of standards-based instruction, it is important that you perceive the Common Core State Standards as a road map for developing your own curriculum that is relevant to your unique students and classrooms, their prior knowledge and diverse social and cultural settings (Saifer, Edwards, Ellis, Ko, & Stuczynski, 2011). Additionally, you will need to build on your own state's or district's previous curriculum that may consider the unique demographic makeup of your students (@ = Countries' and states' literacy standards and plans to address the CCSS).

Kyle's resolve to address the curriculum she was teaching greatly strengthened during the teaching of one of the required texts, *The Adventures of Huckleberry Finn*.

In my classroom there was one black student, no Asians, no Native Americans, no Latinos—there were white kids and lots of them. White walls. White kids. White curriculum. As we began reading *Huck Finn* my students began deferring questions about Jim and racism to the one black student, expecting him to speak on behalf of all people who have dealt with that kind of discrimination. I knew this was trouble; my students needed diversity in their literature, especially if they couldn't get it in their school surroundings.

As she struggled to address her situation, Kyle began to engage in research. She read several articles she found online, including "Developing a Multicultural Curriculum in a Predominantly White Teaching Context" by Richard Milner (2005). Milner set forward a model of levels of multicultural curriculum integration taken from James Banks, the contributions approach, the additive approach, the transformation approach, and the social action approach. Kyle conducted surveys of her students that showed that 78 percent "would like to read about different cultures more often." She spoke with her six departmental colleagues, all of whom wanted to teach more multicultural literature, but all indicated that they just didn't have time in their curriculum to do so.

Kyle's careful consideration of her students' needs and the perspectives of her colleagues was a starting point for helping her to bring in new curricular resources and instructional strategies for her students and for helping her know where to begin advocating for curricular change with her colleagues. As an English language arts teacher, this kind of attention to your specific teaching context will aid you in developing truly relevant instruction.

ACTIVITY: THE INFLUENCE OF STUDENT POPULATIONS ON CURRICULUM AND INSTRUCTION

How does and how should the student ethnic and social class population of a school impact language arts curriculum and instruction? How might reading research about instruction be helpful to a teacher in Kyle's situation? How might the surveys of student and colleague thinking be helpful to her?

CASE STUDY: ENGLISH DEPARTMENT CHAIRS' HALLWAY (UNDERSTANDING THE COMMON CORE STATE STANDARDS)

One of the primary challenges in developing curriculum based on standards is that different teachers differ in their beliefs about what should be taught in a school's shared curriculum, given their own interests, knowledge, and previous instruction.

In this case study, you will learn about the different English curricula at high schools within the same district. Teachers at each of these three schools believe they have the right to teach according to their own passions, knowledge, and interests, and are therefore reluctant to adopt the CCSS into their curricula. Due to the tension felt within the three departments, the English Department Chairs are meeting to discuss how they can get teachers to understand how they can maintain autonomy in exceeding the standards.

You, as a recent graduate who is familiar with the standards, are called upon to share your ideas in this meeting. The Department Chairs are hoping to pick your brain in developing a plan for gaining teacher buy-in. Ultimately, you will be asked to revise an existing curriculum based on the CCSS that foster diverse instruction and teaching styles.

Find two or three peers and go to the LiteraryWorlds.org site, and then to the *Teaching to Succeed* link, to go to this case study in Chapter 1.

FUTURE CHAPTERS: THEORETICAL FRAMEWORKS/FOUNDATIONS OF ENGLISH LANGUAGE ARTS INSTRUCTION

In this first chapter of Part I, Foundations and Theoretical Frameworks for English Language Arts Instruction, we described the development of the Common Core State Standards as well as some of the potential problems when implementing a standards-based approach. Whether you recognize it or not, the way you implement standards is profoundly shaped by your existing beliefs about what should be the focus of English language arts. Given the importance of your defining your own beliefs about teaching English language arts instruction, in Chapter 2, we describe the frameworks that have shaped English language arts instruction based on skills, content, forms, and processes/strategies approaches. Then, in Chapter 3, we propose an alternative English language arts approach based on teaching literacy practices. And, in Chapter 4, we provide you with a framework for planning instruction designed to teach literacy practices.

Formulating Your Beliefs about Teaching English Language Arts

---

CHAPTER OVERVIEW

Traditional English Language Arts Curriculum Frameworks

A Literacy Practices Approach

Case Study: The Teachers' Lounge Hallway (Formulating Beliefs)

How you and others interpret and implement the Common Core State Standards will depend on basic beliefs about teaching and learning in English language arts. Beginning teachers sometimes assume that the most important skills to acquire from methods courses, professional preparation, and in-services are specific techniques or teaching methods—the famed "silver bullets"—guaranteed to ensure the learning of all students with whatever content at any time and place. Yet, as experienced teachers know, high-standard teaching requires complex, informed, and carefully situated professional knowledge. Outstanding English language arts teachers understand the development and evolution of curriculum and instruction in their field and they know what excellent language arts teaching looks like. This kind of knowledge informs local teacher decision-making necessary for high levels of student achievement.

A crucial starting point is to understand the philosophical and theoretical underpinnings of the various language arts curricula encountered in secondary schools. This knowledge can support you in the thoughtful development—through experience, research, and scholarship—of informed beliefs about content knowledge and best teaching. What is, and what should be, English language arts? How will students learn best in your classroom?

Implementing the Common Core State Standards requires thoughtful and informed answers to those questions. Answering these questions involves understanding different theories of learning—learning as acquiring content, employing skills, using cognitive processes, learning forms, or employing literacy practices (@ = Different learning theories).

Whether you realize it or not, you draw on various learning theories every day as you develop your instructional goals and plans. For example, in teaching a literary text you make more or less conscious decisions about whether to focus on teaching content about literature, teaching comprehension skills, modeling interpretation strategies, teaching the form of the short story, and/or fostering the social practices involved in sharing responses.

Having a clearly defined set of beliefs about teaching English will help you justify your use of innovative curriculum and instruction in your student teaching and in your own classroom. During their initial years of teaching, teachers who acquire a well-defined set of beliefs are less likely to conform to the traditional teaching practices operating in the schools than those teachers who do not have a well-defined set of beliefs and attitudes (Smagorinsky, Gibson, Bickmore, Moore, & Cook, 2004). For example, if you believe that English language arts should not be defined simply as a set of preexisting conclusions about established classic literary texts, then you might work to develop means of productively resisting curriculum mandates based on that approach.

TRADITIONAL ENGLISH LANGUAGE ARTS CURRICULUM FRAMEWORKS

In your teacher education program, you may have encountered the Interstate Teacher Assessment and Support Consortium (InTASC) Standards related to the knowledge, skills, and dispositions of effective teaching. Standard 4 addresses the importance of understanding "the central concepts, tools of inquiry, and structures of the discipline(s) . . ." In this book, we propose implementing the Common Core State Standards based on a deep understanding of the content, tools, and structures of our discipline. In our discipline, different curriculum frameworks for teaching English language arts have evolved throughout the years. As we review these frameworks we note their strengths and weaknesses as they inform our development of a literacy practices/critical engagement framework that we believe is vital for success in implementing the standards.

English Language Arts as Literacy Skills

One prevalent curriculum framework for teaching English defines reading or writing as a set of literacy skills. For example, in a skills-based curriculum framework, reading is defined as a category consisting of an extensive set of "subskills"—decoding, word-attack, inference, etc. Writing is defined as a set of skills consisting of outlining, organizing information, defining a thesis, revising, and editing. One limitation of a skills framework is that it fails to recognize "reading" or "writing" as social practices that vary considerably according to the different contexts or purposes for which they are employed. Thus, the notion that one teaches students to "read" or to "write" as generalized sets of skills ignores the variations in how "reading" and "writing" are employed. For example, reading requires the ability to respond to a wide range of different types of texts for different purposes in different contexts. Reading digital texts differs in some important ways from reading print texts: while reading a print text is often a linear process, responding to a website requires readers to follow non-linear cues or links that may best serve their specific purposes—consider, for instance, the non-linear types of reading required in selecting and booking a flight on a travel website. Researchers looking at the online comprehension strategies used by skilled 6th grade readers found that they employ scan-and-skip processing without reading every word. The way they actually read online texts required them to draw on more complex applications of prior knowledge, inferential strategies, and self-regulated reading processes than when reading texts on paper (Coiro & Dobler, 2007). Similarly, writing and producing texts requires complex social understandings of purposes, audiences, and contexts. For instance, writing rap lyrics to perform to a group of peers involves quite different social practices than writing a legal brief for use in a court case.

In her critique of this skills-based framework for teaching English, Shannon Carter (2008) notes that it is futile to reduce reading or writing to one singular set of skills or curriculum content. She draws on David Russell's (1995) example of the category "ball-handling" as involving quite different practices in different types of sports—that ball-handling in ping-pong differs from ball-handling in football or basketball, suggesting that there is no one generalized skill constituting ball-handling that can be applied to all sports. Rather ball-handling "exists as a recognizable practice only within the particular communities of practice using the ball—the game for which the ball is intended . . . literacy education must be treated as entirely dependent on context" (p. 65).

Defining English language arts as a set of decontextualized skills also presupposes a individualist model of learning—that an individual is assumed to either have or not have certain skills, often as determined by their performance on a standardized reading or writing test (Street, 1995). Generalizing that because a student does not do well on a reading or writing test she is therefore not a "good reader" or "good writer" fails to consider all of the different ways in which readers or writers may be considered "good." This concern is particularly relevant to the discipline of English language arts, since language itself is always social and contextual. Typically, a skills framework does not consider how skills vary across different social contexts. A literacy practices framework substitutes the idea of literacy practices for skills, practices whose meaning are grounded in social contexts. Students learn best to be strong readers and writers in contexts and situations that call for engagement and have meaning.

English Language Arts as Content Constituting Shared Cultural Knowledge

Another curriculum framework for teaching English stresses the idea of the language arts as content or shared cultural knowledge essential for an understanding and appreciation of one's heritage and participation in society. This approach is also associated with "cultural literacy" (Hirsch, 1987). In this framework students are assumed to need to know specific information about particular authors or classic works of literature in order to participate in civil society. This model presupposes that certain texts, cherished by certain groups—often those of white, Western, upper-middle-class people—should be considered as more essential for "cultural literacy" than those of other groups. An interesting example: to maintain its authority over India in the mid-19th Century, the British government—rather than resort to the use of only military control—developed a British literature curriculum designed to subtly impose British/Christian values and provide examples of virtuous Englishmen to the religiously diverse people of India exploited by English colonizers. This curriculum was, in fact, the first time English literature was used as school curriculum anywhere in the world (Viswanathan, 1989).

This model of English language arts as shared cultural content privileged by a certain community or society fails to recognize the range of different communities that each value different norms and practices associated with literacy learning. For example, while Hirsch (1987) posits that all students should be familiar with certain classic works of American literature, it is also the case that his proposed list excludes many works by women, writers of color, writers of young adult literature, graphic novels/comics, rap songs, and digital literature—literature that is valued by different cultural communities. Assuming that one can agree on the shared cultural knowledge that all students should acquire does not consider the wide range of different literacy practices operating across these different cultural communities and in different social contexts.

Hirsch's cultural content model also privileges acquisition of specific and isolated bits of information as opposed to acquiring rich contextualized knowledge, or skills of critique or critical inquiry. Especially given the dramatically more culturally diverse school populations of America in the 21st Century, a static cultural literacy model ignores the prior knowledge, experience, and linguistic richness that American students bring to the classroom (Saifer, Edwards, Ellis, Ko, & Stuczynski, 2011).

A "cultural literacy" approach found in many state standards before the Common Core was developed meant that specific content or texts needed to be taught. Although the Common Core State Standards do emphasize quality and appropriate complexity of texts, and mention Shakespeare (no specific works) and mythology, the standards intentionally avoid prescribing specific texts that must be covered. Following the Common Core State Standards means that there are no required texts on which students will be tested. The Common Core State Standards do include a list of "Exemplars of Reading Text Complexity, Quality, and Range" (Appendix B), although these texts "expressly do not represent a partial or complete reading list" (CCSS, 2010, Appendix B, p. 2). The Common Core State Standards stress that "texts need to be selected around topics or themes that generate knowledge and allow students to study those topics or themes in depth" (CCSS, 2010, p. 58). (We discuss selecting literature for meaningful topic and thematic analysis in Chapter 7.)

While students certainly need to know how to read and understand complex texts, it is equally important that the texts and themes you choose are engaging and relevant. Some canonical texts may require knowledge or "cultural capital" not available to all of your students. Additionally, it is important to remember that there are many kinds of complexity that our students need to experience—not only complexity of language structures, but also complexity of plot and character, and complexity of historical and cultural context. This means that, in developing curriculum, you need to move beyond the Common Core State Standards list of exemplar works to select texts and materials that will be engaging to your students based on their particular cultural backgrounds and interests. Every class you teach also has significant variation in reading background and ability. As a teacher you want to attend to your students' backgrounds and prior knowledge, and to support them as they extend to new ideas and information. While raising standards is critical, too much difficulty, without adequate support, can also be devastating. Tom Newkirk (2010) raises concerns about:

The universalization of "advanced placement." The framers of the common-core standards have consistently taken a level of proficiency attained by the most accomplished students and made it a general expectation. Many of the objectives for persuasive writing at this age level describe the work I do with advanced college students—particularly the handling of multiple perspectives on a topic, a very complex skill for young writers. (p. 3)

The literacy practices approach we set forward in this book allows you to think about cultural literacy in a more powerful and meaningful way than simply a list of "great books" that "every American should read." Rather than knowing *about* literature, language, composition, or media, a literacy practices approach emphasizes knowing *through* engagement in texts and activities.

A literacy practices framework therefore shifts from defining English language arts as something that students *acquire* to something one *does* as literacy practices (Sperling & DiPardo, 2008) or what Applebee (1996) defines as "knowledge-in-action." It values and builds on student prior knowledge, and focuses on assessing what they can actually perform. In this sense "cultural literacy" becomes an ability to participate, understand, and critique rather than to recall or reference. This allows for a pedagogy that approaches texts in an engaged way.

Your teaching should never be "dumbed down," nor should you underestimate the capacity of your students for complex, high level thinking. However, you need to be smart and thoughtful about how to get your students to high-level thinking, and about how you create curriculum and instruction that will engage them where they are and take them where you want them to go. As we will illustrate, a focus on literacy practices is a powerful approach for high-expectations teaching.

The lack of a focus on varied cultural perspectives shaping responses to literature in the Common Core State Standards led New York State to add a separate set of literary response standards addressing the need for students to adopt different cultural perspectives. In reading, they emphasize "employing knowledge of literary language, textual features, and forms to read and comprehend, reflect upon, and interpret literary texts from a variety of genres and a wide spectrum of American and world cultures." In the writing standards, they emphasize the need for students to "develop personal, cultural, textual, and thematic connections within and across genres as they respond to texts through written, digital, and oral presentations, employing a variety of media and genres." We see these additions to the Common Core State Standard as useful for teachers in all states in avoiding a focus on dominant forms of content and cultural literacy.

English Language Arts as Knowledge of Literary and Rhetorical Forms

Another traditional model evident in many state standards describes English language arts as knowledge of literary and rhetorical forms specific to understanding and producing texts. The number of genre types and rhetorical structures that secondary students attempt to learn, often by rote in many English classes, is remarkable. Literary types include: sonnets (Shakespearean, Petrarchian, Spencerian), epics, ballads, lyrics, odes, villanelle, haiku, ghazal, novels (autobiographical, detective, dime, dystopian, epistolary, fantasy, graphic, historical, hypertext, picaresque, romance, science fiction, series, etc.), plays (comedy, tragedy, historical, masques, closet, burlesque, musical, sentimental), and more. Similar lists can be created for both rhetorical structures (e.g., comparison-contrast, classification, process analysis, description, narrative, cause and effect, assertion/justification, etc.) and terms (e.g., alliteration, anacoluthon, anaphora, antithesis, aporia, apostrophe, archaism, assonance, asyndeton—to mention only a few starting with "a"!). Students not only rapidly lose interest in "formalist" teaching, but also fail to gain deeper understanding of texts and ideas as a result.

As previously noted, when Liz Boeser inherited her College Composition class, she recognized the limitations of the "formalist" approach based on teaching the "five-paragraph theme" (Figure 2.1), in which students are provided with a template—often in the form of five boxes with an "introductory paragraph," three subsequent boxes, and a "concluding paragraph" box. This formalist composition instruction was popular in the 1950s and 1960s until it was challenged by the rise of "composing process" instruction in the 1970s and 1980s (Emig, 1972) that focused more on instruction of the various composing processes— prewriting, drafting, revising, and editing. The "composing process" movement posited that focusing on teaching various forms placed too much emphasis on creating a single draft that conformed to the desired format without engaging students in the prewriting and revising processes involved in creating that draft. It emphasized that the five-paragraph paper is an exclusively academic form that doesn't help students learn to write in the real world, or communicate with others beyond the teacher. Liz found that when she gave these assignments students would

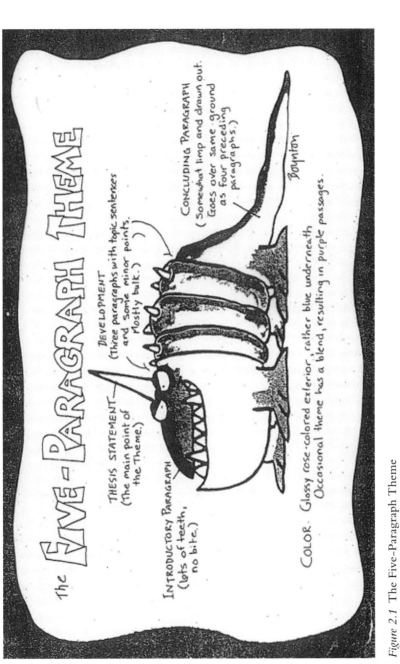

Figure 2.1 The Five-Paragraph Theme
Used with permission of Sandra Boynton

simply "fill in" material into the different parts of their essays and assume that they had completed the assignment. Focusing primarily on the organizational structure of one single draft often limited the degree to which students employed composing processes and engaged in multi-draft revision/self-assessing.

While writing teachers certainly want their students to be able to generate organized, coherent essays, mastering a particular form should not be a goal in and of itself. The formalist approach fails to foster a sense of engagement in the authentic goals of writing—communication of ideas for particular purposes and audiences. And a focus on producing a single "well-organized" draft may limit students' engagement in extensive revision essential to learning to improve writing (Hillocks, 1995).

Liz also recognized that students needed some purpose for their writing other than submitting an essay for her to grade. She perceived the online role-play activity as providing her students with an actual purpose and audience for writing that was far more engaging for students than simply writing essays for her.

One of the fundamental ideas of a literacy practices approach is that form follows content—the key to meaningful instruction in reading or writing is to focus on what the text is about, and then examine how the form of the text is relevant to that content. From a literacy practices perspective, students will learn about the importance of genres and forms, not simply as more facts to memorize or another worksheet to fill in, but as structures deeply related to the sense and significance of texts.

One limitation of the Common Core State Standards is that they sometimes lend themselves to be interpreted as focused on learning forms rather than meaning. For example, the writing standards are organized around knowledge of the conventions for argumentative essays, informational/explanatory essays, and narratives. And, the literature standards are organized around study of types of figurative language in poetry and narrative structure. For analysis of "craft and structure" of literary texts, students are expected to be able to "analyze how an author structures a text, orders events within it (e.g., parallel plots), and manipulates time (e.g., pacing) to create mystery, tension, or surprise." The speaking/listening standards are organized according to different ways of communicating in discussions or through use of media. Within these formalist structures, the standards are then defined based on processes or strategies involved in using different forms.

One possible explanation for the formalist orientation of the standards is that it lends itself more readily to standardized testing and scoring than other orientations might. The definition of a specific formalist term can be the basis of a multiple-choice question. The use by students of certain formal writing structures can be easily identified, even without attending to their argument or language. Literary analysis can be recognized, perhaps even by a computer reading student essays, when a student names a specific literary term or, in writing argumentative essays, formulates a position statement with supporting reasons or counterarguments. As Todd Farley (2011) argues, many of the Common Core State Standards are quite similar to state standards that focus on knowledge of forms, because of the need to match those standards to existing state exams. He cites the example from the Common Core: "Determine a theme or central idea of a text and analyze in detail its development over the course of the text, including how it emerges and is shaped and refined by specific details; provide an objective summary of the text" that involves multiple-choice test items based on inferring the "theme or central idea of a text" found on state assessment. As he notes:

That question is also being marketed as one aligned to work with the Alabama standards ("Drawing conclusions from recreational reading texts"); the Arizona standards ("Analyze the author's use of literary elements/theme"); the California standards ("Compare works that express a universal theme . . ."); the Colorado standards ("Read a given text, identify the theme, and provide support from the text"); the Florida standards ("Identify and analyze universal themes and symbols across genres . . . and explain their significance"); the Georgia standards ("Applies knowledge of the concept that the theme or meaning of a selection represents a universal view . . ."); the Illinois standards ("Explain relationships between and among literary elements including character, plot, setting, theme, conflict and resolution and their effectiveness of the literary piece"), etc. etc. etc. (p.2)

However, even if the Common Core State Standards appear to represent a formalist approach, this does not mean that you need to implement them by adopting a traditional, reductionist, formalist approach that puts meaning and context second, and memorizing of formal names or structures first. In fact, doing so will limit student learning, an issue we consider further in Chapter 3. For the moment, it is enough to note that the standards can be interpreted in ways that go beyond memorizing and naming when you design instruction that engages students in understanding purposes and meanings that are constructed by various forms. Students can study forms both through reading various texts and by constructing their own writing and oral presentations. For example, students might examine how mystery writers deliberately withhold information about certain crimes or plant "red-herring" clues designed to challenge readers. Or, students can listen to oral narratives and identify language designed to heighten the unusual, extraordinary nature of the event (thus adding to what William Labov [1972] defines as a story's "tellability"). Then, they can write their own mystery stories or share heightened oral narratives, building on knowledge of these important strategies that characterize different literary forms.

English Language Arts as the Use of Reading/Writing Processes or Strategies

Critiques of the skills, content, and formalist English language arts frameworks led to new orientations toward ELA instruction in the 1970s and 1980s. Drawing on research on literary response processes (Holland, 1975; Bleich, 1978) and composing processes (Emig, 1972), English educators developed curriculum frameworks based on teaching composing processes. And, based on Louise Rosenblatt's (1978) transactional model of literary response related to use of "aesthetic responses," educators developed different processes or strategies involved in responding to literature. For example, teachers involved students in different processes of "envisionments" in responding to literature— "being out and stepping into an envisionment, being in and moving through an envisionment, stepping back and rethinking what one knows, stepping out and objectifying, the experience" (Langer, 1995). And, teachers taught the "composing-process model" of writing, focusing on prewriting, organizing, revising/editing drafts, as well as self-assessing (Figure 2.2).

However, educators recognized the limitations of just going through the motions of employing response or composing processes without a sense of an engaging purpose or audience (Marshall, 1987). Students were simply completing the different "phases" of the process with little sense of purpose and audience—they would complete their prewriting or revise/edit their drafts, but without a sense of the rhetorical purpose for making choices in revision or language.

Similarly, a cognitive strategy approach for teaching reading and writing gained popularity in the 1970s and 1980s (Flower & Hayes, 1981), based on research identifying how students made specific decisions about topics and revisions. Likewise, an approach for teaching reading focused on teaching comprehension strategies of applying prior knowledge, contextualizing words, predicting story outcomes, inferring main ideas, etc. became the basis for reading instruction (Pressley, 1985).

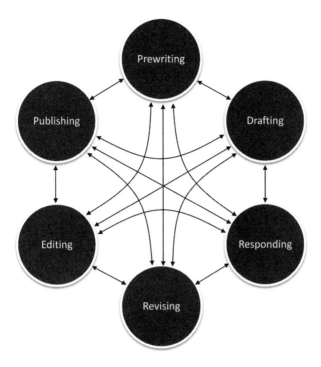

Figure 2.2 The Writing Process

However, in the 1990s, literacy theorists recognized the limitations of focusing on teaching these strategies without a more complete sense of how students engage in writing and reading (Guthrie, Taboada, & Wigfield, 2011).

While attention to reading and writing processes is important to language arts teaching, recent scholarship focuses more on the importance of purpose and audience. For instance, persuasive writing is enhanced when students are thoughtful about using writing to convince audiences to support their positions on a particular issue. At the same time that the process movement was impacting instruction, a number of other innovations were improving English language arts instruction. Writing teachers increasingly employed peer feedback groups as a means to help students reflect on how their writing engaged their peer audiences. Teachers adopted workshop/small group approaches as evident in the publication of Nancie Atwell's (1987) *In the Middle*. This coincided with an increased attention to students' reading interests and "individualized reading" activity related to the growing popularity of young adult literature.

ACTIVITY: RECOLLECTION OF YOUR PREVIOUS TEACHERS' BELIEFS ABOUT TEACHING ENGLISH LANGUAGE ARTS

Think back over your English language arts experiences as a student and list examples of teaching or curriculum that you experienced that appears to you now to reflect the teacher's belief that the focus should be on: 1) drilling on specific skills; 2) reading a text because its author was famous, rather than because the text had meaning to you or your world; 3) memorizing the names of forms, genres, or terms; and, 4) going through stages of a writing or reading process. Then, describe your own level of engagement and learning in these classes. How did differences in the teacher's beliefs impact your engagement and learning?

A LITERACY PRACTICES APPROACH

As a teacher, you have probably discovered that each time you teach a class your experience is different. Differences in your students' backgrounds, interests, attitudes, small changes in your approach and methods, even the space in which you are teaching and the point in the semester—all can impact instruction. Sometimes there are differences between the beliefs and techniques you acquired in your teacher preparation and how you actually teach in your school. Teaching, just like any literacy practice, varies according to context.

The English language arts curriculum frameworks discussed above—skills, content, forms, and processes—share a common limitation. They typically do not account for differences in how people use language and texts in differing contexts, depending on social and cultural circumstances, events, and purposes. And, they do not focus first on issues, topics, or themes that emerge from students and the world.

In this chapter, in addition to reviewing established English language arts curriculum frameworks, we want to introduce a literacy practices framework. This literacy practices approach builds on the strengths of the skills, content, forms, and processes frameworks, while grounding English language arts activities in specific, local, social contexts or communities (@ = Literacy practice theories for teaching ELA).

What are Literacy Practices?

A literacy practices framework defines English language arts as the actions students perform to understand and produce texts for classroom events (Barton, 2006; Baynham & Prinsloo, 2010; Street, 1995; Street & Lefstein, 2007).

Literacy practices are always *social* because they involve relations between the self and others. In our everyday actions we employ a great variety of literacy practices for many different social purposes. In the online role-play activity, Liz's students were adopting roles for the social purposes of developing believable personas and convincing administrators to change their school's Internet policies. A literacy practices perspective highlights the ways in which literacy involves social relations by providing:

The link between the activities of reading and writing and the social structures in which they are embedded and which they help shape . . . Literacy practices are the general ways of utilizing written language which people draw upon in their lives. In the simplest sense literacy practices are what people do with literacy. However, practices are not observable units of behaviour since they also involve values, attitudes, feelings, and social relationships . . . this include[s] . . . how people talk about and make sense of literacy. (Barton & Hamilton, 2000, p. 7)

Literacies are social practices mediated by language. Many activities that people perform individually are, in fact, social. For example, when cooking, people employ written recipes or draw on oral traditions to select, measure, and process different ingredients and create dishes often shared with others. And, of course, what we cook and how we cook it is impacted by culture, economics, and family practices. Specific oral or written recipes emerge from these complex social practices. In defining language as a local, social practice, Pennycook (2010) argues that, rather than language operating as a system that people draw upon to engage in social practices, it is the social practices themselves that determine the meaning of language—"language is the product of social action, not a tool to be used" (p. 8). He describes language as a practice rather than a tool or isolated skill, something to be "used," because the word "use" "suggests that language exists out there in the world and can be taken up and put to some use" (p. 8). From this perspective language does not stand alone but is "a product of the embodied social practices that bring it about" (p. 9), requiring us to ask "how it is that the things we do with words produces language?" (p. 17). For example, students are actively involved in posting on Facebook, using language as a literacy practice for creating their identities, editing their profiles, friending people, sharing their statuses, writing on their walls and the walls of others, posting and tagging pictures, creating links, joining groups, posting videos, and so on.

In teaching English in a Michigan high school, while she loved her work, Steffany Maher began to wonder if "something was missing":

Our discussions were primarily "me" focused. I was imparting all my "teacher wisdom" unto my students, but they were not fully engaged in the conversation. My teacher-led discussion method was not allowing students to respond to the literature, and no matter how many times I told them that any response to what they were reading was valid, they were always looking to me for the "right" answers. Incorporating concepts from my graduate studies, I knew I wanted to take a reader-response approach to the next novel I would be teaching—To Kill a Mockingbird. I have read Louise Rosenblatt's classic Literature as Exploration. She argues something that all of us as teachers and readers understand: when our students read, they bring their own history, experience, emotions, and education to the text. As Rosenblatt puts it, "[t]he literary work exists in the live circuit set up between reader and text: the reader infuses intellectual and emotional meanings into the pattern of verbal symbols, and those symbols channel his thoughts and feelings" (25). Therefore, according to Rosenblatt, our task as teachers is to "foster fruitful interactions—or, more precisely, transactions—between individual readers and individual literary works" (26–27). How could I help my students to find their own meaning in the literature they were reading? How could I help them to engage with the text and discover the relevance of its historical and social contexts?

ACTIVITY: REFLECTION ON LACK OF STUDENT ENGAGEMENT

Have you been a student or teacher in classes where students were not engaged with texts or with each other? What are some ways in which you can foster student engagement?

Perceiving literacy practices as social moves us from a focus on individual acquisition of literacy to literacy as a community resource serving the collective goals of a group engaged in an activity. As members of groups or communities, people learn literacy practices as they contribute to achieving collective goals. As students put on a school play, they learn specific literacy practices needed in their collaborative performance.

The Centrality of Events for Framing Instruction

A literacy practices framework shifts the focus from framing instruction in terms of teaching skills, content, forms, or processes to creating engaging classroom *events* that result in students developing and using literacy practices to produce language or texts (Bloome, Carter, Christian, Otto, & Shuart-Faris, 2005).

Ethnographic researchers use the word "event" to identify a particular occurrence in place and time, for example, a sales transaction, interview, or meeting (Bloome et al., 2005). Participants in events employ the literacy practice of *framing events* to define the goals, plans, roles, norms, and beliefs operating in an event. Different people may frame the same event in different ways (Burke, 1969). For example, while a 16-year-old may frame obtaining a driver's license as a "step towards freedom," a parent may frame that event as "requiring some curfew rules." And, people may frame events in terms of larger cultural and historical forces, perceiving obtaining a driver's license as part of adolescent initiation into adulthood, perhaps similar to initiations in ancient cultures. People can also interrogate how and who framed events and examine ways that such framing creates power hierarchies or exclusionary boundaries—for example, the fact that someone isn't allowed to participate in an event.

Students learn this literacy practice of *framing events* by having the opportunity to frame events themselves as active participants. This suggests that in planning instruction, you and your students co-plan events so that students have some ownership and a voice in determining their meaning.

In studying events in their own lives, and as portrayed in literature, students can reflect on how events are framed in terms of goals, plans, roles, norms, and beliefs, as well as how, in topic, issue, or thematic units, historical, institutional/civic, cultural, psychological, and economic forces shape the framing of events. For example, students might study how adolescent initiations have evolved over time from an historical, cultural, and psychological perspective.

Rather than thinking of events as a background where previously acquired literacy knowledge or skills are used, Pennycook (2010) argues that participation in specific events produces literacy practices and creates meaning in a specific context. Liz's online role play was an event that involved a range of literacy practices—framing the online interaction in terms of goals, plans, roles, norms, and beliefs; constructing identities; identifying issues; formulating arguments; critiquing the status-quo policies; and recommending changes to those policies. So many things we often do in English classes can be seen as events. Examples include book club or literature circle discussions, role plays, hotseating (where a character is put under a spotlight and is asked questions from the audience), spoken-word performances, writing conferences, digital video productions, and many others, as we shall see throughout this book.

Issues and topics that emerge from and/or connect to students' lives can be shaped to constitute classroom events. Addressing historical and cultural contexts in a way that relates to or raises questions about the present can also constitute an "event." In some measure thinking about curriculum as "events" suggests what is often in English called "thematic" teaching, though with the caveat that the themes have engaged meaning and are not handed down by teachers or textbooks in predigested ways. The idea of "events" also implies "active learning" but specifically in ways that relate individuals to each other; that is to say, they invoke literacy practices.

The meaning of literacy practices in events is also shaped by the physical or virtual "affinity spaces" (Gee, 2004) in which they occur. Social interactions in affinity spaces are based on shared, common knowledge and interest, evident in, for example, participants in an online game such as *World of Warcraft*, playing on a volleyball team, attending a church retreat, or attending quinceañera parties. In events, literacy practices create or embody identities and put them into social interaction with others. (Pennycook, 2010; Leander & Sheehy, 2004; Soja, 1998). In constructing their profile roles and interacting on the Ning social networking site, Liz's students' literacy practices created a shared "affinity space" based on a common interest in fostering change in their school's Internet policies.

From a literacy practices perspective, one of the critical tasks of the English language arts teacher is the creation of meaningful events that foster rich, complex literacy practices. Often this involves thinking about how students interact in literacy events outside the classroom. In such events participants are typically invested in making the event a success because they have a role in shaping the activity. For example, members of book clubs are invested in contributing to discussions in part because they have helped select the reading; participated in decisions about how, when, and where the group should meet; and so on. Similarly, in the classroom, you can set up book clubs or literature circles in which students choose books and topics and become motivated participants. For example, in her second year Kyle determined she would create a more diverse curriculum:

I decided to use my *Adventures of Huckleberry Finn* unit to insert multicultural texts because of my past experience with the novel in the classroom and the fact that so many [mistakenly] view it as a multicultural text because one of the characters is a minority.

Kyle settled on a plan to utilize literature circles while reading the anchor text:

Students in my class would have the ability to choose a book from a list of contemporary multicultural titles that interest them. I wanted to make sure the additional book would be interesting to students, since it would have the burden of adding to their classroom workload. Through self-assignment, students would be more likely to engage with the text and learn about a culture they were interested in. Students would read the additional text in tandem with the anchor text, ending the unit with a group class presentation on their literature circle text and an individual project connecting the themes in each novel. With the help of the media specialist at my school and suggestions from peers in my graduate class, I was able to identify a number of texts that would work to "complicate" the ideas of racism presented in our anchor text and in our own community. I also used information I gained from student surveys to help me determine what students would enjoy learning about. I had students choose their book groups, limiting each to a maximum of four members. All received their first or second choice for the books they wanted to read; the excitement in the classroom left me with the impression that my crazy schedule might actually work.

ACTIVITY: ENGLISH LANGUAGE ARTS FRAMEWORKS SHAPING KYLE'S INSTRUCTION

What English language arts frameworks appear to be guiding Kyle's approach to teaching literature? How is she extending or going beyond those frameworks? What else might she do?

Acquiring Dispositions

Through fostering student autonomy as active, contributing members of classroom events, students acquire certain dispositions of perseverance, dependability, responsibility, emotional stability, and openness to novel experience related to success in life and college (Schmitt et al., 2009). For example, granting students autonomy for the success of their classroom book club through co-planning and collaboration with their peers fosters dependability and responsibility. By participating in drama activities in which they adopt different roles and perspectives, students can learn to experiment and cope with experiences new to them.

Teachers can invite students to reflect on the literacy practices they engage in. For example, having participated in a service-learning project working in local schools and social service sites, students reflected in their journals about how coping with challenges provided them with a sense of perseverance, responsibility, and openness to novel experiences (Beach, Campano, Edmiston, & Borgmann, 2010).

The Importance of Multiple Literacies

Literacy practices vary across different domains or institutions as well as across cultures and social groups; for example, school literacies, workplace literacies, media/digital literacies (Pullen & Cole, 2010). However, the boundaries between these domains or institutions supporting these literacies are often not defined; for example, the difference between school and home literacies, where parents may assume that they need to emulate or model school literacies for their children (Street & Street, 1991). And, because certain domains or institutions have more power, certain literacies are perceived to be more powerful or privileged than other literacies (Barton & Hamilton, 2000). While the literacy practices associated with producing and consuming rap music, for example, may be highly valued in certain non-school communities, those literacy practices are not typically valued in schools. (Though a language arts teacher might experiment with changing such values!)

Traditional English curricula have also privileged print literacies over media or digital literacies. However, because literacy practices are constituted by historical and cultural forces, the practices and their status are always changing. Media and digital literacies are rapidly being recognized as more important for language arts teachers to address, given the importance of students joining our online and digital "participatory culture" (Jenkins, Clinton, Purushotma, Robison, & Weigel, 2006). The National Council of Teachers of English (2008) has defined 21st Century literacy as involving multiple literacies, particularly the following digital literacies:

- Develop proficiency with the tools of technology.
- Build relationships with others to pose and solve problems collaboratively and cross-culturally.
- Design and share information for global communities to meet a variety of purposes.
- Manage, analyze, and synthesize multiple streams of simultaneous information.

- Create, critique, analyze, and evaluate multi-media texts.
- Attend to the ethical responsibilities required by these complex environments (p. 2).

The Value of a "New Literacies" Perspective

From a "new literacies" perspective (Lankshear & Knobel, 2003), students are immersed in a digital landscape constituted by multimodality, interactivity, intertextuality, and remixing shaping their use of literacy practices. Understanding and producing multimodal texts entails framing events in terms of the cultural meaning of signs (Kress, 2003). Students need to know how to read, write, collaborate, communicate, "visually represent," and engage in research/publication in this increasingly important digital landscape. Knowing how to interact with others on social networking sites entails use of relating to and collaborating with others in "affinity groups" (Gee, 2004). Knowing how to make intertextual links involves making connections between texts for social purposes. And, remixing involves producing texts by combining diverse sources.

Students are now accustomed to engaging with websites that are highly multimodal. The Internet they interact with employs images, color, and sounds to engage users; builds intertextual connections to different sites and media; and fosters social relationships between users as members of "affinity groups" associated with a particular topic, brand, music, film, TV program, etc. (Stone & Schowen, 2010). It is also important that students become critical thinkers about the Internet. For example, they might critique the ways that sites for teen magazines for girls foster consumerism and adoption of stereotypical gender roles.

Connecting School Literacy and Digital/Media Literacy

In discussions of the engagement of young people with the new technologies, the focus has been on out-of-school digital/media literacies. In the future it will be increasingly important to English language arts instruction to integrate the new literacies, preparing students for the workplace and democratic citizenship of the future (Figure 2.3).

Sometimes curriculum mandates and school cultures position teachers in contradictory ways—while new literacies are proclaimed, resources and curriculum fail to address the need.

In this book we recommend meshing media/digital literacies with print literacies through what Kevin Leander (2009) defines as

Figure 2.3 Practicing Digital Literacy

"remediation." Leander identifies four stances toward incorporating media/digital literacies that teachers might adopt: 1) "resistance" to media/digital literacies; 2) "replacement" of print literacies with media/digital literacies; 3) using media/digital literacies to validate or "return" to print literacies; and 4) "remediation" that combines print literacies with media/digital literacies through "parallel pedagogy." For example, in his teacher preparation course, preservice teachers created digital video adaptations of literary short stories. These adaptations brought together critical analysis of the stories along with the integration of digital production.

CASE STUDY: THE TEACHERS' LOUNGE HALLWAY (FORMULATING BELIEFS)

In this chapter, we've described a number of different learning theories on how students learn English language arts. Based on your reading of this chapter and your own experience as as student and as a teacher, what are your own beliefs about how students learn English language arts?

This case study will engage you in thinking about how your own beliefs and the beliefs of other educators influence the literacy practices we employ in our classrooms. In observing and speaking with teachers after observing their 10th grade English classes, you realize they each espouse very different theories about the nature of English, with some focusing on the need to teach content; others, on the need to teach rhetorical forms and structures; and others, the need to engage students in critical literacy. You will then find yourself in the Teachers' Lounge where you will overhear more conversations that illuminate teachers' beliefs. Sarah Pancost's comments strike you as intriguing, so you even set up an interview during which she speaks about her beliefs and how they inform her classroom planning, teaching, and assessing of student work. You will finally engage in discussion with your peers regarding your own beliefs about English language arts and how these beliefs will manifest themselves in the literacy frameworks you intend to employ as a teacher.

Please find two or three peers and go the LiteraryWorlds.org site and then *Teaching to Succeed* to find this case study for Chapter 2.

In the next chapter, we describe ways of implementing the Common Core State Standards through adopting a literacy practices approach that builds on traditional English language arts frameworks described in this chapter while, at the same time, addressing their limitations. We describe different types of literacy practices associated with achieving particular standards and illustrate how a critical engagement approach helps students identify issues, formulate arguments, and critique and redesign systems.

CHAPTER 3

A Literacy Practices Framework for Implementing and Exceeding the Common Core State Standards

Premises and Principles

CHAPTER OVERVIEW

Adopting a Literacy Practices Approach

Types of Literacy Practices

Critiquing Systems

Case Study: Principal's Hallway (Literacy Frameworks)

In the last chapter, we described different English language arts curriculum frameworks, and made a case for the value of a literacy practices approach. In this chapter, we describe implementing the 6–12 English Language Arts Common Core State Standards through literacy practices and critical engagement.

ADOPTING A LITERACY PRACTICES APPROACH

In adopting a literacy practices approach, you will often need to translate the Common Core State Standards to address writers', speakers', or characters' uses of literacy practices in specific situations. Rather than beginning with the idea that students first need to acquire skills, content, forms, or strategies/processes prior to engaging in activities, in a literacy practices model you begin with a focus on meaningful issues, topics, themes, activities, experiences, and events that will engage students in learning.

To think about this, let's return for a moment to the story of Liz Boeser's students, frustrated by the strict Internet policies at their school. Their concerns arose when, in studying issues of gun control, they wanted to search for the National Rifle Association site—and the site was blocked. Further, when they wanted to find Diane Hacker, a prolific writer of writing handbooks, her page at the Modern Language Association (MLA) style site was also blocked (Doerr-Stevens, Beach, & Boeser, 2011). As Liz's students participated in a role play about these frustrations, she recognized that, although they had legitimate complaints about Internet access, they didn't know how to translate those complaints into effective action to address school policy. So Liz used this event to help her students *establish identities* as reasonable change agents, *distinguish issues, formulate arguments,* and *critique the system.* Each of these elements that her students learned are literacy practices that flowed from the activity they were engaged in as part of classroom learning and connected to broader issues in the school. They also directly address the Common Core State Standards for argumentative writing.

Liz's teaching was not about whether or not her students employed a certain writing form. It was not simply learning *about* argumentative writing. Her teaching entailed actually *engaging in* literacy practices about an issue they cared about to attempt to make a real change in the status quo. These students undertook critical inquiry combined with action.

Our familiar example illustrates a most important point. Rather than using the Common Core State Standards to provide a template for organizing curriculum standard by standard, Liz used meaningful issues and activities to create opportunities to engage in literacy practices that allowed students to meet the standards. From the point of view of planning instruction, one might say that teachers have two very different paths they can follow. They might follow Option A—break down the standards item by item, perhaps in precisely the order they are written, and organize curriculum accordingly. Or Option B, developing meaningful issues and events in which students engage in literacy practices, thus addressing standards:

Option A: Common Core State Standards → direct instruction → guided practice

Option B: Constructing classroom events and spaces for meaningful activities → Common Core State Standards → instruction in the use of literacy practices → using literacy practices to change the status quo

Clearly, in this book, we are proposing Option B.

To help you develop the kind of meaningful activities that engage students in relevant literacy practices, it is first important to think more fully and specifically about that phrase "literacy practices." Given the multitude of different literacy practices in the world, we have identified several crucial types that are most relevant for implementing the 6–12 English Language Arts Common Core State Standards. Within each of these general types, there are many specific variations. The remainder of this chapter further illuminates these literacy practices. The next chapter focuses on drawing on these practices to plan activities to address the standards.

TYPES OF LITERACY PRACTICES

The following different types of literacy practices will help you design and enrich the activities your students engage in so they can meet and exceed the Common Core State Standards. Our approach is based in critical literacy and includes identifying issues, critiquing systems, and redesigning systems.

Framing Events

As we noted in the last chapter, adopting a literacy practices framework involves creating classroom events and addressing topics and issues that endow literacy practices with their meaning. A literacy event involves recognizable, consistent actions shaped by boundaries in terms of space and time (Bloome et al., 2005). These events are unfolding and dynamic, organized around accomplishing a goal; they therefore have a point and are not just rote exercises.

The meaning of actions is always unique to the particular event in which they occur and depends on differences in how people *frame* that event. People *frame events* in terms of goals, roles, plans, norms, and beliefs shaping actions in those events (see Figure 3.1) (Goffman, 1986). Readers or viewers *frame events* in literature or films by inferring the goals, roles, plans/scenarios, norms/boundaries, and beliefs shaping characters' actions (@ = Framing events).

This focus on events is consistent with education philosopher John Dewey's emphasis on learning as doing. In other words, by suggesting that you center your teaching on events, we are emphasizing the importance of actively engaging students in your classroom. Through their active participation, students are responsible for collaborative negotiation

Figure 3.1 Components Involved in Framing Events

of framing goals, plans, roles, norms, and beliefs operating in those events.

In creating classroom events, students employ literacy practices unique to your classroom space. Steffany Maher wanted to find ways to help her 10th grade students engage with and construct meaning from their study of *To Kill a Mockingbird* (Lee, 1960):

I focused on several cultural studies issues inside one piece of literature. I wanted to help students connect their personal responses to the issues prevalent in the text and then relate these issues to their own lives. I noticed that Atticus was a single parent and it occurred to me that the issue of single parenting may shape the daily experience of many of my students' lives. As teachers we know that single parents and blended families are common in our nation today. I assigned the first several chapters of *To Kill a Mockingbird* for the students to read at home. When they came to our next class, before discussing anything, I had them write a free-response journal entry about their reading for that day. We then spent that class time focusing on single fathers. We looked at clips from the films *Finding Nemo, The Pursuit of*

Happyness, and *To Kill a Mockingbird*. Each clip focused on a single father and his interaction with his child. During our discussion, Jenna said, "I feel bad for all single parents trying to raise children and make a living at the same time. That can be a lot of stress and really hard trying to balance both jobs alone. You don't have anyone to help when you need it." Jamie added, "It's not easy for any single parent, but I think it's harder in different ways for moms and dads who are single. Men usually have a harder time opening up and showing their emotions, but kids need that. Plus they have to work, which can be difficult leveling it out sometimes. Atticus seems to have leveled it out pretty well, though." Faith, whose mother recently remarried after being a single mom for several years, said she thought the film clips showed "the real struggle actual families go through every day."

Because I wanted to know how my students were responding to the literature and to the issues on which we were focusing, I gave them each a reader-response journal and assigned prompts that pertained to these issues. Some were as simple as "Write down any thoughts you had from the video clips we watched in class on Wednesday. Any and all thoughts are appropriate! Write whatever comes to mind." Others were more specific: "Think of a father-figure in your life—it could be your father or an uncle or a close friend's father, someone you know well. How is Atticus like this father figure? How is he different?" Several of them told me they liked these journal entries and hoped that we would continue using them after this unit. When I asked them why, one student said, "[The prompts] helped me to focus my thoughts and figure out really what I thought about the reading before you asked me in class. Then I wasn't so afraid to tell everyone else what I thought."

ACTIVITY: STEFFANY'S USE OF LITERACY PRACTICES

In this lesson, what literacy practices did Steffany's students use in responding to the novel in this classroom event? What did Steffany do to foster these literacy practices in the event? How did she focus on the family as the source of discussion? To build their relationships, what literacy practices do adolescents and parents use and in what events might they use them? How could you draw on students' uses of those practices and events to build connections to portrayals of family relationships in literature?

As people *frame events*, they often define goals and purposes. Defining goals helps us identify specific plans and actions. For example, if you plan to sell your car, you will adopt a plan that meets your goal of negotiating a good deal. You will set the price so that you can get the most you can for your car, but you will also aim for a price that will be perceived as fair for your buyer. People come to understand how best to set goals through experience employing and assessing their actions. From your past experience selling another car, you might have learned that setting the price too high will not work because your buyer may lose interest.

Having students define their goals and plans for participating in an event can serve to motivate their participation. Rather than you attempting to motivate them, the fact that they have some say in framing an event in terms of their goals and plans means that they have some ownership in the success of an event. For example, if you allow your students to define their purpose in creating a project—for instance, creating a video about traffic problems surrounding their school—they will be more motivated to complete the project than if you had simply assigned a project with your own purpose in mind.

Having defined goals and plans, people also *frame events* in terms of relevant and appropriate roles and norms. Again, if you are selling your car, you know that as the seller there are certain norms for negotiating a deal. If you are selling to a friend, for instance, you know that you will be perceived as someone who will be accountable for the car being in good condition; you will not want to jeopardize your friendship by selling a clunker!

Beliefs about an event shape people's actions. Based on the success of your negotiations, both you and your buyer may frame your negotiations as a "fair deal." As our simplistic example illustrates, beliefs are constituted in language: a "fair deal." Students could reflect on how use of language or metaphors in framing events reflects certain beliefs (Goffman, 1986). Metaphors reflect underlying cultural models shaping the meaning of actions (Lakoff, 2002). People may use metaphors of madness to describe being in a love relationship (being "crazy" or "out of my mind" about someone) or metaphors of war to describe sports (being in a "battle," throwing "bombs," or "launching a counteroffensive").

Effective English language arts instruction can be developed by creating classroom events/activities that involve students in framing, establishing roles, and determining beliefs. Steffany framed the study of characters in *To Kill a Mockingbird* (Lee, 1960) by the topic of single parenthood. Discussion of additional texts allowed students to *frame specific events* from the novel or the films. Different people *frame events* in different ways, based on their own experiences and knowledge. For example, some students may have viewed Calpurnia as a surrogate mother, and others might not. Student interest in the subject might have led to further research and sharing what they learned. Students could have established and taken on roles in the research, including some students interviewing single parents, others researching websites, others viewing additional films or reading young adult novels. Class discussion, writing, even publishing on the web, would address their beliefs. What were they learning about single parenting and parenting in general? How did this perspective lead them to see their own parents and themselves differently? The unit might have led to group or individual actions: How could we share what we are learning with others? How might I behave differently with my own parents?

Your students will need your help in learning to *frame events*. In *framing events*, adolescents may adopt what William Perry (1970) defines as a "dualist" perspective, framing events by adopting simplistic, either-or explanations. In doing so, they fail to recognize the competing perspectives or complexities required to interpret social practices, to understand difficult texts and situations, or to engage in thoughtful work in school or work environments.

Similarly, in responding to literature, students may assume that they can readily identify one defined reason for a character's actions, while there may be multiple, competing reasons for that character's actions. As Sheridan Blau (2003) notes, "Readers who read texts looking for secure and certain answers to their questions may also read the world with a similar passion for certainty and with a similar intolerance for the moral complexity and ambiguity that resist simplistic formulations" (p. 213). In addressing the Common Core reading/literature standards, you can help students move beyond a "dualist" perspective by modeling or encouraging them to develop multiple, alternative explanations for characters' actions. Adopting multiple perspectives for responding to literature is also related to the reading standard of being able to "assess how point of view or purpose shapes the content and style of a text."

Constructing and Enacting Identities

Another literacy practice related to framing events involves *constructing and enacting identities* or roles in events. For instance to be a daughter/son, friend, student, sports team member, sales/wait person, neighbor, club member, etc., involves particular social practices, traits, beliefs, and attitudes. These "identities are not fixed and stable attributes of individuals, but are produced through language (and other) practices . . . [they] are the products rather than the precursors of our language practices" (Pennycook, 2010, p. 125). For example, you *construct your identity* as a teacher through facilitating discussions, scaffolding activities, and praising students (@ = Constructing and enacting identities).

People *construct their identities* through adopting certain discourses or ways of knowing and thinking—what Gee (2008) refers to as "identity tool kits." These discourses may include acquiring specific uses of academic language associated with thinking and communicating as scientists, historians, lawyers, doctors, business people, government officials, psychologists, etc. As students take academic subjects such as social studies, science, math, or art beginning in late elementary school and going through graduate school, they acquire academic languages or discourses associated with specialized disciplinary or professional literacy practices. As a teacher, you are acquiring discourses of curriculum and instruction as well as English studies, and perhaps educational psychology, philosophy, sociology, and anthropology. These discourses constitute your professional identity as teacher, and mark you as someone whose expertise is valued by others.

The ability to acquire and employ these discourses may ultimately make a difference in people's professional success. James Gee (2011) argues:

Traditional literacy (reading and writing) has and still does come in two grades. One grade leads to working class jobs, once a good thing when there were unions and benefits, but now not such a good thing when it means low pay and no benefits, usually in service work. The other grade leads to more meaningful work and more financial success. What distinguishes these grades of literacy? The premium grade involves mastery of so-called "academic language," the forms of language used in research, empirical reasoning and logical argumentation. Now, I am well aware that nearly everyone hates "academic language" (things like "Hornworms exhibit a significant amount of variation," rather than "Hornworms sure vary a lot in how well they grow"), but when they are in good jobs, they are there because they got through their high school chemistry book and argued and debated their way out of a good college. (p. 1)

You can help your students acquire these academic languages or discourses by having them actively engaged in thinking, reading, and talking, and using different disciplinary texts and topics. For example, by having students read and discuss texts representing different critical perspectives, students begin to acquire uses of different academic languages and discourses.

Students also adopt identities constituted by discourses of gender, class, and race within certain communities of practice or "figured worlds" (Holland, Lachicotte, Skinner, & Cain, 1998). Pennycook (2010) explains how such discourses and identities are linked through an examination of gender:

Rather than viewing gender as the prior identity which gives rise to gendered language use, gendered language practices from this point of view give rise to identities. Communities of practices are not therefore just groups of people who happen to be doing the same thing, but rather people whose communities are constituted by the language practices they engage in. (p. 124)

In other words, rather than understanding gender as simply biological, it is important to help students consider ways that gender identity (as well as identities like race and social class) is developed socially as people participate in specific language practices.

You can engage your students in experimentation with *constructing and enacting different identities* through drama, simulations, or games. In a description of "participatory cultures" (Jenkins et al., 2006), online networking is constituted by a number of different literacy practices: "play—the capacity to experiment with one's surroundings as a form of problem-solving; performance—the ability to adopt alternative identities for the purpose of improvisation and discovery; and simulation—the ability to interpret and construct dynamic models of real-world processes" (p.12). As people *experiment with identities*, they learn to adopt those identities best designed to achieve certain goals.

People are also socialized to adopt identities constituted by certain ways of reading, writing, speaking, and listening consistent with the literacy practices valued in certain groups or cultures. For example, in adopting the identity of a minister, priest, or rabbi, a person acquires a certain way of reading texts consistent with their particular religious beliefs. As Gee (2010a) notes:

People learn a given way of reading or writing by participating in (or at least coming to understand) the distinctive social and cultural practices of different social and cultural groups. When these groups teach or "apprentice" people to read and write in certain ways, they never stop there. They teach them to act, interact, talk, know, believe, and value in certain ways as well, ways that "go with" how they write and read . . . So, for example, knowing how to write a "game FAQ" (a strategy guide for a video game)—or how to read one—requires that you know how game FAQs are used in the social practices of gamers, practices that involve a lot more than just reading and writing. You need to know how gamers talk about, debate over, and act in regard to such things as "spoilers" and "cheats" and "cheating," all defined as gamers define them, not just in general terms . . . People don't just read and write in general, they read and write specific sorts of texts in specific ways, and these ways are determined by the values and practices of different social and cultural groups. (p. 16)

The literacy practice of *constructing and enacting identities* is related to the reading standard, "analyze in detail where, when, why, and how events, ideas, and characters develop and interact over the course of a text," in that students draw on their own experiences of *constructing and enacting identities* when they interpret characters' traits, motives, knowledge, and beliefs. Michael Ben-Chaim (2010) describes the ways in which students' cultural identities shape their responses to a Billy Collins poem, "Divorce":

The reader's decision is a function of her interests, concerns, and values and pertains primarily to her cultural identity rather than to her neurological or psychological makeup. Pervasive problems in reading comprehension in contemporary education pertain to the function students assign to texts in relation to their cultural identities. Consider, for example, two high school students in an American poetry class who are asked to read Billy Collins' "Divorce",

> Once, two spoons in bed,
> now tined forks
> across a granite table
> and the knives they have hired.

It takes a couple of minutes for the two students to realize that the two spoons refer to a married couple resting intimately in bed, that the two forks represent a marital conflict, and that the knives are the lawyers who are finally hired to settle the couple's divorce.

One student, for whom the poem confirms the conviction that poetry is a useless game with words, is now eager to put the poem aside and return to the much more serious business of managing his social affairs on Facebook. The other student reads "Divorce" as a critique of modern life in which the space of intimate relationships is transformed into a battle field. Inspired by Collins' work, he decides to write an essay on other modern conditions whereby peace is transformed into war. For this student, then, poetry is a means of engagement with ideals, ideas, and institutions that shape our lives. (p. 2)

Relating to and Collaborating with Others

Another set of literacy practices involves *relating to and collaborating with others*. These literacy practices are relevant to all standards, but might be especially associated with the speaking/listening standard, "participate effectively in a range of interactions (one-on-one and in groups), exchanging information to advance a discussion and to build on the input of others" (@ = Relating to and collaborating with others).

Learning how to *relate to others* requires the ability to empathize with others' perspectives, share one's own feelings and perspectives, and negotiate differences of opinion. There are many ways students can relate to and collaborate with others in an English language arts classroom. In participating in classroom discussions, for instance, students learn to relate to each other through acknowledging each other's perspectives and feelings and being respectful in stating disagreements with others. In leading classroom discussions, you can help students recognize the use of these literacy practices by modeling metacognitive reflections, for example, "Rhonda, I like how you described Bill's positions on this issue before stating your own position."

Relating to others also involves the ability to engage in online social networking to *interact with others*, acquire relevant information, and share expertise associated with collectively addressing problems. Advocates of "connectivist" learning posit that knowledge now resides in connections people make in online networks. As George Siemons (2010) notes:

We don't, after all, make sense of our complex world as individuals. We make sense through connections . . . and these connections create our identity and help us to find our sense of belonging and our sense of humanity . . . To collapse education, knowledge, teaching, and learning to connections is to give individuals the control and freedom needed to effectively change education. And to change education is to change society.

The new ways that people can relate to each other using online networking have dramatically changed both how knowledge is made and how we learn. People can now readily contribute to and acquire knowledge from many sources including: online databases; open-source courses; blogs; wikis; podcasts; social networking tools such as Facebook, MySpace, or Twitter; and online gaming and simulations (Second Life, SimCity, Project Courts, Quest Atlantis, Whyville, etc.). According to boyd (2009, p. 9), engagement in these "networked publics" is constituted by "persistence" (communication is recorded and stored);

"searchability" (people can readily locate each other and information); "replicability" (material can be copied and moved); and "invisible audiences" (it is difficult to identify one's potential viewers or readers). Online networking allows students to readily move across previously distinct boundaries between home, school, peer group, and workplace, a reflection of "circulating literacy practices" across these different contexts (Vasudevan, Schultz, & Bateman, 2010).

The value of the literacy practice of *relating and collaborating with others* was evident in recent research analyzing problem-solving abilities by groups (Davidson, 2010; Johnson & Johnson, 2009). This research found that the success of a group does not depend on individual members' intelligence or skills; it depends on "collective intelligence"—group members' ability to empathize with each other's emotions, to honor individual differences in the members' diverse abilities, and to have other members acquire these abilities, as well as leaders who listen to and enact others' ideas. Clay Shirky (2009) argues that online collaboration can lead to collective action in which "the cohesion of the group becomes critical to its success . . . collective action creates shared responsibility, by tying the user's identity to the identity of the group" (p. 51). Engaging in collective action requires "some shared vision strong enough to bind the group together, despite periodic decisions that will inevitably displease at least some some members" (p. 53).

Synthesizing and Connecting Texts

Another crucial literacy practice for helping students meet the Common Core State Standards is the ability to *synthesize texts* by putting into one's own words summaries, paraphrases, key points, or positions for the purpose of analyzing written, spoken, or visual texts (@ = Synthesizing and connecting texts).

One problem with decontextualized instruction in synthesizing and analyzing texts is that students often have no sense of the social purpose and audience that can shape the focus of their synthesis and analysis. As a result, rather than synthesizing the key points or ideas in a text, students often recopy or regurgitate the wording of a text and fail to reformulate the points or ideas in their own words. To help students engage in the literacy practice of synthesizing texts, students can write short "microthemes" synthesizing texts for sharing with others on a class blog or wiki (Jacobs, 2010). In doing so, it is essential to provide them with some social purpose and audience for their "microthemes."

To help students go beyond recopying or regurgitating language of a text, you can also model synthesizing by identifying differences between the primary idea, subordinate points, and supporting details and by noting the use of key transition words, such as "for example," that signal a supporting idea or detail. You can also have students employ "tags" as keyword syntheses of blog posts or online articles that they can use in searching for material for writing and organizing essay drafts (Jacobs, 2010). To help students learn to employ tags (key words or terms that stand for specific knowledge or information) as a bottom-up "folksonomy" (a collaborative classification system for creating and managing tags), you can have students review tags employed for a certain blog post or article and discuss how and why those tags are appropriate.

Based on their syntheses of texts, students can then *make connections between texts*. Of course, there are many meaningful ways to *develop connections* between a diverse range of literary, informational, and multimedia texts in our English classes. As they make intertextual connections, students can consider thematic relationships between different texts. Through the use of hyperlinks in online documents, blogs, websites, or wikis, such linking can be explicit, and include images or videos that illustrate the ideas in a written text.

In teaching *To Kill a Mockingbird*, Steffany was aware of the value of using video to provide students with connections to the historical context shaping the threatened lynching of Tom Robinson, and the scene where he is saved from a mob by Atticus and Scout. Steffany wanted to make this crucial event meaningful to her students, so she *connected* the novel with documentary film, related literary works, and postcard images.

I showed them a clip from the video *Eyes on the Prize* that told the story of Emmett Till. Till, a 14-year-old Black boy from Chicago, who went to visit family in Mississippi in 1955 and was brutally beaten and lynched for either whistling or saying, "Bye, baby," to a white woman (accounts differ). That night the woman's husband and another man took Till from his uncle's home, beat him, gouged out his eye, shot him, tied a cotton gin fan to his neck, and threw him into a river. His body was found days later and taken back to his mother.

When the video showed Emmett's body in the open casket, several of my students had to look away. We discussed how this event contributed to the Civil Rights Movement. After we viewed the video, I read aloud *A Wreath for Emmett Till*, a heroic crown sonnet written by Marilyn Nelson. To be honest, I was expecting several students to be bored by the end of the poem. It is lengthy, and it is poetry. Any English teacher knows what that can mean. However, as I looked around while I was reading, I was surprised to see that every student was paying—if not rapt—at least polite attention to me. After my reading, several of them expressed their amazement of the poetry and of Nelson's skill at including such difficult material in a poem.

I finished this topic by presenting the website www.withoutsanctuary. com, a collection of nearly 80 postcards and photographs taken as souvenirs of lynchings and put together by collector James Allen [see Figure 3.2 for one example from the collection].

My students were appalled. When I told them that these were actual postcards sent in the mail, Stacy said, "How could anyone mail that to a relative and say, 'Look what I did this weekend!'?" Laney added, "I think I'll stick with my postcards of unicorns." Although she was making light of the situation, I could see that they were all deeply affected by the pictures. Tanya had looked away, disgusted, when they had come up on the screen, and many others had looks of horror on their faces.

Immediately afterward, I had them open their reader-response journals and free write on what they had just seen and heard. For several students, it was an eye-opening experience, as Jenna expressed: "Our world is so messed up! I don't know why God lets things like this happen." Many of them wrote of how it made them feel. Hope said, "Who could possibly have that much hatred in their heart, killing human beings like that! The

Figure 3.2 Postcard of a Lynching

Used with permission from the National Center for Civil and Human Rights.

video made me angry, terrified, and heartbroken . . . I felt sick to my stomach with anger, horror, and sadness." Some even identified with the people who had committed these crimes simply because they were also white Americans. Jamie wrote: "It just makes me sick to my stomach thinking about what they did. I mean what possessed *us* to think these things [emphasis mine]. God didn't make us to be killers."

Because we had taken the time during class to look at what had happened to people in history, they better understood the gravity of the situation as they read about what could have happened to Tom Robinson in the novel. Dan wrote, "Atticus was in great danger when he decided to protect Tom Robinson from the mob, and Scout and Jem also put themselves in danger when they ran to Atticus. If Scout hadn't spoken to Mr. Cunningham there might have been some killings that night." He also recognized the nature of a mob: "When a mob comes together, they are angry about one thing, and everything else is forgotten."

ACTIVITY: UNDERSTANDING THE VALUE OF VISUAL TEXTS AND DOCUMENTARY HISTORY

Why are visual texts and documentary history important dimensions for creating meaning from *To Kill a Mockingbird*? How might Steffany have further developed the study of lynching, including of the postcard image above (Figure 3.2), in ways that would involve her students with a range of literacy practices?

In well-designed curricular units, it is common for students to use their responses to new texts to make connections and reinterpretations of previous texts. Related to reading *To Kill a Mockingbird*, students can also read *Narrative of the Life of Frederick Douglass: An American Slave* (Douglass, 2005), *Incidents in the Life of a Slave Girl* (Jacobs, 2006), or the original *Confessions of Nat Turner*. You can also ask students to study incidents of racism in their own communities. For example, after an African-American family moved into a house in Minneapolis, on July 16, 1931, one thousand people protested in front of the house, demanding that the family move out. However, the family refused to move and were defended by an African-American attorney and President of the local NAACP. Studying such local incidents helps students recognize that racism occurred throughout the country and not only in the South.

Students can also *synthesize* multiple sources on issues by working in groups as both researchers and presenters—examining archives, crafting displays and websites. Linda Christensen (2009) frequently has her students conduct "tea parties," where they research, take the roles of historical or fictional characters, and engage in interactive discussion and writing.

Constructing Multimodal Texts

Another literacy practice involves the ability to *create multimodal texts* that combine images, video, voice, print, and/or music. From mass culture and advertising to film and the Internet, students are immersed in a fully multimodal world. Traditional forms of high culture are also multi-modal—consider opera or Shakespearean theater. Digital storytelling, slam poetry, YouTube videos, graphic novels, and many other multi-modal forms are highly popular with teens (@ = Constructing multi-modal texts).

Throughout this book we will discuss and give examples of students *constructing multimodal texts*. In Chapter 9, we will specifically explore how the ability to *create multimodal texts* involves the specific digital literacies of multimodality, interactivity, modularity, automation, and collection/appropriation (Lankshear & Knobel, 2003). *Creating multimodal texts* involves making aesthetic and critical judgments about how images, the use of camera shots and angles, music, sound effects, and editing serve to rhetorically engage audiences' emotions. *Creating multimodal texts* also calls for knowledge about how images, print, videos, music, and/or sounds engage audiences in social and cultural ways. For example, students created a video about a teen transported into a music-video world where his peers mimicked different music-video groups dancing to music in the school hallways, and making intertextual references to various pop music stars. In the video the main character has difficulty understanding how and why he was transported into this world—at the end of the video, he attempts to explain events by reading a graphic novel, and is transported into the graphic novel itself as a character, and only then returns to the real world.

Employing these intertextual references involves appropriating, parodying, and remixing popular culture material as evident in the popular MAD TV video parody Nice White Lady (available on YouTube: http://youtube.com/watch?v=ZVF-nirSq5s) that pokes fun at the Hollywood movie genre of the white teacher "savior" figure portrayed in Hollywood films who suddenly transforms her students from resistant to engaged learners. Such appropriation raises questions about the need for students to be concerned about creating *original* texts, when they play with, juxtapose, manipulate, alter, and rearrange *existing* texts to create *new* texts, a practice reflecting a postmodern challenge to traditional notions of "originality" (Beach & Swiss, 2010).

Through engaging in multimodal productions, students have the opportunity to adopt new aesthetic notions of visual rhetoric, performance, and embodiment constituting identity construction (Beach, Hull, & O'Brien, 2011). As they produce and share images of the body, they are exploring how the body is portrayed through dress, posture, language use, gestures, etc. For example, in creating avatars on sites such as Second Life or Whyville, students have to make decisions about purchasing body parts, dress, hair, or faces.

Adopting a Critical Engagement Perspective

In this book, we also advocate for adopting a critical engagement perspective that emphasizes critical analysis and inquiry (Dockter, Haug, & Lewis, 2010; Wohlwend & Lewis, 2011). A critical engagement perspective involves literacy practices of *critiquing and representing issues, formulating effective arguments, critiquing systems*, and *redesigning and transforming systems*. Critical engagement literary practices are essential to meet the Common Core State Standards goal of preparing students to become citizens in a democratic republic. While critical engagement and inquiry are important to all of the standards, it is especially relevant to responding to literature and the media (@ = Critical literacy and engagement).

A critical engagement perspective builds on critical literacy practices of disrupting the commonplace, interrogating different viewpoints, focusing on issues, and promoting social justice (Lewison, Leland, & Harste, 2008). Critical engagement includes critiquing how texts position readers and readers position texts based on discourses and cultural models. Critical engagement considers the emotional/engagement aspects of literacy in ways that in involve "critical distance *and* immersion, a process both analytic and playful, resistant and emotional" (Wohlwend & Lewis, 2011, p. 189). For example, this perspective applied to students' engagement with digital media and popular culture might focus on adolescent production and consumption of digital/popular culture texts. In teaching the animation film *Pocahontas* in a high school English class, the teacher wanted her students to critique the stereotyped representations of Native Americans (Lewis & Dockter, 2011). Interviews with two African-American students in the class in particular developed strong responses to the hypersexualization of Pocahontas, a critique that reflected their prior knowledge of stereotypes of African Americans and drove their adoption of a critical stance. This suggests the importance of tapping into students' emotions as triggers for engaging in critical inquiry.

From their experiences, students can identify tensions or contradictions between the way things are and the way they should be; in other words, students can be asked to examine situations in which they sense that something is "just not right" (Bruce & Bishop, 2008). For example, if students value participating in team sports, but they know that their schools' athletic program is being cut due to declining tax revenues, then they have identified a tension or contradiction. Or, as Steffany found, if students learn about the violence of lynching, it conflicts with their prior sense of the importance of justice for all.

Identifying tensions and contradictions can lead students to ask important questions such as, "How come?" and "Why is it this the case that . . .?" as a means of "disrupting the commonplace" (Lewison et al., 2008, p. 7). In a series of "Critical Research Seminars" offered during the summers from 1999 to 2004 at UCLA, high school students recounted some of the problems they experienced attending some of the poorest public schools in the nation in Los Angeles (Morrell, 2008). By asking "How come?" they recognized that a major problem had to do with the lack of funding for their schools. Identifying these tensions evoked certain emotional or ethical reactions—doubt, frustration, puzzlement, concern, indignation, and anger.

Adopting a critical engagement framework is also useful in helping your students examine issues of literacy and power—how, for example, language can be used to deceive people to perpetuate inequalities within power structures. In her model of critical literacy, Hilary Janks (2010) identifies four key aspects associated with the relationship between literacy and power (pp. 23–26):

- *Domination*: how do language and other literacy tools serve to maintain and reproduce dominant relationships?
- *Access*: how can marginalized people access dominant forms or power associated with language or genre use?
- *Diversity*: how do people acquire different, diverse ways of using social practices and literacy associated with alternative ways of doing, being, and thinking?
- *Design*: how can students employ literacy tools to design alternative texts and systems in ways that redesign or transform texts and systems?

These components need to be connected in a critical literacy curriculum, otherwise, imbalances can occur. For example, Janks (2010) argues that "celebration of diversity without a recognition that difference is structured in dominance and that not all discourses/genres/languages/ literacies are equally powerful". (p. 26)

Kyle describes some of the challenges and opportunities created by her approach as described in Chapter 1 for exceeding the curriculum and the standards she was given:

Students have been successful in their *Adventures of Huckleberry Finn* discussion and quizzes, as well as their reading and quizzes for the choice books. The connections between the books are starting to become more evident for the students, though we have found some difficulty discussing these connections as a whole class. Since no more than four students are reading the same book and there are eight different books being read in the class, students have experienced confusion when groups discuss how the themes of *Adventures of Huckleberry Finn* connect to a novel not everyone is reading. I've also found it difficult as a teacher to provide supplementary material to all groups; however, I have had groups start to create some of that material themselves. Students created character charts, lists of literary devices used in their novel, and charts of themes and connecting ideas. Students have become effective in their groups, as they discuss confusing portions of the texts, guide each other in their reading, and talk about issues that give them pause and make them question the text and the author's motives. Class has changed a great deal during this unit. I've seen an increase in student engagement and excitement; students are willing to take on the pressures of an extra text if it means they have the opportunity to read texts that they get to choose and are relevant to their lives. Students have seen lives outside their own experience and sparked a passion for making the world the way they want it to be.

ACTIVITY: KYLE'S USE OF LITERACY PRACTICES

What literacy practices and activities are Kyle's students employing in her classroom? How might she, in future semesters, further develop those tasks, practices, and activities? How might the changes you propose impact student learning?

CRITIQUING SYSTEMS

Related to formulating arguments are literacy practices involved in *critiquing systems*—there are many systems students can critique in our language arts classes: educational systems, the economic/class system, media/digital communication, transportation/travel, environmental, agricultural/food production, housing, financial/banking, healthcare, law enforcement/legal, higher education, government/political systems, retail/business, military, research/science, and so on. Literary, informational, and multimodal texts of all kinds offer representations of systems that can become starting points for analysis and connections to other works, topics, and issues (@ = Critiquing systems).

Identifying and interpreting actions and events as shaped by these larger systems will be a challenge for students, particularly middle school students, though research, collaboration, and participation in appropriate classroom events can help all students develop their critical skills.

As illustrated in Figure 3.3, students can extend how they frame actions in events by applying various perspectives to define the meaning of actions related to goals, plans, roles, norms, and beliefs. There are certainly numerous other perspectives students could adopt to analyze systems; we believe that historical, institutional/civic, cultural, psychological, and economic forces are especially important.

Students can adopt a variety of different perspectives to analyze how spaces and systems shaping events are constructed through historical, institutional/civic, cultural, psychological, and economic forces. For example, in adopting a cultural perspective, students may consider how

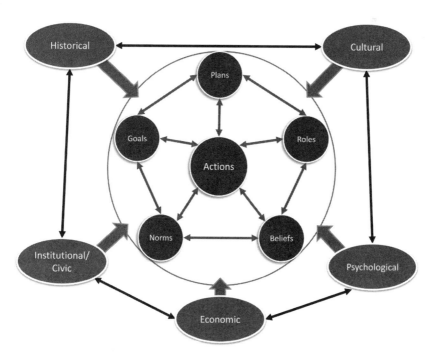

Figure 3.3 Framing Actions

spaces are constructed through gender, race, or class—for example, how spaces may be defined as "working class" or "upper class."

Historical Perspectives

One way to analyze actions in systems is by framing systems within the context of certain historical periods, a perspective that's important for addressing the history reading/writing standards. In adopting an historical perspective, students can examine people or characters as "persons in history" (Holland & Lave, 2001) whose goals, plans, roles, and beliefs are grounded in those particular periods. For example, many people who experienced the Great Depression of the 1930s developed beliefs regarding the importance of being frugal, as well as a positive attitude towards the role of government associated with New Deal legislation that created institutions designed to assist people.

By teaching your students to employ an historical perspective to *frame events*, you will be addressing the language standard "use grade-appropriate general academic vocabulary and domain-specific words and phrases purposefully acquired as well as gained through conversation and reading and responding to texts." For example, in reading a series of essays related to a particular historical event, you might ask students to consider what particular kinds of language and beliefs are common across the essays and how they are reflective of that time period.

In studying literature or films, students could study historical forces operating in the period in which a novel, story, play, or film occurs. As previously noted, Steffany employed the documentary *Eyes on the Prize* to provide her students with the historical context for *To Kill a Mockingbird*:

I showed them a clip that presented the trial and acquittal of the alleged murderers of Emmett Till and their subsequent confessions. From there, we jumped right to the "Mississippi Burning" trial. I read them a synopsis of the events leading up to the case and the trial of the alleged murderers of three Civil Rights activists.

A discussion of our nation's system of trial by a jury of our peers and how it functioned during this time period ensued. From our discussion, I could see that their sense of justice was bruised. Students expressed their anger at jurors who knew what was right and yet ruled otherwise. This transitioned smoothly into a discussion of the court scene in *To Kill a Mockingbird*. I told them that I was going to allow them to lead the discussion and that I would offer comments only in the last few minutes. Because the students had already written in their journals and discussed in

small groups their thoughts on the assigned reading, each one had
something to contribute to the discussion:

Stacy: "Even though they had the evidence, they still completely ignored it
    because of their own bias. I chucked the book at the wall when I read the
    verdict!"
Laney: "You always chuck the book at the wall when you don't like something
    that happens."
Stacy: smiling, "Yeah, well . . . I do tend to do that. But I was *really* mad this
    time!"
Catey: "I got really mad, too, and was like, 'I'm never going to read this book
    again!'"
Hope: "It was just so unfair! This sweet little dude didn't do anything, and they
    said he did, and that was all they needed [to convict him]."
Catey: "Yeah, but I did read the book again—I finished it *and* watched the
    whole movie!"

The conversation continued, and students brought up such topics
as Tom's obvious innocence, Mayella's motivation, Bob Ewell's
despicable character, and Jem's response to the verdict. Then, without
needing to call on him as I have always had to do in the past, Jesse
added:

"I thought it was important—Scout's reaction to the verdict—because
she said all these people were people she'd grown up with and
trusted, and then they just convicted someone who was—obviously—
innocent. I thought that was pretty powerful, her reaction."

And *I* thought it was a pretty powerful discussion. Finally all my students
were contributing their ideas, including Jesse. We finished this issue by
watching the court scene from *To Kill a Mockingbird*.

As this experience illustrates, acquiring an historical perspective
is a key means of helping students to understand and critique systems
that are at play in literature and life. Other ways to tap into historical
perspectives include asking students to interview their parents or grandparents about their autobiographical recollections of living in previous
decades. They could ask parents or grandparents to contrast their past
and present lives—for example, their experiences as daughters/sons
during their childhoods and their current experiences as parents or
grandparents.

Institutional/Civic Perspectives

Another perspective involves focusing on the different institutional/civic forces shaping students' lives as members of families, schools, communities/neighborhoods, organizations, or workplaces. Helping students acquire an institutional or civic perspective will aid them in understanding how their identities are constructed through membership or citizenship in particular institutions. To help students take on this perspective, you might ask them to examine how actions are shaped by institutional discourses that represent specific ways of knowing and thinking (Gee, 1996). People adopt or "double-voice" different discourses (Bakhtin, 1981) related to various institutional contexts and norms. Examples of such discourses include legal, scientific, psychological, religious/spiritual, educational, and business management. For example, you might imagine asking students to write letters to their city council to address issues of higher levels of air pollution due to increased traffic surrounding a new retail development. In order to effectively write such a letter, students would need to adopt not only a scientific discourse related to presenting objective data about air pollution, but also an economic discourse related to "growth" to argue against new retail development.

In adopting an institutional or civic perspective, students can consider ways in which these institutions shape actions and events both at a larger societal level and in their own lives. For instance, in writing the letter discussed in the previous paragraph, students might learn how the political forces operating in their neighborhood shape attitudes towards issues of sprawl, traffic, transportation, redevelopment, and pollution (Beach & Myers, 2001).

Students can connect issues in almost any text they read to problems in their community and institutional or civic groups working to address them. Students reading Steinbeck's *Of Mice and Men* (1982) or Tomas Rivera's *And the Earth Did not Devour Him* (2007) might engage in service learning related to migrant workers. Students reading *The Taming of the Shrew* or Laurie Anderson's young adult novel *Speak* might learn about and work with women's shelters, hotlines, and YWCA programs supporting survivors of abuse or sexual violence.

Cultural Perspectives

Adopting cultural perspectives involves examining how certain cultural models or unconscious beliefs about the world operate among various groups of people in various "figured worlds" (Holland, Lachicotte, Skinner, & Cain, 1998). Studying cultural models can shed light on reasons why certain actions and beliefs are valued over others in particular contexts. For example, working-class parents in some communities may value their roles as parents over their workplace roles, while the reverse may be the case for upper-middle-class parents in some communities. Or, in examining political or government systems, you would find that the cultural model of the "strict father" (who values top-down mandates related to controlling citizens' social practices) guides some political systems, while the cultural model of the "nurturing parent" (who provides government support for citizens) guides others (Lakoff, 2002).

You can teach your students to understand various cultural models by helping them examine the unconscious or unstated beliefs about what is valuable or normal that are found in various institutions, and social and media worlds. For instance, students could consider values underlying the day-to-day functions of their school—promptness, individual merit, reserved affect, etc. Or, you could ask students to examine cultural models of romance that are portrayed in the advertising of "beauty products" that serve to emphasize physical appearance in shaping relationships.

Psychological Perspectives

You can engage students in psychological perspectives by asking them to reflect on ways that people adopt actions based on needs, desires, and perspectives associated with particular systems. For example, within a family or workplace system, parents' or managers' literacy practices are defined by their roles as nurturers, supporters, and role models. Adopting these roles depends on parents' or managers' ability to empathize with others or express certain emotions associated with support and guidance.

Students can critically analyze instances of breakdowns in family or workplace systems as they are related to failures of expressing needs, desires, or emotions. Students may discover that such breakdowns are often due to parents' or managers' inability to effectively employ certain social practices.

Economic Perspectives

In adopting economic perspectives, you can help your students examine how actions in systems are shaped by economic forces. For example, students might study how class status in their neighborhood affects one's ability to effect changes in his or her neighborhood. Or, on a larger scale, students might consider how capitalist economic systems designed to foster economic growth damage ecological systems and lead to resource depletion. For instance, students could read ideas by scholars such as

James Gustave Speth (2008), who argues that individuals in the environmental movement itself have had little success in reversing expansive growth and consumption by attempting to work within a capitalist system, "Indeed, the system will seek to undermine those efforts and constrain them within narrow limits. Working only within the system will, in the end, not succeed. Transformative change in the system itself is needed" (p. 28).

Speth argues for the need to move away from a consumption, pro-growth economy driven by the need to continually produce more goods and consume more energy. For Speth, identifying the limitations of a consumption, pro-growth economy as a system leads to envisioning a transformed, "postgrowth" society that focuses on quality of life as opposed to increasing the gross national product through consumption. Reframing the environmental movement therefore requires thinking in terms of larger economic forces perpetuating a pro-growth, consumption economy/system, as opposed to an economy designed to reduce consumption of energy, natural resources, and water in ways that are destructive of the environment (McKibben, 2010).

To encourage her students to adopt an economic perspective on issues of class differences in *To Kill a Mockingbird*, Steffany had her students examine the issue of the status of the Ewells and the Cunninghams as white, working-class people in the novel:

I started class by instructing the students to write in their journals what they thought of when they heard the word "poor." Their responses varied:

> Jenna: "If you're poor it could be because you're irresponsible and you don't use your money wisely."
> Jesse: "I think of not having food or good clothes. I also think of Michigan right now. The economy is causing poverty in a once great state."
> Carissa: "People don't have much food. Ragged clothes. Living in dark, dirty alleys. Starved people, working hard all day for only a few dollars. People sitting on street corners with old, rusty cups, begging for money."

I then showed them a large poster of the famous photograph, *Migrant Mother, 1936*, taken by Dorothea Lange. This is a picture of a woman holding one of her seven children while two others lay their heads on each of her shoulders. I had my students do a focused free write for 10 minutes, writing whatever came to their minds while looking at the photograph. Their responses were insightful.

Hope wrote: "I wonder if the kids have a father/the woman has a husband. Their clothes look very worn. They look poor, and the mother looks worried. The mother looks like she's had a tough life."

Liza wrote more scattered thoughts: "Sad, dirt, poor, tired, frustrated, hard working mother, looking for relief, at wits end, the picture makes you have pity on this family."

After writing, when I told them all that she was only 32 years old, they were shocked. Many thought she was much older. We talked about what life was like for many people during the Great Depression, touching a bit on "Hoovervilles."

We then listened to the song "Coal Miner's Daughter" by Loretta Lynn and, once again, I had them free write on whatever came to mind as they listened closely to the words. Afterward I asked them to share what they had written. Many students were struck by how proud she was of her modest beginnings and how thankful the family was for the "little things" in life, like a new pair of shoes after not having any all summer long. They also noted how hard the father and mother both worked. Catey wondered aloud how anyone could function, working all night as a coal miner and all day as a farmer.

After sharing our thoughts on this topic, we moved to a discussion of the novel. I asked them to think about the similarities and differences between the Ewell family and the Cunningham family in *To Kill a Mockingbird*. They shared details from the text that informed them how poor the two families were:

Catey: "The Cunninghams were poor because they couldn't pay Atticus except with things like chestnuts."

Alyson: "Yeah, and Walter never had lunch to eat."

Dan: "But the Cunninghams would never take something they couldn't pay back somehow, while Bob Ewell would drink away any money they got."

Carissa: "Mayella had to take care of the kids and the house. Her dad was just a drunk and beat them."

Catey: "But Mr. Cunningham was respectable and paid back his debts the best he could."

Robert: "Except when he was in the mob."

Catey: "Well, yeah. Maybe he wasn't respectable then." Everyone laughed.

Robert: "But he wouldn't even get into debt unless he couldn't help it. And his kids went to school. The Ewells just went the first day every year and then didn't go back. The description at the beginning of what the Ewell kid looked like showed how poor they were. They didn't have any shoes or anything."

If we had had more time, I would like to have gone further into discussion about poverty in our world today, perhaps making connections between the novel and the conditions of life in our own community.

ACTIVITY: IDENTIFYING MATERIALS FOR TEACHING ABOUT WEALTH AND POVERTY

If you wanted, like Steffany, to have students consider issues of wealth and poverty in their community, what other literary texts or films might be used to initiate the unit? How could you make such a unit authentic and meaningful for your students?

Redesigning and Transforming Systems

After you have led students through critique of problems in existing systems, it is important that you ask them to consider ways to redesign and transform events or systems in order to address their critiques. This may involve taking action, what Engestrom (2009) defines as "expansive learning." The cycle of expansive learning involves questioning the way things are, leading to analysis and perhaps resistance, and resulting in developing, modeling, and testing out of revised social practices or alternative uses of tools.

In a study of preservice English teachers' development of critical literacy curricula for their student teaching, Paula Wolfe (2010) found that a number of the preservice teachers engaged students in taking action. One preservice teacher, Angela, asked her students to:

Write a newspaper report focused on "raising social awareness about a particular newsworthy situation or event . . . The group newspapers will be displayed in an area of the school which is designated as a display area for student work." Beyond simply posting the newspapers in the designated display area, several students chose to submit their stories to a local newspaper. (p. 328)

In a journal reflection Angela wrote,

All students loved exploring their own opinions while studying editorial writing. Several of their articles were published in a local paper, which sent the ultimate lesson that newspapers give everyone—even middle schoolers—the opportunity to have their voices heard . . . They also did a fantastic job thinking about contemporary social issues and how those issues affected their lives. (p. 328)

ACTIVITY: REFLECTING ON YOUR OWN USE OF LITERACY PRACTICES

Given these different literacy practices, reflect on a recent event you have been part of—a social activity, classroom discussion, project meeting, presentation, workplace encounter, etc. Identify different literacy practices that were occurring in these events. For example, many social activities include the sharing of narratives. What did you need to know to be able to label something a "literacy practice"? How were the literacy practices you came up with social—how did they involve interaction between people? How effective were people employing these practices? Why or how did people vary in their ability to employ these social practices? How might you create classroom activities to engage students in uses of these literacy practices?

CASE STUDY: PRINCIPAL'S HALLWAY (LITERACY FRAMEWORKS)

In this chapter, we've described our notion of a literacy practices curriculum framework. The challenge that remains is how to put this framework into practice—how can it be implemented in a specific school context?

After you are hired on the spot to teach English to students in grades 6–12 at a new, small, rural school, you are told that you will be responsible for developing a new curriculum framework for the school's English curriculum. This case study will guide you through the curriculum development process as you work to design a plan that will best serve the student population, half of whom are white and half of whom are Latino, as you discuss which literacy practices you will emphasize for grades 6–8, 9–10, and 11–12. You will then defend your newly designed curriculum at an Open Board Meeting, as you entertain questions from a retired teacher, a concerned parent, an elementary teacher, and two board members in an open question-and-answer session.

Please find two or three peers and go to the LiteraryWorlds.org site and then the *Teaching to Succeed* link to engage in this case study for Chapter 3.

CHAPTER 4

Using a Literacy Practices Framework to Plan Instruction that Meets and Exceeds the Common Core State Standards

Putting Theory into Action

CHAPTER OVERVIEW

How Much Say Do I Have in Interpreting and Enacting My Own Curriculum? Respecting My Autonomy as a Professional

Who Am I Working with in My Classroom? Thinking about Students' Knowledge and Experiences

How Does Knowledge of My Students Influence How I Plan? Non-Linear Planning through Student Collaboration

What Do I Want My Students to Learn? Selecting and Integrating Common Core State Standards to Formulate Learning Objectives

How Do I Apply Different Curriculum Frameworks in Planning Instruction?

How Can My Students Learn Literacy Practices? Learning Literacy Practices through Socialization, Imitation, and Reflection

How Do I Select and Assign Texts Based on Consideration of Student Interests/Ability and Text Complexity? Weighing Different Factors in Selecting and Assigning Texts

What Literacy Practices Will My Students Be Using to Address These Common Core State Standards? Unpacking and Translating Standards Documents

Case Study: Ric Shahin's Hallway (Planning)

As we argued in Chapter 1, the Common Core State Standards provide a general framework for developing curriculum and instruction. Meeting and exceeding the standards will require you to make independent, informed choices about how you create, modify, interpret, and enact curriculum. Your knowledge, interests, and passionate commitment to what you are teaching are vital to the success of your students. In this chapter we describe ways to foster students' uses of literacy practices and address key questions for planning curriculum and instruction that will be further illustrated in the rest of this book by specific examples in teaching literature/reading, writing, speaking/listening/media, and language—the four major categories of the standards. Further resources for curriculum planning are also available on this book's website, www. routledge.com/cw/beach as well as at this specific link (@ = General resources for planning instruction).

HOW MUCH SAY DO I HAVE IN INTERPRETING AND ENACTING MY OWN CURRICULUM? RESPECTING MY AUTONOMY AS A PROFESSIONAL

As we noted in Chapter 1, a limitation of standards-based curriculum development is that, even as a professional teacher, you may be asked to adhere to a pre-packaged curriculum or scripted textbooks marketed by for-profit corporations to address standards. Presented with such materials claiming to be "proven by research," you may be tempted or encouraged to simply adopt a curriculum in its most literal form, following the written script to the letter. Although you certainly need to plan instruction based on the scope and sequence of your school's existing curriculum, in order to achieve the high expectations called for by the standards, you need to tailor the curriculum to your own knowledge and beliefs and to your students' needs, interests, and abilities. For any curriculum and instruction to be successful, it is essential that you have a sense of ownership over how it is implemented in your classroom.

Therefore, we believe that districts and schools with high expectations for their students should encourage teachers to approach the Common Core State Standards with a spirit of autonomous professionalism. For instance, teachers should be able to make a certain number of text selections that are tailored to their specific classrooms, as opposed to be asked to strictly adhere to a list of mandated texts (remember, the Common Core does not *mandate* any specific texts, although it lists a series of exemplars). At the 2010 Annual Convention of the National Council of Teachers of English, NCTE members supported a resolution strongly supporting teacher decision-making:

The development and adoption of the Common Core State Standards and its inclusion of exemplar texts heightens the concern that the authority of teachers as professionals who make decisions regarding materials and practices in literacy education will be diminished . . . Resolved that the National Council of Teachers of English reaffirm the rights of teachers and their students to draw from many diverse and dynamic sources—not only a list of exemplar texts—in the selection of classroom texts and materials; continue to endorse a school curriculum that honors cultural and socioeconomic backgrounds, language variety, and the interests and needs of the individual student; and continue to support and advocate for the inclusion of teachers at all levels of educational decision-making.

When you have opportunities to modify and supplement your curriculum and design your own instruction, you are able to respond more authentically to your students—for instance, changing course when they seem disengaged or allowing extra time when more depth or practice is needed with a particular concept. Designing curriculum is exciting and important work that requires time and modification based on experience. High-quality curriculum is not static, but is always evolving.

We certainly realize that, particularly during student teaching, you may have limited opportunities to develop your own curriculum. This means that you will need to balance your desire to develop and teach your own curriculum with the constraints and dictates of your cooperating teacher's and school's existing curriculum. However, by developing thoughtful curriculum units prior to student teaching, you can provide your cooperating teacher with concrete evidence of your own ideas. This kind of dialogue may create opportunities to employ or modify curriculum in your student teaching. With growing experience, your ability and opportunity to develop curriculum should continue to expand. Master teachers don't allow supposed financial limitations on purchasing of materials to limit their curriculum; instead they find ways to creatively develop, beg, borrow, and innovate to bring to their students the resources they need for outstanding success.

WHO AM I WORKING WITH IN MY CLASSROOM? THINKING ABOUT STUDENTS' KNOWLEDGE AND EXPERIENCES

As we argued in Chapter 1, the meaning of literacy practices for your students will be specific to the local context in which you teach, your knowledge and passions, your students' prior knowledge and experiences, and the unique purposes and needs that literacy practices fulfill for students in your community.

You can begin by tapping into students' experiences outside of your class. Carol Lee (2007), for instance, suggests that teachers make connections to students' knowledge and experiences by linking the familiar (students' cultural knowledge) to the new (instructional content and ideas you want to teach)—a concept she refers to as "cultural modeling." In her use of "cultural modeling," Lee (2007) drew on her African-American students' experiences with rap lyrics and "signifying"—ritual taunting that involves the use of symbolic meanings. She then drew on her students' experiences to help them interpret the symbolic meanings of figurative language in Toni Morrison's (2004) *Beloved*. Students drew on their knowledge of "signifying" to develop literary interpretations.

You can encourage students to draw on their knowledge and experiences to *frame* classroom events and make connections to their readings. Making these intertextual links addresses the standard that asks students to "analyze how two or more texts address similar themes or topics in order to build knowledge or to compare the approaches the authors take." Understanding issues young adults in your community face might lead you to develop relevant curricular units that begin with resonant ideas and move into various young adult and classic novels, films, writing assignments, and school or community actions that address and provide thoughtful, new, and empowering perspectives on those issues.

Knowledge of your content area and students should be coupled with awareness of what is going on in the larger world. Jeff Paterson, teaching in a rural alternative school, noted that military recruiters frequently visited his students, that many of his students knew soldiers serving in Iraq, and, indeed, that two of his seniors were already married to American soldiers stationed in the Middle East. Drawing on these connections, Jeff designed a curriculum unit addressing literature from the Iraq War, including the young adult novel *Sunrise over Fallujah* (Myers, 2009), blogs from young Iraqis, student research, writing, and film-making (Webb, 2011b).

HOW DOES KNOWLEDGE OF MY STUDENTS INFLUENCE HOW I PLAN? NON-LINEAR PLANNING THROUGH STUDENT COLLABORATION

As you learn more about your students and the issues in their lives, it is useful to consider *how* students engage in learning outside of the classroom. Take, for instance, a student who wants to learn more about how to snowboard. She may interact online with peers for their advice; search for useful sites about snowboarding, seek out how-to resources such as YouTube videos; check map or weather sites about where to snowboard; and discuss questions in online forums about challenges associated with snowboarding. In doing so, she is employing the literacy practice of *relating to others* as a novice snowboarder, as well as producing a text in the form of advice to her other novice peers about snowboarding. She is *framing this event* in terms of her goal of learning more about snowboarding using online tools.

Engaging in these non-linear, online learning processes is a recursive process different from the often structured, sequential learning students experience in traditional classrooms. When students—accustomed to framing learning events in non-linear ways in online spaces—enter the classroom, they may experience a linear, hierarchical, even lock-step model of learning. This model of learning is reflected in the traditional lesson-plan template of learning objectives, anticipatory set, materials, tasks, closure, and assessments. It reflects a teacher-driven way of learning shaped by what Stevens and Dugan (2010) refer to as the "grammar of schooling" based on familiar structures of planning and organizing classrooms.

As a teacher in the 21st Century, you may want to rethink familiar notions of classroom instruction, instead involving students as co-learners operating in a redefined workspace. Rather than simply absorbing knowledge from the teacher and returning that knowledge on tests or papers, students can become creators of knowledge and develop resources for others. Contemporary technology and the Internet make this all the more doable. For example, in Stevens and Dugan's (2010) study, a high school English class was organized as a media lab in which groups of students collaboratively produced four genres of videos: a commercial, public service announcement, interview, and documentary. The media lab learning space fostered collaborative, hands-on learning driven by the goal of producing a winning video shown on the school's TV news. In this class, when students asked the teacher, "What are we doing today?" the teacher asked the students "What are you doing today?" (Stevens & Dugan, 2010, p. 64). The students knew that producing successful videos depended on their ability to effectively collaborate through co-planning with each other and the teacher. This model of "autonomy support" results in increased engagement, motivation, and achievement (Patall, Cooper, & Robinson, 2008). As Alfie Kohn (2010) notes, "What matters is not what we teach; it's what they learn, and the probability of real learning is far higher when the students have a lot to say about both the content and the process" (p. 17).

WHAT DO I WANT MY STUDENTS TO LEARN? SELECTING AND INTEGRATING COMMON CORE STATE STANDARDS TO FORMULATE LEARNING OBJECTIVES

In a standards-based model, planning curriculum and instruction begins by selecting the particular standards that you want your students to learn. With the Common Core State Standards some states have added their own additional 15 percent of standards, so each state's standards may be different. (As previously noted, New York has added a major additional standard related to the cultural aspects of responding to literature, while Minnesota added media/digital literacies standards.) The website for your state's department of education will have information about the Common Core State Standards in your state (@ = State departments of education CCSS sites).

The 6–12 English Language Arts Common Core State Standards are organized according to four basic categories: reading/literature, writing, speaking/listening/media, and language for each 6–12 grade level. In many cases, these standards are similar within the grade-level spans of 6–8, 9–10, and 11–12. You therefore need to refer to the specific grade level with which you are working to address the appropriate standards. At the same time, you also need to recognize that standards assigned to certain grade levels may be either too challenging or not challenging enough given your students' abilities. Moreover, the extent to which your students are able to address certain standards is more a function of the instructional activities you develop than the specific grade level assigned to individual standards.

ACTIVITY: TRANSLATING STANDARDS INTO CURRICULUM AND INSTRUCTION

In planning classroom activities based on addressing certain standards, you'll be translating those standards into curriculum and instruction related to your specific classroom context. To do so, you'll need to identify specific activities that will best serve to implement a standard by unpacking the verbs in a standard to identify those tasks students will perform and the purpose/value for employing those tasks. You also need to select the tools and texts students will use. And, you'll need to formulate directions for, and model, those tasks, the amount of time they'll devote to completing those tasks, and criteria you'll use to evaluate students' learning.

Select a particular grade-level Common Core State Standard based on an actual or imagined classroom/grade level. Then, devise a lesson plan based on your purposes, tasks, tools, texts, directions, modeling, and criteria. For example, for this 8th grade reading standard, "compare and contrast how two or more authors writing about the same topic shape their presentations of key information by emphasizing different evidence or advancing different interpretations of facts," you may focus on the key actions—"compare and contrast" to focus students' analysis of texts with conflicting analysis of the same information or events. You will also need to select texts consistent with 8th graders' interests and prior knowledge, as well as criteria for what constitutes effective use of evidence to support students' comparisons and contrasts of competing texts.

Addressing Grade-by-Grade Learning Progressions

Grade-level-by-grade-level standards are based on a developmental hierarchy of *learning progressions* involving increasingly more complex, sophisticated ways of addressing the core standards. For example, for the core standard related to interpretation of point of view or perspective, "assess how point of view or purpose shapes the content and style of a text," there are increasingly more difficult standards for grades 6–12. The learning progression for this standard begins in the 6th grade with being able to describe point of view in a text leading to describing competing points of view in grade 7 to interpreting how disparities between reader and character perspective result in dramatic irony in grade 8. Then, for grades 9–10, students focus on how an author develops her own perspective or stance in a text, and, for grades 11–12, how authors employ satire, sarcasm, irony, or understatement to convey multiple meanings.

The concept is that, when working with students at particular grade levels, you should be able to draw on these learning progressions to refer back to what students have previously acquired in earlier grades to prepare them for addressing standards at their current grade level. If students are having difficulty achieving their grade-level standard, you may also revert back to earlier-grade standards to create activities based on those earlier standards. If, for example, students are having difficulty contrasting different characters' perspectives at the 8th grade level, you may need to develop activities related to inferring characters' perspectives associated with achieving grade 7 standards.

However, there are a number of problems with the concept of a "learning progressions" continuum that identifies certain standards as appropriate for certain grade levels. This continuum is based on cognitive stage development models that presuppose that, at different age levels, students are cognitively capable or incapable of employing certain literacy practices. For example, based on notions of early adolescents' presumed egocentricity—that they have difficulty adopting perspectives other than their own—assumptions are made about their ability to adopt multiple, alternative perspectives. These cognitive stage models fail to consider how students' ability to employ literacy practices varies according to differences between students, texts, activities, and contexts. For example, students' ability to adopt characters' perspectives may vary according to individual differences within your class as well as differences due to the complexity of a text's language or students' understanding of, or motivation to participate in, your activity. Given this variation, it is difficult to make generalizations about your entire class's ability to address particular standards based on a continuum.

While it may be possible to identify a continuum in a subject such as math, in which students need to have specific knowledge as a prerequisite for solving challenging problems, learning literacy practices in English language arts requires a more holistic, recursive experience. Framing the English language arts curriculum from a literacy practice perspective, we are not presupposing that students' abilities to employ certain literacy practices are specifically or necessarily tied to grade levels. While certain literacy practices such as the ability to critically analyze institutional systems may be difficult for middle school students, this does not necessarily mean that middle school students are not able to engage in critical analysis of institutional systems. In fact, we urge you to never sell short what younger students are able to accomplish.

Assuming that students, based on a certain "learning progression" continuum, may not be able to engage in certain literacy practices may underestimate students' abilities, especially when they are engaged and motivated. Holding high expectations does not mean, for example, that 6th grade teachers should only address "how an author establishes the point of view." Sixth grade teachers need to be aware of the whole range of complexity of meaning, up to and including the 12th grade standard of understanding "various layers of meaning." In English one kind of knowledge does not always lead step-by-step to the next kind of knowledge. While these learning progressions may have logical appeal, they typically have no basis in empirical research and oversimplify students' literacy learning. Indeed, the specific progressions laid out in the standards are not necessarily related to how skills and learning are actually acquired. For instance, suggesting that "dramatic irony" is somehow age appropriate for 8th graders and "taking a stance on a social issue" is age appropriate to 9th or 10th graders has no logical basis. Moreover, the idea that "taking a stance on a social issue" is an intellectually more advanced skill that somehow follows or is dependent on prior knowledge of "dramatic irony" is equally illogical. Students of all ages need to consider how authors take stances on issues and how the knowledge of the reader or audience may differ from the knowledge of characters in a story (dramatic irony). In this sense, we recommend caution in applying learning progressions established by a presumed continuum of development in planning instruction.

Rather than making instructional decisions based on simplistic grade-level-by-grade-level learning progressions, we recommend that you view the entire set of language arts standards holistically and focus on designing those activities or events that you believe are most likely to engage your particular group of students based on their unique needs, knowledge, abilities, and interests. Evoking student motivation by engaging in rich, complex, relevant, and meaningful learning is the best way to set high standards and to meet and exceed the Common Core State Standards.

HOW DO I APPLY DIFFERENT CURRICULUM FRAMEWORKS IN PLANNING INSTRUCTION?

In Chapter 2, we described the different curriculum frameworks that have traditionally shaped English language arts instruction: content, formalist, skills, strategies/processes, and literacy practices. As illustrated in Figure 4.1, adopting a *content* framework means focusing your instruction on knowledge about literature as evident in survey courses or textbooks organized according to national traditions, chronological survey of authors, literary periods, and key texts. Adopting this means a *formalist* framework, organizing instruction around teaching the features of different literary or genre forms, the supposed structure of narrative, or the presumed form of an argumentative, comparison and contrast, or five-paragraph essay. If you adopt a *skills* framework, you will focus on teaching specific skills—word-attack/decoding or inferring the main idea of a text—often in isolation of any larger context. If you adopt a *processes/strategies* framework, you will focus on teaching the cognitive strategies, reading processes of synthesizing the meaning of a text or predicting outcomes, or

Frameworks	Curriculum Focus
content	knowledge about literature
formalist	forms and structures
skills	decoding and comprehension skills
processes/strategies	synthesizing, predicting, stages, etc.
literacy practices	uses of texts and talk for social practices

Figure 4.1 Frameworks/Curriculum Focus

writing processes as a specific set of stages from prewriting to publication. And, if you adopt a *literacy practices* framework, you will be—in contrast to a skills or strategies/processes framework—focusing on how students are writing or using texts to engage in social practices.

You will likely find each of these frameworks operating in any school in which you observe or work, often depending on the standards being emphasized. Teachers may also adopt certain frameworks depending on the students with whom they are working. For example, in thinking about her English instruction, Polly, a 20-year veteran teacher in a suburban school, asks herself, "how do I decide what to teach?" and her answer is "it depends entirely on who my students are" (Brooks, 2010, p. 96).

Given Polly's recognition of differences in her students' interests and needs, rather than simply formulating curriculum in terms of what she believes her students *should learn*, she also considers what she senses her students *want to learn*. This means that, in defining your purposes or goals, you need to go beyond simply thinking about possible activities or topics you want to include in a unit or course to, instead, determining what students may want to learn from engaging in these activities or topics and, how you will gain their passionate commitment meeting and exceeding standards and expectations. Saying that you want your students "to respond to images in a poem" simply states the nature of your activity. You are not defining the larger purpose—why are you doing that activity? To define your purpose or objective, you need to consider *what* students will be learning from responding to the images in a poem—and ask yourself why that learning is important.

At the same time, you will also need to think about *how* your particular group of students may best learn literacy practices in terms of activities or events most likely to foster that learning. For example, to help students understand how images have symbolic meanings, you might have them use Flickr or Google Images to find images evoked by a poem they are reading and then have them describe how and why they selected those images based on their readings. Such images and explanations could be hyperlinked to the poem as part of a multilayered response.

HOW CAN MY STUDENTS LEARN LITERACY PRACTICES? LEARNING LITERACY PRACTICES THROUGH SOCIALIZATION, IMITATION, AND REFLECTION

The meaning and use of literacy practices is specific to certain situations or events. Gee (2008) defines this sort of learning as "situated cognition." For example, students learn that certain specific literacy practices are associated with auditioning for a school play. They know that they need to be familiar with the play, the role they want to assume, and how to read aloud certain lines associated with that role.

Learning literacy practices in these situations or events is supported by socialization into communities of practice—groups of people who share a common interest or passion for addressing certain issues, topics, or themes (Wenger, 1999). What distinguishes a community of practice from simply a group or network of friends is that the community shares a strong commitment to a "shared domain of interest" (Wenger, 1999). For example, imagine that a group of young people is playing *World of Warcraft* together as a team. To do so, they acquire certain shared practices through active participation in playing the game, sharing game "cheats," and reflecting on how to cope with challenges or losses. Through conversing about their experiences, they develop stories and descriptions as a shared knowledge base for effective game playing. And, veteran members provide newer members with this knowledge to socialize them into membership in the community.

When you construct your classroom as a community of practice, you are shifting from an expert/novice model in which students are dependent on you, to a more collaborative model in which you and your students are mutually grappling with issues, themes, or topics. You can do this by sharing your own interests and passions as well as determining those of your students in order to set instructional goals for your teaching. Your curriculum then would be not simply "teacher-centered" or "student-centered," but focused instead on identifying those literacy practices that you hope your students will acquire through active participation in events in your classroom as a unique community of practice (@ = Learning in communities of practice).

For example, in her 9th grade English class at Roosevelt High School in Minneapolis, Rebecca Oberg fostered a positive sense of community (Beach & Dockter, 2010). Roosevelt is dedicated to a digital media program (DigMe) where students in all classes across the curriculum:

- Develop and use critical thinking abilities
- Participate in daily reading, writing, analyzing, and discussion activities
- Complete exercises to stretch their creativity
- Design and produce projects which demonstrate learning in a variety of ways, often involving the use of digital media tools (Digital Media Program, 2011)

Rebecca encouraged students to assume leadership roles in computer use. She provided positive feedback that enhanced confidence and agency. And, she built social relationships with students so that they were comfortable working with her. For example, one student who initially adopted a defiant, withdrawn stance, by chatting with Rebecca during lunch hour shifted her stance to becoming an active class member. Students in this class, with the support of the teacher, took on particular identities constituted by their uses of language practices specific to the context of their community of practice.

Rebecca also fostered students' sense of ownership by having them create their own personalized blogs in which they added images, videos, links, and color, and changed names and templates. Students used their blogs to share images of themselves with friends around the school and engage in the social practice of *networking* with peers in ways that served to *define their identities* within the DigMe program. Ms. Oberg also continually modeled literacy practices, *showing* students *how* to engage in activities within their "zone of proximal development" (ZPD) (Vygotsky, 1986)—the space in which they are able to perform certain tasks easily and attempt to perform complex tasks with further assistance—versus simply *telling* them what to do (see Figure 4.2). She demonstrated ways of relating to and collaborating with others through *how* she interacted with students and *how* she responded to challenges in the classroom.

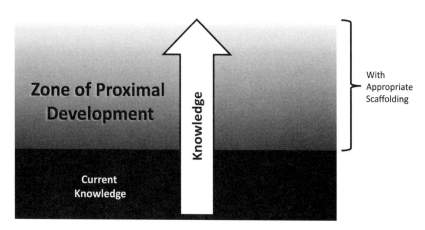

Figure 4.2 Zone of Proximal Development

Imitation of Others' Uses of Literacy Practices

Within communities of practice, new members observe veterans using literacy practices to accomplish certain goals in certain events. For example, when you model the use of open-ended inquiry questions in talking about literature, students may observe and imitate you, learning how to construct, pose, and consider inquiry questions related to literature and other kinds of texts. Likewise, students will observe and imitate one another. You may, therefore, want to assign students with particular kinds of expertise to serve as peer mentors or tutors to assist other students. These kinds of peer mentoring experiences can benefit both parties.

Students can also imitate others' writing or video/artistic productions—what Dyson (2010) refers to as "copying" from popular culture or the media—a practice evident in hip-hop sampling or remixing of online texts. Rather than discourage such copying as representing a lack of originality or potential plagiarism, you can show students how writers, artists, or musicians often draw on others' work in creating their own work. Publishing outstanding student work both on paper and/or on the web creates models that future students and classes can learn from and imitate.

Metacognitive Reflection on Uses of Literacy Practices

As your students experiment with literacy practices, they need opportunities to reflect on what they are doing. For example, if a student has difficulty reading her lines in a class readers' theater enactment of a dramatic work, she may then reflect on reasons for her difficulty relative to the situation. Based on this reflection, students then recognize the need to make changes in their uses of literacy practices in the future.

In doing so, they are reflecting on *"uptake"*—the effects or reactions of others to their uses of speech acts or social genres (Freadman, 2002). For example, students engaged in a mock trial or online role play in your classroom attempt to persuade others to accept their position on a certain issue. As they do so, they may reflect on their audiences' responses or "uptake" to their positions to determine if they have been convincing. They might recognize, for example, that they needed to appeal more to their audience's positions, beliefs, or needs, as well as provide more concrete supporting evidence for their own positions. Students are more likely to engage in this reflection if you provide them with opportunities to debrief with one another and consider which tactics and specific arguments were most effective.

Students may reflect on the *significance* of their use of certain literacy practices—whether or not engaging in a certain practice is a big deal or important to them. Actions that may not seem important from an adult perspective are often highly significant to an adolescent. The fact that a relatively shy, reserved student can perform in a classroom poetry slam activity and receive positive responses from peers may be highly significant. Or, the fact that a student interviewed a grandparent for a family history project and uncovered new information about that grandparent's life may be highly significant. Considering the consequences of successfully employing a literacy practice can help students recognize that it has impacted their sense of self-worth, thus fostering their motivation. Students may also reflect on *appropriateness* of their use of literacy practices within specific social contexts. Certain social contexts call for a degree of formality that others do not—wedding ceremonies, business meetings, court hearings, job interviews, etc. People who do not recognize that they are operating in a more formal context may employ literacy practices that violate contextual norms and seem inappropriate to audiences. For example, in the television series *The Wire* (Simon, 2002–2008), the head of a drug gang, Stringer Bell, demands that his gang members follow Robert's Rules of Order during a meeting of the gang. When one gang member stands up and starts shouting, Bell declares that the member is "out of order," and the incident serves as a humorous commentary on differences between language use in formal and informal contexts. In studying various kinds of writing found in print and digital forms, students can begin to judge the tone, voice, and formality of conventions appropriate for various forums and audiences. As we discuss in Chapter 11, on language use, students whose home language differs from the language of power and broader communication need to learn how to code-switch.

Acquiring Metalanguage for Reflection

Reflection can provide students a way to understand how literacy practices develop over time. To help students engage in reflection on their uses of literacy practices, you can model the use of metalanguage and ask relevant questions. For example, based on the concept of a pedagogy of "rhetorical dexterity," Shannon Carter (2006) has college composition students examine notions of, and experiences with, literacy in their different communities of practice. Students address questions related to their uses of literacies in social contexts:

1. How do I put literacy to use in my own life among people that matter to me in places I know and understand, especially in those places and

among those people where I am taken most seriously, as a meaningful
member with ideas that matter?

2.   How can I reuse (and reclaim) these strategies in new places and for
new people who may have different needs and expectations for their
lives and for their communities? (p. 102)

Students also reflect on how they learned these literacies:

What are the activities that make up a community of practice with which
you are deeply familiar? How did you learn them? What identities are
constructed via these activities? In other words, how is who you are
shaped by your experiences within this community of practice? What
artifacts are produced via the activities of this community of practice and
how might those compare with the artifacts produced in academic
communities of practice? (p.102)

How to plan classroom activities to implement the Common Core State
Standards through literacy practices is the focus of the next chapter.

HOW DO I SELECT AND ASSIGN TEXTS BASED ON CONSIDERATION OF STUDENT INTERESTS/ ABILITY AND TEXT COMPLEXITY? WEIGHING DIFFERENT FACTORS IN SELECTING AND ASSIGNING TEXTS

In developing curriculum and instruction to meet the Common Core
State Standards, you should have opportunities to select relevant and
effective texts. In some schools, you may be asked to employ a mass-
marketed textbook supposedly geared to specific grade levels and coded
to specific standards. Although these textbooks can provide convenient
starting points, it is important that you approach standardized textbooks
with knowledge of their limitations.

Textbooks are manufactured to sell and generate profits. National
textbooks companies are big businesses dominated by an increasingly
small number of publishers. (For example, the highly profitable Pearson
Publishing owns Allyn & Bacon, Heinemann, Longman, Scott Foresman,
Simon & Schuster, Penguin, and Prentice Hall, among others.) Many
textbooks are organized by old-fashioned approaches to literature and
the language arts (see Chapter 2) that are no longer supported by university scholarship or expressive of current understandings of literacy.

Textbooks may include a wide diversity of excerpts (rather than complete texts) that do not cohere around meaningful themes or issues. They are often censored (including Shakespeare's *Romeo and Juliet* and *Macbeth*!). The questions and activities provided by these textbooks may not be consistent with your own goals and plans. The sales imperative means that textbooks are designed to be acceptable to highly conservative boards of education in those few large states that adopt these at the state level, in particular Texas. (For instance, the former chairman of the Texas state Board of Education, Don McLeroy, is a creationist who believes teaching of evolution is inconsistent with Christianity and argues that "we need to start teaching our children about the Biblical origins of America" [Bernier, 2010]). So textbooks avoid controversy— yet it is exactly controversy that energizes the study of reading and writing, and engagement in literacy practices.

Textbook publishers have jumped on the Common Core State Standards bandwagon—look to see old familiar materials now "aligned" and cross-linked with the new standards. These textbooks make it appear that based on "research" the "experts" have thoroughly figured out what your students need to learn. But ask yourself: Will following this mass distribution textbook chapter by chapter really be the best way to engage my students, fire their creativity, and challenge them to exceed expectations?

Even if marketed and pre-digested, many textbooks do contain valuable and useful material. Therefore, we suggest that if you and your colleagues are expected to use a textbook, you carefully select pieces that will connect to the literacy events and themes that will engage your particular students and are consistent with your particular goals and plans. You will likely not want to follow the textbook in the order in which it is presented. As you gain further experience, you will want to supplement textbook excerpts with a wide range of other materials including not only traditional texts, written documents, and print media, but also digital forms, that will add depth, breadth, relevance, controversy, and meaning to your curriculum. Finding supplementary texts has become much easier for teachers as more non-copyrighted literary texts have become available online. And the "Fair Use" doctrine gives teachers more latitude than others when it comes to copyright for educational purposes (Aufderheide & Jaszi, 2011). For instance, you might search the many texts available on Google Books (http://books.google.com); Bartelby (http://bartelby.com); Literature archives (http://www.literature.org); or Poets.org (http://poets.org). One advantage of using online texts is that your students can share their responses to texts using annotation tools such as Diigo.com and make links to materials from their blogs and wikis. Using online texts and tools allows you to select from a range of different materials, combining literary texts with nonfiction, videos, and images so that students perceive connections across different modes. Finally, the breadth of texts available online can provide a means for student selection of texts, indeed for student creation of textbooks, that they see as consistent with the issue, topic, or theme your class is studying (@ = Using online texts).

In selecting texts, you may encounter censorship issues. If you select a text that is considered controversial in your community, you might encounter parental objections. Some of these objections stem from the assumption that reading controversial texts leads students to adopt objectionable behaviors or problematic beliefs. For example, parents sometimes worry that reading about drug use will lead students to take drugs. When you select texts, it is important to weigh these understandable (though often ungrounded) concerns against your goals as a teacher. Preparing students to become democratic citizens—a goal of the Common Core State Standards—means tackling controversial questions and weighing various perspectives on difficult issues. There are many resources for teachers facing censorship questions, including the NCTE Anti-Censorship Center (http://www.ncte.org/action/anti-censorship), the Electronic Freedom Foundation, the American Library Association, the American Civil Liberties Union, and teacher unions including the National Education Association and the American Federation of Teachers (@ = Coping with censorship).

In responding to censorship challenges, you are not alone. Many districts have established policies for parents to challenge materials and following those policies typically helps protect teacher decision-making. In meeting and exceeding the standards, you will sometimes need to take risks. Thoughtful risk-taking is necessary for growth, learning, and exceeding the standards. We believe that the greatest risk is self-censorship—an avoidance of risks that comes out of fear. We are not suggesting that taking risks should jeopardize your career. Instead we believe it means choosing texts that you think matter, that meet your objectives, and that you are willing to defend. When you select texts with these goals in mind, you will be ready to rationally and passionately provide reasoning for your use of controversial texts if concerns are raised in your community.

Selecting Texts Based on the Common Core State Standards "Complexity" Criteria

A major focus of the Common Core State Standards involves encouraging students to read increasingly complex texts as they advance through grade levels. The goal of this focus is to help students to "read independ-ently the kinds of complex texts commonly found in college and careers." Specifically, the standards ask that students "read complex texts inde-pendently, proficiently, and fluently, sustaining concentration, moni-toring comprehension, and, when useful, rereading."

Designers of the Common Core State Standards believe that college success requires reading of complex texts, and they cite research indi-cating a presumed decline in the complexity of texts and in the number of nonfiction texts students are asked to read. They propose a set of criteria for assessing text complexity based on qualitative, quantitative, and reader/context features and set forward different "grade band" recommendations for levels of text complexity for grades 6–8, 9–10, and 11–12. For example, for the 6th to 12th grades, it is generally recom-mended that 70 percent of the texts students read will be at a complexity level for those grade levels, with some texts being even more difficult and requiring some instructional support.

We certainly agree that students need to learn to read "complex" texts. We applaud the Common Core designers for recognizing the importance of contextual factors shaping "complexity." However, we also believe that, given the highly subjective nature of individual students' transactional experiences with texts, it may be difficult to derive any valid and reliable measure of grade band "complexity." A text may have high or low appeal for students based on their own interests, needs, and cultural backgrounds. For example, some of Walter Dean Myers' young adult novels that are set in urban neighborhoods may have high appeal for students living in those neighborhoods and low appeal for students living in suburban neighborhoods, and may be easier for one group of students to read than for another.

Ultimately you will need to decide, based on a host of factors, which, if any, of the "complex texts" on the Common Core list of recommended texts are appropriate for your particular students. Faulkner's (2000) *As I Lay Dying*, for instance, not only is a difficult text, but also fails to be engaging for most high school students. The novel addresses a narrow social group in the South and family issues specific to that context and historical period. It may lack relevance for students who have little prior knowledge of the context. As a teacher, you will need to balance the benefits of teaching a text like this one against the potential frustrations that students may face in trying to make sense of it.

In a similar vein, we want to point out that determining appropriate texts for your students cannot be adequately accomplished by relying on their "grade-level" reading ability. For example, knowing that Sue, a 9th grader, is reading at a "5th grade level" as determined by scores on standardized reading tests does not provide you with enough information to assess Sue's reading abilities. These reading level categories do not consider variations in students' engagement with certain genres and modes of texts, their prior knowledge about a given text's content, or their purposes for reading.

Gaining a true sense of your students' reading abilities requires both taking the time to get to know your students and also a certain amount of trial and error. If time permits, you might consider surveying your students and meeting individually with them to begin to understand their interests and reading preferences. You might begin your school year with a range of shorter texts such as poetry, short stories, essays—of course connected to meaningful literacy events and themes—that you can use to gauge how well the content engages your students' interests and to what extent the complexity of each text serves to challenge, but not frustrate, your students. Activities like these will give you information for determining the kinds of texts that are at the right level of complexity for your students.

Moreover, differences in students' understanding or engagement with a text are also a function of the kinds of activities you develop for responding to that text, activities that themselves may vary in their complexity (Jacobs, 2010). For example, while the Cinderella fairy tale is not a complex text, having students apply a poststructuralist or feminist analysis to Cinderella is a relatively complex task. In planning activities, you should therefore be considering the complexity of both the text *and* the activity for responding to that text relative to your students' "zone of proximal development" (Vygotsky, 1986).

There is a great deal you can and should do to support students reading complex texts. Previewing the context and content, reading initial or difficult portions of the text aloud, having students write about what they read, preparing knowledge of key terms or vocabulary, reading sections together from the data projector, teaching reading strategies and modeling your own, providing knowledge of the genre of texts, using teacher- and student-created study questions, incorporating readers' theater events, creating scripts, and using drama activities—these and so many other techniques can help your students with difficult texts. Yet remember that, above all, what creates student success with difficult texts is having a meaningful and relevant curriculum so that students clearly understand why a difficult text is worth the effort. As this book argues, it is the literacy practices and events you organize that will develop your students' passion and carry their reading forward.

Thoughtful teaching includes recognizing complexity—there is no one "right way" to develop engaging, challenging instruction. It is therefore important for you to seek out and learn from veteran teachers in your building and district who are employing more innovative instruction; they have an important role to play as mentors and supporters as you begin your career.

WHAT LITERACY PRACTICES WILL MY STUDENTS BE USING TO ADDRESS THESE COMMON CORE STATE STANDARDS? UNPACKING AND TRANSLATING STANDARDS DOCUMENTS

Unpacking and translating the Common Core State Standards involves identifying those literacy practices that are relevant to certain standards. For example, one of the reading/literature standards relates to character development: "analyze in detail where, when, why, and how events, ideas, and characters develop and interact over the course of a text." To address this standard, students may employ a number of different literacy practices. Characters develop through constructing or enacting different identities in different contexts or through relating to others. And, characters develop through resisting or critiquing status quo systems, leading to attempts to redesign systems. For example, Rebecca's 9th grade students studied *The House on Mango Street* (Cisneros, 1991) by reflecting on how the main character, Esperanza, developed through enacting different identities in her interactions with various characters and through negotiating and overcoming conflicts related to the existing realities of poverty in her Chicago Latino neighborhood (Beach & Dockter, 2010).

Transfer of Familiar to Less Familiar Literacy Practices: The Example of Framing Events

To help students understand social practices and how to frame events, Rebecca developed a connection between the students' community and the novel *The House on Mango Street*. She worked with the geography teacher so that in geography class students learned to gather data from city databases about their neighborhood's crime and employment rates, level of education, schools, retail establishments, public transportation, and parks. Next, students reflected on the following questions: "What is a neighborhood? How do neighborhoods change over time? and How does the individual impact his/her neighborhood?"

Students then transferred their experience with the literacy practice of framing their own neighborhood to *framing* the goals, plans, roles, norms, and beliefs in the Mango Street neighborhood in the novel. The transfer of this literacy practice aided students in noticing instances when cultural norms regarding gender, class, and race influenced and limited characters, leading Esperanza to perceive both the strengths and narrowness of her neighborhood. As they analyzed the database material in their geography class, students engaged in the literacy practice of *critiquing systems*. Understanding the economic forces shaping lives in their own neighborhoods, such as institutional poverty, unemployment, and racism, equipped students with tools for critiquing similar systems at play in the Mango Street neighborhood.

Rebecca also fostered use of the literacy practice of *collaboratively sharing* both their interpretations of *The House on Mango Street* and their analysis of their neighborhoods on "neighborhood blogs" (via Blogger), as well as the literacy practice of *constructing identities*. In their blogs, students responded to prompts designed to foster reflection on their identities as members of their neighborhoods:

•   How do environment and neighborhood shape our identity? What identities, if any, are permanent and which do we have the power to change? What roles do neighborhood and community play in shaping who we become?
•   What is your identity? Make a top 10 list of words to describe.
•   What is your neighborhood? Make a top 10 list of words to describe.

As the culmination of this unit, to foster use of the literacy practices of *identifying issues*, *critiquing systems*, and *redesigning systems*, students completed an "oral history" project and interviewed a neighbor asking questions such as "What are the best parts of your neighborhood and why? What needs improvement in your neighborhood and why? How have you impacted your neighborhood and how has your neighborhood impacted you? How has your neighborhood changed over time?" Students also created interview questions relating to their neighbor's social life, education, economic forces, occupations, avocations, skills, passions, political roles, ethnic/cultural identities, and personal lives. Students then wrote a two-page reflection essay on what they learned from the interview, including a comparison of their own perspective with their interviewee's perspective on their neighborhood by drawing on their analysis of database information in their social studies class.

In her teaching, Rebecca was consistently translating standards into literacy practices that would engage her students and foster a high level of learning.

CASE STUDY: RIC SHAHIN'S HALLWAY (PLANNING)

In this chapter, we've described different components for planning instruction. The challenge that remains is how to use these components to create engaging classroom activities.

This case study calls upon you to help social studies teacher Ric Shahin, as he prepares to teach an English class for the first time in 20 years. You will learn about the context of Ric's situation as you watch and listen to him speak about this new class entitled "Current Language and Literature," the demographics of the class, and his beliefs about teaching English. After choosing a current work of literature to anchor a unit for the course, you will then design a unit around this text that corresponds with Ric's vision and that you believe will engage his students. In designing this curriculum, you will work to employ literacy practices that align with Ric's aims for the course, as well as your beliefs and ideas about such a course.

Please find two or three peers and go to the LiteraryWorlds.org site and the *Teaching to Succeed* link to engage in this case study for Chapter 4.

PART II

Implementing and Exceeding the Common Core State Standards

CHAPTER 5

Interpreting Nonfiction/ Informational Texts

CHAPTER OVERVIEW

Teaching Reading Literacy Practices
Purposes for Reading: Framing Texts within Curricular Contexts
Students' Self-Concepts as Readers
Addressing the Standards for Reading of Social Studies and Science
Fostering Reading Literacy Practices through Integrating Reading, Writing, and Talking
Interpretation as Critical Inquiry
Learning Online Reading Literacy Practices
Case Study: Mr. Plot-a-long's Hallway (Teaching Reading)

One of the major shifts in the Common Core State Standards for secondary English language arts teachers is an increased focus on nonfiction, informational texts—essays, reports, articles, historical and cultural documents, blog posts, reviews, etc. In this chapter we provide strategies to teach your students the kind of close and careful reading of language, ideas, and arguments that are required by the Common Core State Standards. We will show you why knowledge of literacy practices is essential to teaching reading at a high level of complexity and we will explain and illustrate how to effectively integrate nonfiction and informational texts into a meaningful language arts curriculum.

All teachers share in the task of teaching reading. Each discipline or content area has its own types of texts, vocabularies, organizational structures, forms of argument, and necessary background knowledge. The Common Core State Standards recognize the importance of reading across the curriculum and provide additional reading standards for social studies and science.

Reading is a complex process. It involves not only decoding words or understanding sentences, but also drawing on prior knowledge, recognizing and interpreting textual forms, analyzing arguments, inferring ideas, and integrating new concepts with previous understandings. Readability studies by Edward Fry (1977) and others establish textual difficulty as a measure of the length of sentences and the length (number of syllables) of words. While this kind of information about a text is a factor to consider in determining its difficulty, equally or more important is your students' prior knowledge of and interest in the subject of the reading and the context in which your students read. While we want students to be able to understand texts with long words and sentences, the Common Core State Standards point us toward a more complex understanding of arguments, issues, and questions.

Constructivist Learning Theory

New knowledge develops in relationship to what we already know. Students are not blank slates that teachers simply write on, nor are they empty vessels that information from texts can be poured into. Student prior knowledge shapes the way reading is understood, and new knowledge from reading, or any source, influences the way previously ideas are interpreted. This process of building new knowledge in relation to existing knowledge reflects a constructivist theory of learning—knowledge is not "out there" as some package to be delivered, but instead is continually being made in relation to what is already known (@ = Constructivist learning theories).

We therefore posit the need to shift the focus of reading instruction from simple comprehension of texts to uses of reading for constructing knowledge through building connections between people and texts. For example, because their region of the country experienced more extreme weather patterns—high incidents of cold and hot temperatures, as well as more storms—a group of 8th grade students studied the relationships between climate change and extreme weather patterns. Most of the students knew a few things about climate change—that average temperatures have been rising and that the Arctic and Antarctic ice packs are melting—and they had experienced extreme weather patterns in their region, but they knew little about any relationship between the two: is climate change related to more weather patterns, or are these weather patterns occurring because of other factors? Students had limited knowledge of the scientific approaches to studying such relationships;

that determining a scientific relationship requires empirical evidence that demonstrates either a statistical correlation or a causal effect.

One initial step in helping students investigate weather patterns involved finding relevant reports on this issue—empirical reports that went beyond personal opinion or experience. This required students to activate relevant prior knowledge of keywords or topics for searching online. It also required students to know which databases or sites to access to find these reports.

As the students read reports on the relationship between global warming and extreme weather patterns, their teacher asked them to share their prior knowledge and continually make explicit what they were finding in their research on a wiki. Students were 1) defining what they already knew, and 2) sharing what they knew for the benefit of others. The teacher also modeled this process for the students by having them go to the relevant Wikipedia entries on the topics of weather and climate change. By making explicit their prior knowledge, students were then able to identify new knowledge that built upon and challenged their prior knowledge. As students acquired new information from their reading, they added that new information to the wiki, noting instances in which their new knowledge built upon or confirmed their existing knowledge and instances in which their new knowledge conflicted with or contradicted existing knowledge.

As students built their shared knowledge, they noticed certain consistent patterns from their readings that suggested that different scientists agree that there in fact may be a relationship between climate change and more extreme weather patterns.

In English language arts the possibilities for applying this shift toward the collaborative creation of public knowledge are endless. In the 21st Century, students can create a wide variety of relevant informational texts, including websites, wikis, blogs, videos, Prezis, podcasts, VoiceThreads, or contributions to sites such as Thinkquest.

Connecting Literary and Informational Texts According to Themes or Issues

Given the fact that most English teachers are accustomed to teaching primarily literary texts, the easiest way to integrate informational texts is to develop thematic units for literary works that call for an exploration of historical and cultural contexts, as well as ethical, political, philosophical, and controversial questions, through the reading of nonfiction and informational texts. You can expect your students to engage in truly in-depth thinking when you are engaging them with a thematic curriculum that puts literary works and connected informational texts into dialogue with each other. Informational texts that could be important to your units include historical documents, news articles, essays, editorials, speeches, biographies, autobiographies, social science research, advertisements, documentaries, websites, Wikipedia articles, blogs, and more. Remember that still images, films, and podcasts are all forms of informational texts; in our media-saturated society, language arts students need to learn to critically read and creatively write these genres as well as more traditional print forms. Students need to learn how to engage in research and to find, evaluate, and utilize texts relevant to themes or topics they are studying.

TEACHING READING LITERACY PRACTICES

All of the specific Common Core State Standards for analyzing key ideas and details, craft and structure, and the integration of knowledge and ideas can be brought to bear on both literary and informational texts. Putting multiple works together into a coordinated and comparative curriculum facilitates engagement in the literacy practices of *synthesizing and connecting texts*, *critiquing and representing issues*, and *formulating effective arguments*. The standards urge teachers to consider returning to founding documents of American history, documents that address themes of liberty, justice, and fairness for all. Situating literary texts in a thematic curriculum rich with closely related informational texts facilitates critical inquiry, opens questions for debate and controversy, and prepares young people for democratic participation and national and world citizenship (@ = General reading literacy practices).

Teaching in a small town on the shores of Lake Michigan, Tracy Becker developed a 12th grade English language arts course around Thomas Friedman's (2005) book, *The World is Flat: A Brief History of the 21st Century*. Friedman argues that globalization caused by historical events and new technologies has created a world economy that is more than ever a "level playing field." Tracy explained:

To jump start our year and first unit, students will be introduced to *The World is Flat*. In brief, it suggests we are all living co-dependently as countries, where connections are continually made all over the world. Because we are in a time where we can consider our world to be "flat," voices from around the world are important to our social, political, and economic understanding and outlook as future leaders.

After Tracy's students closely read Friedman's complex text and considered its rhetoric, they engaged in a number of explorations to more deeply understand his ideas and how they might be relevant to understanding world literature. On the website Tracy created about the class (@ = Tracy's website for teaching *The World is Flat*), she emphasized that:

Each unit specifically addresses a social justice issue within our world today, preparing students to be more compassionate, empathetic, culturally aware, and attuned to a world that is more connected now than ever before . . . Ultimately, it is the aim of the course to educate global citizens, to prepare them for a future they can both understand and help lead.

The first unit, which she called "Voices from the Middle," involved a study of diverse texts—literary, informational, and visual—from the Middle East. The students all read *Baghdad Burning: Girl Blog from Iraq* (Riverbend, 2005), a collection of blog posts made by a 24-year-old young woman in Iraq starting four months after the American invasion. This collection provides insight into the experience of the Iraq War from the point of view of an Iraqi family. A work like *Baghdad Burning* creates openings for many additional informational texts. It also illustrates the power and impact of blogging, as Riverbend's blog was read and commented on by people around the world.

Reading this book, Tracy's students began their own blogs, connected to one another by a class "blog roll" that made it easy to respond to each other. Tracy's school, in an experiment to save money on textbooks, provided all her students with Apple iPads, but any student with web access could easily create a blog. Blogs began as a form of web commentary, a place for linking to and writing about news and events on the web. However, Tracy's goal in creating blogs for her class was to have her students respond to their readings, and link to issues in the news and background information that could be found on the Internet—just the right kind of work for a blog format (and a further illustration of Friedman's argument about technology-based connections). Going far beyond simply turning in a paper to the teacher, the student blogs became a resource for others, both commenting on and adding to information accessible on the web. As literacy practices, participation in the blog assignment let the students *frame events* as they situated the readings they were doing in historical and political contexts. They also allowed each student to establish and design their own web presence, thus *constructing texts* and *enacting an identity*. As the blogs were linked and allowed for commentary from fellow students and readers from around the world, they aided students in *relating to and collaborating with others* as they responded and created new knowledge.

After reading *Baghdad Burning*, Tracy's students formed literature circles and read a number of recent Middle Eastern texts, including *Rooftops of Tehran* (Seraji, 2009) (Iran); *War in the Land of Egypt* (Al-Qa'id, 1997); *A Thousand Splendid Suns* (Hosseini, 2008) (Afghanistan); *Year of the Elephant* (Abouzeid, 2009) (Morocco); and *Five Years of My Life: An Innocent Man in Guantanamo* (Kurnaz, 2009). Middle school teachers eager to have their students learn about the Middle East could choose young adult texts such as *Habibi* (Nye, 1999) and *Under the Persimmon Tree* (Staples, 2008), or graphic novels such as *Persepolis: The Story of a Childhood* (Satrapi, 2004) and *Palestine* (Sacco, 2002). These books raise issues that Tracy's students explored in groups, in online research and study of additional informational texts, and in their blogs. Students (and teachers) participating in this kind of curriculum are in a better position to engage in discussion, debate, and analysis about conflicts and transformations in the Middle East, as well as American involvement in the region, an important topic especially for high school students eligible for military service (Webb, 2011b).

As Tracy's students moved on to another related unit, they continued to explore informational and literary texts in a useful way. Friedman's book describes many economic changes that are impacting America and the global economy, such as "outsourcing," "supply chaining," and business collaboration. Tracy's students examined these concepts by looking at a quintessentially American enterprise, the fast food industry.

Her students read *Fast Food Nation: The Dark Side of the All-American Meal* by Eric Schlosser (2001), carefully analyzed its arguments, considered related issues, and compared and contrasted what they found with Upton Sinclair's (2004) classic 1906 muckraking novel, *The Jungle. Fast Food Nation* is compelling investigative journalism interesting to high school students, who not only consume fast food but also work in the industry. Schlosser examines the evolution and marketing of fast food, the exploitation of teenagers, the conditions of meatpacking, the use of immigrant workers, and the globalization of the fast food industry. The book has spawned a film of the same name, and other important films about the health and economics of the food industry including *Super Size Me* and *Food, Inc.* There is also a young adult version of *Fast Food Nation*, called *Chew on This* (Wilson & Schlosser, 2006). For middle school students, *Chew on This* could be combined with other reports, essays, and documents about young adults and eating. Given the crisis of overweight teens, youth-onset diabetes, anorexia, and bulimia, it is valuable for middle school and high school students to have class time devoted to questions of healthy eating and corporate food marketing.

Tracy described her students' study of *The Jungle* (Sinclair, 2004) and how the unit led to a service learning project:

As this book closely aligns with the obvious theme of corruption and capitalistic greed within the food industry, students will also start to explore the inequalities and struggles of working-class immigrants, both yesterday and today. Following in the footsteps of the main character Jurgis Rudkus, students will uncover what it means to stand for change and begin their own projects that center on social justice.

In this service project Tracy's students selected an issue they had read about in the course. Such service projects can become service learning when linked with curriculum and tied to analysis and reflection. Tracy explained:

Feeling propelled and inspired by something they have read throughout the year, students will develop and refine research questions that center upon social justice. Students will choose literature they find relevant to their passion and study, and create a project to address a specific issue. Students will analyze how their project has led them to better understand the texts addressed in our course and share their learning with each other.

Following the Common Core State Standards, Tracy integrated informational texts into her course in ways that significantly enriched the study of literature and English language arts. Her curriculum was relevant to important questions in the world and to the lives of her students. Informational texts are not some kind of "add-on" unit, but need to be meaningfully embedded in the curriculum. Rather than starting with the idea of teaching a specific comprehension skill, Tracy began by thinking about her students' interests and what she wanted them to learn about the world through uses of literacy practices, such as careful reading of both literary and informational texts in the interest of investigating relevant and important subjects.

PURPOSES FOR READING: FRAMING TEXTS WITHIN CURRICULAR CONTEXTS

Tracy's class illustrates one way to build a context for meaningful reading. The meaning of nonfiction or informational texts is not "out there," nor is it "in" the text. Students read to acquire information or ideas relevant to certain purposes, and they employ the literacy practice of *framing* the meaning of texts within events or contexts. For example, if students want to find out how to use GarageBand to remix some music, they go online and search for directions. The meaning of those directions lies in the transaction between the student and the text. The meaning is influenced by the particular knowledge, beliefs, interests, and needs that students bring to the text, as well as the event or context in which students are reading the text. If students know little about GarageBand or about remixing music, the meaning of these directions will be different than if they have extensive experience with GarageBand or remixing music.

Recognizing the Importance of Context as a Way of Knowing

In considering the value of nonfiction/informational texts, in the past we typically focused on their value in terms of the information they provided—the *what* of the content in these texts; what we could learn about difficulties in the Iraq War from reading about that war, for instance. However, with the advent of digital information sources that readily provide such *what* information, there is a shift towards the importance of knowing *where* to obtain certain relevant information from online sites (Thomas & Brown, 2011). In other words, it is important to consider the context that is created for acquiring and understanding knowledge. As Thomas and Brown (2011) note, "Where one chooses to post, where one links to, or where one is linked from does not just serve as a locus for finding content. It becomes part of the content itself" (p. 94). Moreover, rather than assuming that context is fixed and stable, by altering context through remixing or creating multimodal texts, or by recontextualizing content by putting that content in a different context—for example, placing videos in the context of a parody—your students can learn to put attention on the context itself as central to acquiring knowledge. Again, Thomas and Brown (2011) explain:

Meaning, therefore, now arise[s] not from interpretation (what something means) but from contextualization (where something has meaning). The process of making and remaking context is, in itself, an act of imaginative play (what we might call the "how" of information). Understanding that process and being able to participate in it also forms the basis for evaluation in the twenty-first century. (pp. 95–96)

In asking your students to focus on the process of contextualizing or framing texts you will be helping your students to develop a clear sense of purpose for responding to texts. Students will learn to consider *where* to discover new knowledge through making connections with people and/or texts, by posing questions such as "What do I now know about a topic or issue? What do I want to learn more about related to this topic or issue? Where are the best places to discover or learn more about this issue?" Having a clear purpose also motivates students to want to read a text, because they are seeking out information that they consider useful.

STUDENTS' SELF-CONCEPTS AS READERS

Defining reading to learn as an active process of constructing knowledge also requires that students perceive themselves as capable of constructing knowledge and making connections through their reading. To do so, students need to develop a positive self-concept of themselves as people for whom reading is a fulfilling, and sometimes entertaining, experience.

However, with the increased use of mandated standardized reading tests, students have been labeled as "struggling" or "striving," or as reading "above" or "below" grade levels, in ways that may undermine their development of positive self-concepts as readers. These labels presuppose that "reading ability" is a singular phenomenon that applies to all different types of texts and genres employed across different fields or disciplines. However, students' "reading abilities" may vary considerably according to differences in the types of texts and genres they most frequently read, resulting in differences in their knowledge of text or genre conventions, as well as differences between the ability to read print versus online texts. Acknowledging differences in students' abilities to read across texts and genres challenges the singular, normative notion of "reading ability" as based on a reading test score. It is also important to consider that students' knowledge about certain topics or issues influences their "reading abilities." If test items are based on particular topics, discourses, or vocabulary about which students have no knowledge, then they will not do well on those items.

The reading ability labels we have been discussing need to be understood as products of an educational discourse that adopts normative notions of "reading ability." These labels therefore operate within school cultures as a means of sorting students based on hierarchical notions of "good" "reading ability." These normative notions of "reading ability" can dampen the already weak self-confidence of many students and further alienate them from reading (Alvermann, 2001). All of this suggests the need to focus on developing students' skill and self-confidence as readers by enhancing their engagement in reading in ways that provide useful knowledge and an understanding of their lives and world.

Determining and Activating Students' Cultural Knowledge and Experiences

As noted in the last chapter, one of your goals in planning instruction should be to build on students' knowledge and experiences, including their cultural backgrounds. Students bring certain cultural experiences and attitudes to texts that shape the meaning they construct from those texts. Because the Common Core reading standards do not reference students' use of prior knowledge or cultural background as shaping construction of meaning, New York added the following standards: "[Students will use] their experience and their knowledge of language and logic, as well as culture, to think analytically, address problems creatively, and advocate persuasively," and "[Students will read], annotate, and analyze informational texts on topics related to diverse and nontraditional cultures and viewpoints." Given the diversity of students not only in New York but in every state, it is important for all teachers to recognize and support the different cultural experiences and attitudes students bring to reading texts in their classes.

With the right kind of curriculum, these different backgrounds can be seen as an advantage and as resources, rather than deficits or challenges. As students identify and share differing cultural experiences, beliefs, and attitudes associated with certain texts they can enrich the reading of all. For example, if your students are reading Peggy McIntosh's (1988) famous essay "White Privilege: Unpacking the Invisible Knapsack" and connecting this essay in high school to Richard Wright's (2005) *Native Son*—or in middle school to Sherman Alexie's (2009) young adult novel *The Absolutely True Diary of a Part-Time Indian*—you discover that your students of color bring different experiences and perspectives to their reading than your white students. When students share those experiences, beliefs, and attitudes, a rich dialogue may evolve with important learning for all. Many classrooms in the United States have Latino English Language Learners (ELLs). Addressing themes where these students are likely to have expertise, including informational and literary texts with Spanish words that address Latino experiences (for instance, the young adult novels of Gary Soto), can allow Latino English Language Learners to emerge as experts and resources for their classmates.

ADDRESSING THE STANDARDS FOR READING OF SOCIAL STUDIES AND SCIENCE

A primary focus of the Common Core State Standards is developing the ability to read informational texts employed in social studies and science classes by applying social studies analysis or scientific thinking (@ = Reading literacy practices in social studies and science). While language arts teachers can be a resource for collaborating with and supporting their social studies and science colleagues in the teaching of reading, we particularly support the Common Core State Standards approach of fostering the integration of social studies, science, and language arts curriculum (Lattimer, 2010).

If you're working in a middle school, in which you typically plan curriculum with teachers from different disciplines, you can organize readings around topics or issues by adopting a social studies and science perspective on these topics or issues. You can also organize instruction by having students focus on particular topics that they study in depth through adopting these different perspectives. In Kieran Egan's (2011) *Learning in Depth* project (http://www.ierg.net/LiD), students were randomly assigned topics, which they then studied for an entire year or several years. At the end of their studies, the students shared what they learned in a public forum. By doing so, students learned how to construct knowledge through extensive reading about a topic, and were perceived by others as people with expertise and agency. In a similar study, middle school students were randomly assigned topics about challenges facing urban neighborhoods—employment, housing, environmental issues, law enforcement, schooling, retail, entertainment, traffic, etc.—that they studied in their English language arts, social studies, and science classes (Beach & O'Brien, 2003). Students then acquired expertise through their reading that they applied to their study of an actual neighborhood, resulting in final reports to the school.

Framing Texts Constituted by Historical or Cultural Contexts

In reading literary texts or original documents from a social studies perspective, students need to recognize how these texts are informed by beliefs and values of the cultural and historical periods in which they were produced. For example, in reading about the Great Depression of the 1930s, students could read documents about the economic boom of 1920s prior to the Stock Market crash, as well as fictional texts such as *The Great Gatsby* (Fitzgerald, 1991), which portray class differences and inequities of that period. They could then read descriptions of life during the Great Depression written by writers funded by the Federal Writers' Project (FWP) established in 1935, along with fictional texts such as Steinbeck's *The Grapes of Wrath* (Steinbeck, 2006a) or *In Dubious Battle* (Steinbeck, 2006b), or Richard Wright's *Native Son* (Wright, 2005). Along with reading fictional texts, you might ask your students to do research on the period and simultaneously read informational texts, such as Franklin Roosevelt's Second Inaugural Address, which describes "one-third of a nation [as] ill-housed, ill-clad, ill-nourished" and articulates a vision of the distribution of national wealth such that "the lowest standard of living can be raised far above the level of mere subsistence."

Another historical period in which you might engage your students is the 1950s, a period of the post-World-War II boom as well as a period of ardent anti-Communism. Students could read essays about writers such as Arthur Miller (1996), whose 1949 play, *Death of a Salesman*, which critiqued the emptiness of a salesman's life, was perceived to be an enemy of capitalism, resulting in the author being forced to testify before the House Un-American Activities Committee. They could read Miller's (2000) essay about that experience, "Are You Now or Were You Ever?," as well as view films such *Good Night and Good Luck* (Clooney, 2005)—addressing the debate between Edward R. Murrow and Joseph McCarthy—along with foundational documents like the Bill of Rights and essays about freedom of speech and the press. They could then compare domestic suppression and foreign policy actions fueled by anti-Communist hysteria with post-9/11 America by reading texts such as the Patriot Act, newspaper articles on government surveillance and attacks on Muslims, and Michael Moore's (2004) documentary *Fahrenheit 9/11* (Figure 5.1).

FOSTERING READING LITERACY PRACTICES THROUGH INTEGRATING READING, WRITING, AND TALKING

Rather than "correct answer" worksheets, you can employ activities involving students in literacy practices to actively construct the meaning of texts.

"Frontloading" Texts Based on Topics, Themes, or Issues

In providing students with materials that help them understand the background and context of difficult informational texts, you can help

Figure 5.1 America Under Communism

them learn to apply their prior knowledge or cultural beliefs/attitudes to *frame the meaning of texts* based on textual connections between topics, themes, or issues. Providing relevant background information serves to "frontload" texts in ways that help students define and activate their purpose, prior knowledge, and beliefs (Wilhelm, Boas, & Wilhelm, 2009) so that they can effectively construct textual meaning.

Rather than you providing students with all "frontloaded" resources, as is the case with the traditional anthology textbook, you can have students search for their own online texts related to certain topics, themes, or issues. These texts can include a range of different types of texts—essays, videos, art work, blog posts, news reports, letters, etc. By doing so, you will be encouraging them to engage in *collective, collaborative learning* in which they are contributing to building a knowledge base for the class. And, by asking students to work in groups to collect and post texts as links or file attachments to a class website or webquest, students can make intertextual connections between these texts that represent collective construction of knowledge. Using a jigsaw structure, students can teach each other about their own particular expertise. You can also work with colleagues to have students across different classes and disciplines share their texts using a department or school website.

Written Notes/Blog/Journal/Discussion Entries

Writing should be seen as a crucial part of reading; writing can be a process of inquiry into the meaning of texts. The use of electronic discussion before, during, and after class discussion of reading is another powerful way to support students' careful reading of a text. Electronic discussions are a form of writing that allow students to *collaborate with others* as they develop their own interpretations, *synthesize and connect texts, critique issues,* and *formulate arguments.* If you hold such discussions before class you will be able to review and assess student prior understanding of a text and thus organize discussions and class activities specific to student needs and knowledge. When students utilize electronic discussion during or after class, they can return to questions under debate, refine understandings, and extend interpretation. There are a variety of synchronous and asynchronous online conferencing and course management tools such as Nicenet, Moodle, Blackboard, Ning, Google+, Skype, and Open Meeting (Rozema & Webb, 2008).

Think-alouds/Paired Reading

In using think-alouds, students pair up and share their responses to a text as they read, as opposed to summarizing or interpreting a text on their own at the culmination of the reading. Students may also note what intrigues them, connections they find with other texts, or difficulties they are having in reading a text. Partners simply react with positive support and then students switch roles. Because students may have difficulty making their thoughts explicit, you may need to model the think-aloud process for students. Students can also engage in think-alouds before they begin a text, reporting their purposes or expectations for reading a text, what they may expect to learn from a text, and issues on which they may focus (Wilhelm, 2001). Some questions that students can use in think-alouds include "What are you doing?" or "What is going on in your mind?" Recordings of think-alouds, particularly when dictated using speech-to-text software programs such as Dragon Speaking that create transcripts, can be assessed in terms of the range of different responses.

ACTIVITY: ENGAGING IN THINK-ALOUDS

To learn to effectively model think-alouds for your students, it is useful to engage in your own think-alouds. Select a partner and a relatively short text. Then, share your explicit thoughts with your partner as you are reading through the text, what Elbow (1973) described as "movies of your mind" (p. 85), stopping at certain set places in the text. Rather than attempt to interpret the text, share how you are thinking about the text, including difficulties in comprehending the text. Your partner should simply provide you with supportive non-verbal or verbal feedback to encourage you to continue with your think-alouds. Then, switch roles and your partner does a think-aloud. When you're both done, step back and reflect on how you will model the process of doing think-alouds to your students.

After students complete their shared readings, they can discuss whether and how a text fulfilled their purposes or expectations, and how they will apply what they learned to work on a project or activity. Students can work together to formulate questions and respond to key moments in a text (Filkins, 2010). This activity is likely to work best if there is initial modeling by the teacher, or the use of a "fish bowl" to observe and learn from students using the process. Helping students slow down and carefully examine sentences and arguments is especially important for difficult pieces.

Written Annotations/Hypertexting

Students can also write annotations, summarizing what they are learning from a text related to their purposes or questions.

When possible and appropriate students need to learn how to write on and in books and essays—possibly with electronic text readers as well as with paper. Students can be taught to create their own "marginalia," which they can return to and use later to better understand texts. When marginalia are not appropriate, such as in a school book to be used by others, students can also use multicolored sticky notes to comment on and/or thematically link specific passages.

Today many, perhaps most, informational and literary texts that we want our students to analyze are available as digital texts online and in accessible archives. When these texts are downloaded or cut and pasted onto a computer that the student is using, many opportunities are created for annotating, linking, hypertexting, and *synthesizing and connecting texts* in ways that effectively *construct new texts* as well as *critique and represent issues* and *formulate arguments*. Students can cut and paste from electronic texts and create their own commentary (or hypertext) with notes on specific words, ideas, or characters. They can do this using many online tools or even with just word processing software. They can make comments in different colors, perhaps using "track changes" to indicate thoughts on characters or to add to descriptions of settings. Students can also insert pictures to create their own illustrated works and then write about how their images respond to the text and impact its interpretation. The same can be done with music, video, or clips from other kinds of texts to create multi-genre pieces. Because they can create "sticky note" annotations for online texts using tools such as Diigo, or tablet apps such as iAnnotate or Goodreads, students can share their annotations with their peers. Students can then react to each other's "sticky note" annotations, creating a repository of reactions.

Rob Pope (2006) has written extensively about students intervening in texts and analyzing the impact of their interventions as a powerful and creative way to engage in close reading. Allen Webb's students have made many interventions in literary works and the same approach could easily be applied to informational texts:

One student worked with a collection of Garcia Lorca poems, hyperlinking them to each other around key images and metaphors and adding images that the poems referred to. Another student took Poe's short story, "The Tell Tale Heart," and, by linking from a number of words in the work, created a series of the inner thoughts of the narrator and provided a psychological justification for the murder. In a similar way, another student took Nathanial Hawthorne's short story, "The Minister's Black Veil," and, focusing on the character of Elizabeth, linked to a series of monologues she had written that retold the story from Elizabeth's point of view. A student created several different interventions into an Anton Chekhov short story, changing the social class of the characters in one, modernizing the tale in another, and altering the ending in a third. To each of these he added an explanation of the choices he made. (Rozema & Webb, pp. 11–12)

Hypertexting is an excellent way to develop and explore connections between literary and informational texts in an integrated curriculum.

INTERPRETATION AS CRITICAL INQUIRY

According to the Common Core reading standards students must not only understand explicit meaning and summarize texts; they must also be able to analyze, assess, and critically evaluate them. Critical inquiry calls for a question-posing approach to education and leads to an empowered sense of citizenship. In *Pedagogy of the Oppressed* Paulo Freire (1968) argues:

> Education either functions as an instrument that is used to facilitate integration of the younger generation into the logic of the present system and bring about conformity or it becomes the practice of freedom, the means by which men and women deal critically and creatively with reality and discover how to participate in the transformation of their world. (p. 34)

Freire advocates an approach to learning that he calls "problem posing," which emphasizes "acts of cognition, not transferrals of information" (p. 67). Freire believes that "The teacher is no longer merely the-one-who-teaches, but one who is himself taught in dialogue with the students, who in turn while being taught also teach" (p. 67). And that, "In problem-posing education, men [and women] develop their power to perceive critically the way they exist in the world with which and in which they find themselves; they come to see the world not as a static reality, but as one in process, in transformation" (p. 71).

Posing Questions

Engaging students in critical inquiry involves posing questions based on their concerns, interests, and passions about issues in texts and in their lived worlds. Rather than posing questions simply to find certain specific information, students are then posing questions as itself central to learning. As Thomas and Brown (2011) note:

> Our educational system is built upon a structure that poses questions to find answers . . . Yet finding answers and memorizing facts do little to inspire students' passion to learn . . . We propose reversing the order of things. What if, for example, questions were more important than answers? . . . What if students were asking questions about things that really mattered to them? . . . Every answer serves as a starting point, not an end point. It invites us to ask more and better questions. (pp. 81–82)

Students can collaboratively construct questions about a topic or issue by listing questions in groups or as a class. They can then sort the questions into categories or prioritize those questions they perceive to be the most significant or relevant to addressing their concerns, interests, and passions. Posing questions is not only a critical part of close and careful reading, but it invites students into the curriculum making process.

Finding Relevant Texts

Traditionally, of course, when students had questions they wanted to research, their teachers took them to the library. We still think libraries are important and wonderful resources! Nonetheless schools are dramatically cutting back on libraries, and the Internet has come to replace the library as an astonishing and ever-growing repository of information and of texts both informational and literary.

Based on their questions, students can employ search engines or their library databases to find relevant texts that address them. Students often initially go to Google, Yahoo, or YouTube for their searches. In using these tools, it is important that students recognize that certain companies employ "search optimization" tools so that their sites obtain high rankings—sites that often contain ads. They also need to know how to enter more specific search terms by employing "advanced search" strategies. Further, students need to learn to use databases through their libraries' sites such as InfoTrac Junior Edition, Academic Search Premier, Gale Group, CQ Researcher, or General Reference Center Gold. You can also work with librarians who have created "pathfinders" that provide students with directions on how and where to search for specific topics (Valenza, 2005).

Students may also employ Wikipedia to find what they assume to be authoritative information about certain topics. To determine the validity of Wikipedia entries, students can look at the revision histories on entries to note deletions and additions, as well as Talk Pages for discussions of misinformation (Jenkins et al., 2006). Students can learn to be contributors to Wikipedia, creating and updating pages for institutions, programs, or people they know in their own community, including for their school.

LEARNING ONLINE READING LITERACY PRACTICES

Much of students' reading of informational texts now occurs online. Online reading comprehension requires that students employ some literacy practices associated with the specific affordances of online texts (Kress, 2003; Leu, O'Byrne, Zawilinski, McVerry, & Everett-Cacopardo, 2009). While reading print texts involves a left-to-right linear processing, reading online texts involves reading for relevancy in terms of locating icons or links related to certain purposes for reading. This requires that students have a clear sense of purpose for locating those icons or links and "reading for relevancy" (Kress, 2003) (@ = Learning online reading literacy practices).

Central to online reading comprehension is the ability to pose clearly defined questions or problems that shape online searches for relevant information. For example, if students pose the question "Does climate change result in an increased number of hurricanes?," students then need to determine whether their search results address that question as well as evaluate whether those results are based on empirical evidence versus opinions.

You can assist your students in this question-asking and assessment process by modeling your own think-aloud processes as you read online texts. Using a data projector you can display different kinds of webpages and digital texts for your students and, as a group, you and the class can discuss how you find yourselves reading online texts. You can then pose questions such as "How do we best read this kind of page or document? When do you slow down to study specific sentences or images? How do you read the images with the texts? What role do links play in giving this page authority or meaning? If you had this page on your own computer, what might you do with it? How might you keep track of the information on this page?" Reflecting and modeling help students to hone their abilities to make meaning from digital texts.

Informational websites vary greatly in how much support or scaffolding they provide students for reading online or understanding information (Coiro & Fogleman, 2011). Many websites simply provide information without providing students with scaffolding. Others include navigational tips, hypertexted definitions, titles and subtitles, commonly structured sections, summaries, relevant links, source information, bibliographies, etc. As students are researching topics or issues, you can design some specific tasks to help them better understand and utilize this kind of scaffolding. Sites such as Fact Monster (www.factmonster.com), which serves as a reference archive site, provide support for students by providing them with interactive games, word searches, learning tools, and links to standards (Coiro & Fogleman, 2011). Another type of informational website includes virtual situations that scaffold learning. For example, Google Lit Trips (www.googlelittrips.org) lets students traverse the setting of books using Google Earth—for example, going through Afghanistan while reading *The Kite Runner* (Hosseini, 2004)—or Literary Worlds

(LiteraryWorlds.org), which offers online virtual worlds, role plays, games, and museums related to commonly taught literary works (Webb, 2011a).

Critical Analysis of Website Sources

Students also need to critically analyze websites by searching for who created them and studying the "about us" or "who we are" links so that they can determine the sources of the information on websites (Leu et al., 2009). In many cases, a website might be produced by a commercial company selling certain products; the information provided may be designed to promote those products. Of course, many websites offer false or misleading information. One way to start to think critically about information is to look at extreme examples, and then move on to the more mundane. There are many websites projecting a veneer of sophistication that, in fact, are nothing more than hoaxes. Students will enjoy studying such hoax sites and they will begin to develop more critical web-reading skills. Sites can be easily found by searching "hoax sites," but a few favorites include the Federal Vampire and Zombie Agency, Feline Reactions to Bearded Men, AFDB (Aluminum Foil Deflector Beanie), and satirical sites such as The Onion or the Church of the Flying Spaghetti Monster. There are also troubling extremist and hate group sites from Holocaust denial, to Islamophobia, to the site http://www.martinlutherking.org, operated by white racists, that contains racist misinformation about Martin Luther King.

Teaching Online Reading Using Reciprocal Teaching

To teach students these online reading literacy practices, you can employ Reciprocal Teaching methods that focus on your modeling various practices for responding to a text, having students model practices for each other, and discussion and reflection about the use of certain practices (Brown & Palincsar, 1989). The central idea behind Reciprocal Teaching is that demonstration and scaffolding of practices result in a gradual release of responsibility to students for their own learning.

Given differences between print and online reading comprehension, these methods have been modified for use with online texts (Leu, Coiro, Castek, Hartman, Henry, & Reinking, 2008):

- Teachers model questioning, locating, critically evaluating, synthesizing, and communicating practices through formulating questions/problems and reflecting on how they search for and assess relevant material using search strategies.

- Both teachers and students model think–aloud responses to texts for each other, describing the practices they employ to locate, assess, and synthesize what they learn from online material (for videos of students modeling practices: http://www.newliteracies.uconn.edu/iesproject/videos). Teachers and students can share their syntheses on blogs, wikis, Twitter, IM'ing, or class websites. The fact that students assume teacher roles enhances their sense of agency, since they can share their expertise with others.

- Students begin to work on their own through use of individual or collaborative inquiry units based on their own questions in which they are still modeling practices for each other. To assess students' growth in uses of practices, you can have students list those practices they learned, why these practices are important, and how they use them for understanding online reading (for more description of these assessment techniques: http://www.newliteracies.uconn.edu/IRT).

CASE STUDY: MR. PLOT-A-LONG'S HALLWAY (TEACHING READING)

In this chapter, we've described some different methods for teaching reading of both print and online texts. The challenge you now face is how to implement these methods in the classroom, particularly for students who are having difficulty comprehending texts or who aren't all that interested in reading.

You begin this case study outside of a classroom, where you encounter two middle school students discussing their trouble reading a short story for Mr. Plot-a-long's 7th grade English class. You will then observe Mr. Plot-a-long's class, which begins with a reading-check quiz over the story, much to the dismay of several students, including the student from the hallway who read the story but did not understand the plot. In preparing to help Mr. Plot-a-long and his students, you will watch a brief video clip in which Kristin Sovis, former high school English teacher and current English Education doctoral student, discusses a particular struggling reader in her freshman English class and how she both recognized this student's struggles and addressed the struggles through various strategies. Your task is twofold. First, you will "revise the reading check," as you design an alternate lesson plan that will engage the struggling student in Mr. Plot-a-long's class. Second, you are invited by the principal of the school to present to the teaching faculty about how literacy practices can improve students' reading comprehension and engagement, so you will brainstorm for and plan this talk.

CHAPTER 6

Reading and Writing Narratives, Drama, and Poetry

CHAPTER OVERVIEW

Responding to and Creating Narratives

Literacy Practices Involved in Interpreting and Producing Narratives

Constructing Narratives

Responding to and Enacting Drama

Responding to and Performing Poetry

Case Study: Mr. Poetry-Pro's Hallway

As an English language arts teacher, it is important that you think about how reading, writing, speaking, listening, and viewing can be meaningfully and continually integrated rather than treated as separate activities. Even though these activities are addressed in separate standards in the Common Core, effective teaching brings them together in mutually supportive ways. For instance, as students read narratives, drama, poetry, and the whole range of literary and informational genres, they can be invited to engage in the literacy practices of *framing events* as well as *synthesizing* and *connecting meanings* of texts through acquiring knowledge of the conventions—using reading to acquire knowledge and skills that will support their own writing of narratives, drama, poetry, and other genres. And, as they write in different genres, students can use the literacy practices of *constructing and enacting identities* and *creating texts and objects* to learn about the techniques writers employ in creating these texts and to subsequently enhance their ability to read, interpret, and appreciate them.

RESPONDING TO AND CREATING NARRATIVES

It is important that students understand that narrative is a basic way humans understand and organize information. Narratives can be defined as more than descriptions of events. To use E. M. Forster's familiar example, "the king died and then the queen died," is not a narrative, while "the king died and then the queen died of grief" is a narrative because in the latter a reader needs to infer the causal relationship between the king's death and the queen's death—that she died of grief due to the king's death, something that's not invited in the former (Worth, 2008). Through responding to and constructing these causal relationships in narratives, students acquire what Sarah Worth describes as "narrative reason" (p. 55), through which they transform a sequence of events into a narrative where causal relationships make sense of experience (@ = Understanding and creating narratives).

Thus, understanding narrative means understanding the idea of meaning and relationship. To begin teaching about narrative you might have students share stories in class about things that have happened to them recently. Students in Ms. Oberg's 9th grade class studying urban neighborhoods shared their stories about positive and negative experiences with neighbors. For example, some students shared narrative about neighbors who pitch in and help other neighbors in distress, and other shared stories about neighbors who complained about other neighbors.

You can then ask students to reflect about how and why they shared these stories. This activity may help students understand how stories serve as "illustrative anecdotes" (Burke, 1969)—a way of conveying knowledge about, or making a point about, everyday experience (Bruner, 1990, 2002). Ms. Oberg's students used their stories to reflect on what it means to have supportive versus less supportive neighbors and to create a sense of a neighborhood as a community.

How students tell their stories has a lot to do with *why* they are telling their stories—their purposes for conveying certain ideas or points based on what it is like to have a particular experience. In sharing a story about playing in a basketball game against a team with much taller players, a student may simply state, "We played a team with much taller players but we won." Or, the student may elaborate on their description by noting that "We played a team with much taller players but we ran the ball faster than they did, so we won." By providing this explanatory information, the student is conveying the point that simply being physically outmatched does not equate to defeat. Adding the information "but we ran the ball faster than they did" provides the additional information to establish a causal, if-then, explanation.

Defining How Violations of Norms Relate to Inferring Points

The underlying "point" of a narrative emanates from a narrative's "tellability." Tellability is conveyed through focusing on the unusual, extraordinary nature of events using certain cues, repetition, asides, and hyperbole that dramatize how events deviate from the norm (Labov, 1972). For example, in sharing the experience of driving to school, a student may simply state, "I drove my car to school today." This doesn't qualify as a narrative because it simply describes an event without any other related events—it has little or no tellability because nothing unusual or out of the ordinary occurs. However, if the student reported, "I drove my car to school today and almost wrecked it; the fog was really, really thick so I just missed hitting a tree," his narrative has more tellability because he then added another event and emphasized the deviation from the norm in describing the thick fog using the repetition of "really, really" to accentuate and dramatize the deviation from the norm.

Because they emphasize these deviations from the expected, narratives are often used to portray or teach people about certain norms, particularly when they are being socialized into a new community. For example, new members of Alcoholics Anonymous acquire an understanding of norms operating in AA through hearing testimonial stories from veteran members about their experience of "hitting bottom" and restoring their sense of self-worth through following the AA regimen (Wortham, 2001).

In reading narratives, students can acquire the literacy practice of *framing norms* or critically engaging familiar beliefs operating in events or certain social worlds by identifying consistent instances in which characters violate or deviate from norms that result in their being punished or identified as deviants, in some cases because they believed in higher moral values. For example, in responding to *I Know Why the Caged Bird Sings* (Angelou, 1969), students may infer instances in which the African-American characters are continually discriminated against or mistreated given the norms of segregation in the South, or they may examine the implications of sexual abuse, response, and strategies for survival (@ = Responding to and creating narratives).

LITERACY PRACTICES INVOLVED IN INTERPRETING AND PRODUCING NARRATIVES

There are a number of specific literacy practices involved in interpreting and producing narratives. Having students interpret and reflect on these practices as they are responding to narratives transfers to their writing of narratives. In this chapter, we discuss ways of teaching Toni Bambara's (1992) story "The Lesson," which portrays the experiences of a group of young African Americans who live in Harlem, focusing on the main character and narrator, Sylvia (for a copy of the story: http://cai.ucdavis.edu/gender/thelesson.html). An older woman, Miss Moore, who lives in the neighborhood, and who has attended college, is interested in teaching these young African Americans "a lesson" about the economic class structure shaping their lives. To do so, she takes the group to the FAO Schwarz toy store (Figure 6.1) on Fifth Avenue to show them the expensive toys in the store, including a sailboat that costs $1,195. She points out the disparities between the group's own poverty and these expensive toys that are meant for wealthy people, a reflection of economic inequality in America. At the same time, she also wants the group to realize that they themselves could aspire to achieve a different social status.

Sylvia is initially resentful about Miss Moore's recognition of her own family's poverty. However, during the visit to the store, Miss Moore asks the children about why, given the high costs of the toys, only certain people could afford them, leading some of Sylvia's peers to openly express their resentment about economic inequality. Sylvia then begins to rethink her own beliefs, comparing her visit to the

Figure 6.1 FAO Schwarz

store with her plans to conduct a prank in a Catholic church, which never materialized because she was intimidated by the wealth represented by the ornaments and statues in the church. When Miss Moore asks her to express those beliefs, she refuses, but the reader senses that she has learned a lesson about class structure that may influence her future actions.

Interpreting Settings

Rather than treating settings simply as physical places, students need to perceive settings as constituted by social and cultural norms shaping characters' actions. The setting of a story "establishes the rules" that shape and constrain characters' actions (Smith & Wilhelm, 2010). Again, the social norms become evident when characters violate or challenge them. To help them determine how the norms operating in a particular setting might shape their own behavior in lived worlds, Scott Filkins (2010) has his students define those cues or signals regarding appropriate behavior in different classrooms, as well as how those cues or signals are different in other settings, such as a party. Students may note that in classroom A there are strict rules constituting their behavior, while in classroom B there are few, if any, rules. They may then interpret other students' actions based on their behaviors in these two different settings— a student can be perceived as "deviant" or a "behavioral problem" by not conforming to the strict rules in classroom A, but as a "good student" in classroom B that has few rules.

After learning to interpret social norms in various settings, students can transfer their knowledge to reading a text by applying "rules of notice" (Rabinowitz, 1987) to note instances in which characters adhere to or violate norms.

The setting for "The Lesson" involves differences contrasting between the norms of the children's world in Harlem described in the story by Miss Moore as "the slums," and the upper-middle-class economic world of the FAO Schwarz store on 5th Avenue. The children lack the cultural capital associated with the upper-middle-class economic world—this is evidenced by their not knowing the purpose for a paperweight in the store. At the same time, Miss Moore's world, as constituted by her college degree and language use, contrasts with the children's and their parents' world as evidenced by differences in their dialects and knowledge of the world outside of Harlem.

Students can examine the construction of these different worlds by attending to the children's and Miss Moore's actions. For example, the children are intimidated by being in the unfamiliar world of the FAO

Schwarz store and they perceive Miss Moore as being different from the other adults in their neighborhood.

As the teacher, you can pose questions to help students identify instances of conforming to or violating norms established by a narrative's setting:

- What are some instances in which characters are perceived as violating certain norms?
- What are the consequences for their violations?
- What do these violations and consequences suggest about the norms operating in the setting?

Adopting a Point-Driven Stance

Many students have difficulty inferring the thematic meaning of stories—the point of a story or what a story is trying to "say." To understand this meaning is to go to the heart of what makes a story or any collection of facts into a narrative. To infer the point of a text, they need to adopt a "point-driven" stance (Hunt & Vipond, 1992). Adopting this stance requires going beyond a "story-driven" stance in which they are simply determining what happened in a story without inferring the larger point or theme.

Adopting a point-driven stance involves inferring the point of a story in terms of a writer's position or statement about social norms constituting the world—for example, that colonizing people and taking their land and resources represents an immoral act. To infer this point, students then need to determine the social norms operating in narratives, as well as the consequences for adhering to or violating these norms.

Inferring the point of "The Lesson" involves recognizing that Sylvia, while she does not openly admit it, experienced a sense of discomfort in visiting the store. This discomfort was caused by different sets of norms and led her to recognize the economic inequalities shaping differences between her own world and the world of the store.

Predicting Story Outcomes

In responding to narratives, students are also predicting story outcomes—what will happen next? In making predictions, students often focus on how characters cope with problems or challenges, leading to some change in themselves or in their worlds (Ohler, 2007). As part of developing their responses, you might ask students to create maps or graphs that chart characters' coping with a problem or challenge, the behaviors they undertake, and the changes characters make as a result.

When students make predictions, they should also formulate reasons for their predictions based on their knowledge of genre/story conventions, knowledge that, for example, comedies end happily while tragedies do not. To make predictions about crime or detective storylines, they may apply their knowledge of the problem/solution structure in identifying the nature of the crime, how the detective will solve the crime, and what means he/she will use. The typical detective narrative locates evil in a deviant individual, rather than in the larger social order—with this knowledge of the generally conservative nature of the detective story genre, students can critically engage with the social meaning of a particular detective story.

At the end of "The Lesson," students could predict what Sylvia may do next in her life based on what she learned from Miss Moore—whether she'll emulate Miss Moore and go to college or whether she will choose a future limited in some ways by social and economic conditions.

Inferring and Explaining Characters' Speech Acts

Students also need to be able to infer and explain characters' actions based on inferences about their traits, beliefs, and/or goals. In doing so, they are employing the literacy practice of *framing events* in which characters act in certain ways given their traits, beliefs, and/or goals.

Speech acts performed through characters' use of dialogue include requesting, promising, inviting, asserting, praising, apologizing, challenging, etc. (Austin, 1962). In making inferences about characters' dialogue, students can attend to the effects or "uptake" of speech acts; for example, the fact that when character A proposes marriage to character B, and B refuses, they may then make inferences about A's traits—that he/she is perceived by B to not be suitable for marriage, or that A didn't really believe that B would accept a proposal. To help students infer traits, beliefs, and goals, you can ask them to respond to questions such as: "What did the character do? What traits or characteristics influenced what she did? What beliefs or attitudes shaped her decision to do what she did? and What goals were driving what she did?" Students could also adopt the roles of different characters and pose these questions to each other playing as characters. For example, at the end of "The Lesson," Sylvia's friend, Sugar, states that:

"You know, Miss Moore, I don't think all of us here put together eat in a year what that sailboat costs." And Miss Moore lights up like somebody goosed her. "And?" she say, urging Sugar on. Only I'm standin on her foot so she don't continue. "Imagine for a minute what kind of society it is in which some people can spend on a toy what it would cost to feed a family of six or seven. What do you think?" "I think," say Sugar pushing me off her feet like she never done before cause I whip her ass in a minute, "that this is not much of a democracy if you ask me. Equal chance to pursue happiness means an equal crack at the dough, don't it?"

In this exchange, Sugar's act of asserting the disparity in her own family's wealth versus the cost of the sailboat results in Miss Moore's positive uptake affirmation response, leading to Miss Moore's follow-up question resulting in Sugar concluding that inequality of opportunity is inconsistent with democracy.

When Miss Moore then asks Sylvia for her opinion, Sylvia doesn't answer. However, she notes that "somethin weird is goin on, I can feel it in my chest"—an effect of the question that suggests that she, as did Sugar, has actually learned something about economic inequality.

Inferring Characters' Perspectives

Inferring the speech acts and uptakes in this exchange also involves inferring Miss Moore's, Sugar's, and Sylvia's perspectives or inner thoughts. The fact that the story is told from a first person point of view means that readers are privy to Sylvia's thoughts and feelings. Similarly, use of a third person point of view provides readers with certain perspectives or information shared by the omniscient narrator such that characters may not know certain things known by the reader.

To infer characters' or narrators' perspectives, students engage in what Lisa Zunshine (2006) calls "mind-reading," or "our ability to explain people's behavior in terms of their thoughts, feelings, beliefs, and desires" (p. 6). For example, in responding to a mystery/detective story, readers engage in "mind-reading" of the detective's thinking processes in sifting through various clues or interviewing potential suspects. This requires the ability to intuit or ascribe certain thoughts or feelings based on characters' or narrators' observable, explicit actions—that they are crying, so that they must be upset. To help students acquire "mind-reading" practices, they could engage in think-aloud responses to descriptions of characters' actions or dialogue in which they intuit the characters' thoughts and feelings, noting those actions or words they use to make those inferences.

Students could also note instances in which characters begin to shift their perspectives, beliefs, and attitudes over time by keeping a record of characters' perceptions of events or other characters. Because "The Lesson" is told through Sylvia's point of view, a reader experiences her negative reactions to Miss Moore's pedagogical agenda and the fact that the children have difficulty understanding Miss Moore's economic analysis given that "don't none of us know what kind of pie she talkin about" (p. 90). However, Sylvia later begins to pose the kinds of critical questions modeled by Miss Moore, such as "Who are these people that spend that much for performing clowns and $1,000 for toy sailboats? What kinda work they do and how they live and how come we ain't in on it?" (p. 94). And, at the end of the story, Sylvia reveals the fact that she's pondering what she learned through adopting this critical stance that might mirror Bambara's own stance (Heller, 2003).

Responding to Comics and Graphic Novels

You may want to include high-quality graphic novels in your class-rooms—for example, the Maus series (Spiegelman, 1986, 1991), *Persepolis: The Story of a Childhood* (Satrapi, 2004), *American Born Chinese* (Yang, 2008), *Palestine* (Sacco, 2002), and *The Adventures of Johnny Bunko: The Last Career Guide You'll Ever Need* (Pink & Pas, 2008), as well as the Scholastic Comix series for middle school students. These texts are appealing to students because they provide visual support for understanding language and story development, as well as draw on students' experiences with video games (Frey & Fisher, 2008; Wilhelm, 2004). To help students respond to these texts, you may provide students with practices for responding to the multimodal formatting and iconography employed in panels, frames, balloons, gutters, and positioning of readers through close-up versus long shots or different angles (Bitz, 2010; Carter, 2007). As you engage students in responding to comics and graphic novels, you can also ask students to create their own comics using comic-creation software (Comic Life, ToonDoo, MakeBeliefsComix, Pixton, ReadWriteThink Comic Creator).

CONSTRUCTING NARRATIVES

Based on their responses to narratives or drama, students may also write their own narratives or dramas; doing so allows them to explore issues in their lives or communities and enhance their understanding of writing techniques.

Writing Autobiographical Narratives

Writing autobiographical narratives allows students to recall certain past events that shaped their identities in a certain developmental phase or turning points in their lives—for example, moving from accepting others' beliefs to voicing their own beliefs.

Autobiographical writing offers an approachable starting point for composing narratives. To write autobiographical narratives, students can conduct research about their family history or past historical events related to their lives. Teachers often have students create maps of the home or neighborhood where they grew up and mark sites of significant events that could be addressed in their writing. Students can conduct online genealogical searches, find their own photos or photos in digital archives related to their past experiences, or interview people who knew them in their past. In interviewing people, students can elicit other people's perceptions of their past selves in certain cultural contexts (for examples of interviews with 1,750 African Americans: StoryCorps Griot http://www.storycorps.net/initiatives/griot).

Writing is most effective when students flesh out specific past events through use of descriptive details and dialogue. In doing so, they can then describe events through the eyes of their past point of view, a perspective that represents their particular past identity. For example, in recounting her "turning point" experiences, Maya Angelou (1969) assumes the perspective of a young African-American girl witnessing her grandmother being harassed by white racists.

In recalling details about past events, students may be concerned about the need to recall events exactly as they happened. To address this concern, you can help them recognize that their memories of the past often change as they acquire new understandings or ways of thinking about life. They may also even shift or revise the facts to effectively convey their points about the past. As Maureen O'Leary (2007) notes, "I teach them that they can, indeed, they often *should* play a little fast and a little loose with the facts, with the happening-truth, in order to achieve the even truer story-truth" (p. 163). Students can also discuss the ethical dimensions of deliberately distorting the truth of one's past, and the difficulty of making a clear distinction between fiction and nonfiction in portraying the past.

Constructing Identities

In portraying their past selves, students are engaging in the literacy practice of *constructing their identities* as being certain kinds of people with certain beliefs or attitudes shaping their actions. As Holland et al. (1998) note:

People tell others who they are, but even more importantly, they tell themselves and they try to act as though they are who they say they are. These self-understandings, especially those with strong emotional resonance for the teller, are what we refer to as identities. (p. 3)

And, through constructing past identities, they are *framing events* in terms of their ethical beliefs. As Betsy Rymes (2001) notes, "Through telling [stories], people are not creating a merely random identity, rather, they are actively narrating themselves relative to a moral ideal of what it is to be a good person" (p. 498). In "self-making" narratives, students position themselves as having a persona designing their narratives, as with all literacy tools, to accomplish certain actions. In a study of Los Angeles Latino(a) high school students' drop-out narratives, Rymes (2001) describes students' use of narratives to project themselves in a positive manner in coping with threats, violence, mistreatment, or boredom that led them to drop out of school. She cites the example of one student, Rosa, who described the event of a teacher chasing her down a school hallway and then holding her, thereby positioning herself as the victim of the teacher's physical treatment for the purpose of explaining why she dropped out of school. Rymes notes that she tells the story in a manner that conveys her "moral self" to make her "look good" (p. 35) within the setting of an authoritative school culture.

Writing Auto-ethnographic Narratives in Historical/ Social Contexts

Autobiographical writing can help students locate themselves historically and socially. Sometimes this kind of writing is called "auto-ethnography." Auto-ethnography draws on the techniques of ethnography, such as observation of daily behavior, careful study of local beliefs, recording of life history (including kinship, family roles, education, coming-of-age events), and in-depth interviewing. An auto-ethnography emphasizes not only one's own story, but an examination of how one's own experience is situated in culture. An auto-ethnography is a cultural accounting and involves thinking about how one's own experience was similar to or different from others. Auto-ethnography shows "people in the process of figuring out what to do, how to live, and the meaning of their struggles" (Bochner & Ellis, 2006). The Common Core State Standards recognize the importance of narrative elements in the understanding of history. The 6–12 history/social studies writing standard focuses on students' ability "to incorporate narrative elements effectively into arguments and informative/explanatory texts. In history, students must be able to write narrative accounts about individuals or events of historical import."

Students can write biographical, autobiographical, or auto-ethnographic narratives about their own or others' lives as "persons in history" (Holland & Lave, 2001) as shaped by social, cultural, or historical developments or trends. In doing so, they go beyond an individualistic perspective to recognize that their own and others' lives are shaped by larger institutional forces and events. To do so, they can interview family members or friends about their experiences with certain forces and events. For example, parents or grandparents may recall specific events related to how their families coped with living through economic recessions, resulting in changes in their lives and identities.

The history/social studies reading standards focus on analysis of how historians frame events in certain ways reflecting certain perspectives or attitudes, as evident in the standards for grades 9–10: "explain how an author chooses to structure information or an explanation in a text to emphasize key points or advance a point of view," and "compare the point of view of two or more authors by comparing how they treat the same or similar historical topics, including which details they include and emphasize in their respective accounts." Meeting the Common Core State Standards entails analyzing writers' explanations for historical events as well as considering how different writers may provide different explanations for the same events or adopt different perspectives. To meet this standard students are engaging in the literacy practice of *framing events*, as described in Chapter 2. This requires students' ability to analyze the validity of reasons or explanations for events in terms of the relevance or sufficiency of the evidence provided. To do so, students need to learn to infer the underlying assumptions or warrants, inferences described as linking between the description or proposition about an event with the reasons for the event.

To model this process, you can provide students with examples of event descriptions/reasons and have them infer the assumptions or warrants linking the event descriptions and reasons. For example, someone may state, "It will rain today" (event description) "because it's cloudy out" (reason), "gap-filling" the underlying assumption: "When it's cloudy, then it will rain." To test out the validity of this assumption or warrant, students then cite examples of days that are cloudy but when no rain occurred.

RESPONDING TO AND ENACTING DRAMA

Another important genre is drama (@ = Responding to and enacting drama). Because drama texts are solely dialogue, understanding drama texts requires inferring speech acts to frame characters' actions in terms of goals, plans, beliefs, and norms. For example, in responding to *Hamlet*, students infer from Hamlet's speeches whether and how he plans to revenge his father's murder—the fact that he is questioning, pondering, and plotting.

You can help students interpret drama texts, by having them act out specific scenes from plays, then using their performances to interpret the meaning of speech acts. Students can also create videos of certain scenes from a play.

It is also important to have them attend performances or view film versions of the play. Rather than simply sitting through an entire film, it will likely be more effective to have students closely and repeatedly view a single scene, perhaps from recordings of different productions. Students can then analyze the ways in which a director or film interprets the text through how actors perform roles or how a film version uses certain cinematic techniques, settings, music, lighting, editing methods, or actors.

Engaging in Dramatic Inquiry Activities

You may also engage students in dramatic inquiry activities in which you create imagined situations or dilemmas where students adopt roles and attempt to address problems or challenges created by the teacher (Beach et al., 2010; Edmiston, 2000, 2003; Heathcote & Bolton, 1995). For example, students could be told that they are members of a company whose mission is to address issues of homelessness, requiring them to develop some strategies for working with homeless people. Or, students could be told that the gorillas in Uganda are being threatened with extinction due to poaching, requiring them to develop strategies to stop poachers. As these dramas unfold, you as the teacher can continually *frame and reframe events* by posing questions and adding new complications.

This work requires that students continue to develop critical inquiry and problem-solving practices. They also need to conduct research, for example, studying various models for dealing with homelessness or researching the topic of gorillas in Uganda.

In proposing the centrality of improvisation for agency and identity formation, Dorothy Holland and her colleagues (1998) have argued that improvisation is intended action which is not a set response to a situation and that it changes spaces to make them less restricted by, and more playful in relation to, both existing cultural norms and relationships with others. Holland et al. argue that, when they are able to improvise, people achieve agency in social settings within particular cultures, and, over time, shape their identities. People have agency both beyond rejecting or accepting a cultural norm and resisting or embracing a social positioning. People's identities are not fixed but rather change across time as they discover novel ways of acting by playing within appropriate cultural boundaries and as they have new experiences on which they can reflect and tell stories. When students have opportunities to explore new ways to socially position others, and be positioned by them, their agency and identities to develop in classroom interactions.

Writing Drama Scripts

Students may also write drama scripts designed to be performed by their peers based on their concerns about certain issues in their school, community, or society (Chizhik, 2009; Edmiston, 2000; Frey, Hischstein, & Guzzo, 2000; Karakelle, 2009). In writing drama scripts, students portray tensions between their articulated values and their actions, leading to critique of the systemic, structural forces shaping their decisions (Gervais, 2006; Winn, 2010a, 2010b). In doing so, students experience a "doubled" reality related to both their everyday "what is" experience and their "what if" imagined experience that serves to provide alternative perspectives on the "what is." This work constitutes a critical literacy practice leading to awareness of institutional forces or discourses shaping their "what is" experiences (Edmiston, 2003). Further, this work can lead students to reimagine their own "what is" roles, for example, how their role as "student" in school worlds would be different in alternative narrative spaces that involve identity experimentation (Erstad, Gile, Sefton-Green, & Vasbo, 2009). Students may also draw on intertextual references designed to reframe lived-world practices in terms of alternative discourses or cultural models constituting the "figured world" of the text (Holland et al., 1998). Students can begin by writing down conversations, and explore the move from oral to written language. Practice with dialogue addressing issues in the community can evolve into student-created theatrical pieces. For example, two 16-year-olds in an East Los Angeles high school interviewed former student activists who walked out of their classes in 1968 to protest the poor conditions of their schools (Tobar, 2011). Based on these interviews they created the script, *2011 Meets 1968*. In the play, the students portrayed these students as arguing with their parents, confronting teachers who assumed that they shouldn't be educating Mexican-American students, and being humiliated for speaking Spanish, leading to a two-hour production with professional actors.

In a drama production class in a suburban Midwestern high school taught by Sam Tanner, students built their scripts around problems they perceived in their school. Sam explained that writing these drama scripts that lead to play productions involved students in critique of the institutions shaping their lives:

My work, in schools, has been to challenge acts of colonization and, therefore, de-humanization. I have meant to create spaces that allow for a more organic humanity to take shape and grow. These spaces, once established, have given context to the social practices I have employed as an educator through my work in literacy. I have allowed social practices a powerful place in the canon of my curriculum that allows my students to acquire practices through practice.

One script written by Laura (pseudonym) reframes the school world as a prison in which a warden readily punishes deviant inmates, reflecting the application of a "strict father" cultural model (Lakoff, 2002). Both the warden and the prisoners adopt an "incarcerated discourse" of individualized self-degradation and blame for their difficulties as opposed to critiquing public institutions causing these difficulties (Winn, 2010a). In her play, the prisoners ultimately challenge the warden's harsh control through resistance.

Laura also drew on the television program *Jersey Shore* to portray tensions between rival gangs—the female "Mean girls" and male gang "Jocks"—as continually fighting for power in the prison, as well as focusing on physical aspects of gender identity, a reframing of gender roles in school that accentuates gender stereotypes. Laura also employed intertextual links to lyrics to *High School Musical*, when Ms. Warden attempts to have the prisoners celebrate a false sense of unity at the end of the play by singing "We're All in This Together," an ironic comment on the conflicts between the warden/guards and prisoners.

Laura noted that her parody of schooling as a hierarchical system was derived from her own experience as an "outsider" student. She equated the prison staff with the students who benefit from being privileged within the schooling system, and the inmates as those who, like herself, are marginalized by the school, and are therefore punished because they lack power. She noted that "writing the script gave me a more critical eye for the world around me; things that were serious, now seem humorous to me."

Another script, written by Mathew, portrays conflicts between four tribes on an island, a reframing of tensions between the schools' four grade levels as well as an actual homecoming event in which the senior girls engage in a highly physical touch football game with the junior girls. This script was based on intertextual links to the reality TV show *Survivor*, to portray conflicts between the different classes as tribes fighting with each other. The script also reframes the school's senior versus junior female homecoming football game as a "Puff Battle" in which the characters murder each other, a commentary on the violent nature of that game. These reframings mediated by reality TV shows draw on the discourses of competitive individualism.

Mathew perceived his hierarchical "figured world" as a critique of the institution of schooling. Rather than creating a happy ending, he deliberately ended the script with a scene of destruction to make the argument that "these things wouldn't change," reflecting his awareness of the rhetorical effect of the drama production on peer audiences.

In *Theater of the Oppressed* (1993) and *Games for Actors and Non-Actors* (2002), the Brazilian theater director Augusto Boal has developed theory and a number of dramatic strategies that transform audiences into active participants in the theatrical experience. His techniques are especially useful when students are writing their own scripts addressing lived-world events. One Boal technique, as adapted by teachers, involves having student performers freeze actions, and having the audience (or rest of the class) brainstorm different actions or endings that offer various solutions to real world social problems, which are then performed by the students. As students write scripts and engage in this kind of active performance, they are reframing lived-world events in their school to critique their school as a system constituted by cultural models of preferential hierarchies and "strict father" (Lakoff, 2002) authoritative control, as well as discourses of individual competition and self-blame (Winn, 2010a) (@ = Responding to and engaging in drama).

RESPONDING TO AND PERFORMING POETRY

Another important literary genre is poetry. As with narratives and drama, it is important to continually integrate responding or performing with writing of poetry. It is also important to build on students' own experiences with poems in the form of music or rap lyrics, as well as selecting those poems that will engage them through having students search for or bring in poems found on poetry sites, such as the Academy of American Poets (http://www.poets.org) or the Poetry Archive (http://www.poetryarchive.org). It is also important to emphasize the subjective experiences of reading and responding to poems without initially engaging in a lot of instruction about the features or structures of poetry (@ = Understanding and creating poetry) (Figure 6.2).

Reading poetry from online sites immerses students in a world of poetry beyond a traditional textbook. So many of these sites are *alive*, connected to living poets and to poetry lovers. The Academy of American Poets, for instance, features a "National Poetry Calendar" where students can search for poetry events near them. This site also advertises poetry book clubs; accepts manuscripts from contemporary poets; gives poetry awards; produces a free podcast; offers a free newsletter; and provides reading recommendations, lesson plans, and resources for teachers. Other sites let students explore poetry in other ways, beyond what is possible in printed text. The American Verse Project (http://quod.lib.umich.edu/a/amverse/) assembles volumes of American poetry published before 1920 and allows users to search for occurrences of words and phrases throughout the entire full-text archive—thousands of poems. The Poetry Foundation (http://www.poetryfoundation.org/) includes searches by category, occasion, title, first line, and popularity. This site also features articles, audiovisual materials, links to poetry resources on the web, subscriptions to poetry magazines, letters to the site, and more.

In fostering responses to poetry, you can encourage students to initially read aloud or perform a poem to capture and share their emotional or sensory responses using the method of "think-and-feel-aloud" practices (Eva-Wood, 2008). For example, in responding to Shakespeare's Sonnet 116, students could read aloud the poem, performing it in different ways through emphasizing certain words or use of pauses (for one version, Amber Rose Johnson, winner of the National Poetry Aloud award: http://ttbook.org/book/amber-rose-johnson-16-year-old-poet).

Sonnet 116
Let me not to the marriage of true minds
Admit impediments. Love is not love
Which alters when it alteration finds,
Or bends with the remover to remove:
O no! it is an ever-fixed mark
That looks on tempests and is never shaken;
It is the star to every wandering bark,
Whose worth's unknown, although his height be taken.
Love's not Time's fool, though rosy lips and cheeks
Within his bending sickle's compass come:
Love alters not with his brief hours and weeks,

Figure 6.2 Poets.org

Courtesy of the Academy of American Poets

But bears it out even to the edge of doom.
If this be error and upon me proved,
I never writ, nor no man ever loved.

Through performing poetry, students physically perform their particular interpretations of poems using pitch, alliteration, assonance, rhythm, metaphor, pauses, emphasis, sounds, and alternating voices (Reyes, 2006). This requires that they reflect on the meaning of a poem to envision and rehearse how they will convey that meaning through their performance. Students could study online clips of performances from the PBS video *Poets Read: Fooling with Words* (http://www.pbs.org/wnet/foolingwithwords/main_video.html) or *Poetic License* (http://www.itvs.org/poeticlicense), or they might listen to podcasts of spoken-word performances, attend poetry slams, or study examples of rap and spoken-word poetry in various anthologies (Eleveld, 2007; Medina & Rivera, 2001; Pough, Richardson, Raimist, & Durham, 2007). They can also record their own performances using GarageBand or Audacity, or employ tools such iMovie or VoiceThread (http://www.voicethread.com) to create digital poetry that combines audio with images or video.

Students learn to acquire certain voices and authority through their participation in spoken-word performance groups—what Maisha Fisher (2007) describes as "participatory literacy communities" (p. 116) that provide "a neutral space where students were encouraged to maintain a non-judgmental attitude toward their peers [through] a 'culture of listening' and valuing words" (p. 127). Because students may be apprehensive about publicly reading aloud their work to their peers, it is important to directly address students' potential fears as well as describing specific aspects of what they liked about the performances and what they inferred or wondered when they heard certain words (Jocson, 2007; Reyes, 2006).

One of the exciting emerging formats for reading poetry aloud is the "poetry slam." Although slam competitions typically involve performances being judged on a numeric scale by previously selected members of the audience, classroom slams need not involve this kind of judging. Poetry slams can feature a broad range of voices, styles, cultural traditions, and approaches to writing and performance, and have been popular with teenagers.

Responding to Poetry

Understanding poems also requires careful, multiple rereadings through attending to the meanings of certain words or phrases through use of think-alouds. For example, in responding to Sonnet 116, students need to translate some of Shakespeare's language into more current language. In doing so, students benefit from identifying the words or lines that pose difficulties for them, leading them to address those difficulties (Blau, 2003). Formulating reasons for their difficulties can then guide their rereadings designed to help clarify what they don't understand. For example, students may not understand the line "the star to every wandering bark," requiring them to infer that "the star" is the North Star and that a "bark" is a ship that follows the North Star. And, in response to the lines "Love's not Time's fool, though rosy lips and cheeks/Within his bending sickle's compass come," students could infer the reference to aging that may change one's appearance, but not one's love for another.

Students could also draw on genre knowledge of the Shakespearean sonnet itself—the fact that many of his sonnets addressed the topic of the challenges to love. And, they could draw on their own experiences with short-term versus long-term love relationships and reasons for their lasting or not lasting.

Drawing on models from established poets, Linda Christensen (2009) has developed a variety of poetic exercises that facilitate her secondary students' writing and sharing about important events and people in their lives and communities. Her students write poems about who they were "raised by," about activities they were involved in at certain ages, about the people they view as their community, and about how they can heal the pain in their lives. The poems are shared in "read arounds," where students sit in a circle and, as students finish reading, the others write positive comments about their fellow student's work on strips of paper and share their comments with the author. This activity becomes a powerful way for students to develop community in her classroom.

ACTIVITY: CREATING DIGITAL STORIES AND POEMS

Digital storytelling and poetry combine words with images, sounds, music, and video to create an interactive experience for a reader (for examples of digital storytelling, see http://tinyurl.com/45xfohc; for examples of digital poetry, see http://tinyurl.com/3kde43k, particularly the Electronic Literature Association's digital poetry collections http://collection.eliterature.org/1 and http://collection.eliterature.org/2). Using the tools on these two links, including, for example, iMovie, Windows Movie Maker or PowerPoint/Keynote, create a digital story or poem by reading aloud the text and adding images/videos that convey your experience of the text. You may also create hypertext stories or poems using a blog, wiki, or website that include links for readers to select that take them on different pathways through a text.

All of this suggests that responding to and creating poetry does not have to be a dry, academic exercise if students perceive how poetry is related to their daily lives.

CASE STUDY: MR. POETRY-PRO'S HALLWAY

In this chapter, we've discussed ways of teaching narratives, drama, and poetry. The challenge that remains is how to honor and facilitate individual differences in their responses to narratives, drama, or poems.

This case study invites you into the high-energy 7th grade English classroom of Mr. Poetry-Pro at an urban school. In preparing to read Lorraine Hansberry's play *A Raisin in the Sun*, Mr. Poetry-Pro asks students to respond independently and in writing to Langston Hughes' poem "A Dream Deferred," which prefaces the play. You will have the opportunity to read and analyze three students' responses to the poem, discussing what the responses reveal about students' knowledge and how these responses might inform instruction.

CHAPTER 7

Critical Analysis of Literary Texts

CHAPTER OVERVIEW

A "Critical Engagement" Framework

Framing Texts in Terms of Critical Perspectives

Fostering Critical Engagement about Issues or Themes in Students' Lives

Critical Engagements in Literary Worlds as Simulations

Case Study: Mr. Virtual's Hallway (Critical Responses)

Literature allows students to imaginatively step into alternative worlds, both like their own as well as far-distant, and gain understanding of self and others in rich social, cultural, and historical contexts. From this perspective what matters most about the study of literature is not the memorization of different genres or forms or gaining passing familiarity with a canon of cultural monuments. Instead, you can select works that will be effective in helping students understand and address issues in their lives and in the broader world. The Common Core State Standards emphasize a variety of skills that support students gaining this kind of understanding, including careful reading, understanding of characters and how they develop, recognition of point of view, recognizing differences in representation in different media, and connecting literature study to the basic documents and values of a democratic society. The Common Core State Standards don't emphasize an approach that is common in secondary schools, the study of literary terms and genres. The emphasis is on understanding content and on careful and thematic analysis. We believe that students are more likely to become engaged when literature instruction is thematically organized, when a curriculum is not a set of "pearls on a string." Instead, texts in a language arts class should foster imaginative journeys that relate to each other in the context of issues that matter.

To improve reading skills and develop knowledge of texts and the world, students need to do extensive reading. While this chapter will focus on texts read in common, that is not meant to indicate that independent reading of various kinds is not important. We believe that every English language arts class should foster extensive reading beyond common focused texts. English language arts teachers have done this effectively in a variety of ways, including reading workshops (Atwell, 2007), literature circles (Daniels, 1994), and the Accelerated Reader commercial program. All of these approaches can be modified to further develop thematic connections between independent and common reading.

This chapter extends the methods described in Chapter 5 by developing activities for having students engage in interpretations and critical analyses of characterization, themes, and ideological stances. These methods are based on a model of critical inquiry that fosters students' engagement in analysis of literary texts.

A "CRITICAL ENGAGEMENT" FRAMEWORK

An essential component of critical inquiry is student engagement using the critical inquiry perspectives described in Chapter 3. In contrast to a critical literacy framework which "often connotes an analytic distance in relation to texts" (Dockter et al., 2010, p. 418), a "critical engagement" framework "combines critical distance with immersion and emotional investment" (Dockter et al., 2010, p. 418). Research on "students' interactions with varied forms of non-print text and their participation in the production of knowledge through digital technologies" in an urban high school program focusing on digital media "demonstrated that rigor and engagement are inextricably tied to a curriculum that invites emotional investment, immersion, and intellectual challenge" (Dockter et al., 2010, p. 418). Dockter et al. (2010) derived this critical engagement framework from an analysis of a teacher's documentary film class in which students were highly engaged in producing documentary films around issues that concerned them. Students' engagement was enhanced by sharing their documentaries in a film festival with multiple audiences. This sharing enhanced their sense of agency because they knew that they were informing others about these issues.

FRAMING TEXTS IN TERMS OF CRITICAL PERSPECTIVES

As noted in Chapter 3, you can ask students to *apply critical perspectives* that focus on the historical, institutional/civic, cultural, psychological, and economic forces shaping events in literary texts. For example, in inter-preting settings, students need to be able to infer particular historical or cultural norms operating in a story or novel, requiring some background knowledge of the historical period or culture. Interpreting *To Kill a Mockingbird* (Lee, 1960) requires defining the cultural norms operating in the segregated South that created racial and class hierarchies challenged by the Civil Rights Movement. Atticus's principled defense of Tom Robinson based on a vision of a new world of integration challenges the practices of the town's segregated world. And, understanding the portrayal of witch hunts in the play *The Crucible* (Miller, 2003) involves under-standing how Puritan religious beliefs led townspeople to believe that their peers were agents of the devil, a parallel to the 1950s and 1960s as shaped by McCarthyism and anti-Communism. And, in studying *The Kite Runner* (Hosseini, 2004), students can study the cultural world of Afghanistan during the Soviet invasion as shaped by fundamentalist Muslim beliefs associated with the Taliban control of the country.

Any one of these texts could be connected to more in-depth curric-ulum that includes different literary, visual, and nonfiction works that address complementary issues such as racial discrimination (*To Kill a Mockingbird*), religious and political freedom (*The Crucible*), or conflict in the Middle East (*The Kite Runner*). As we suggest at various points throughout this book, there are any number of important cultural studies themes emerging from students' lives that can be used to bring together different literary texts. When a curriculum is organized in this way texts speak to each other and thinking becomes increasingly complex as the semester progresses. Focuses such as homelessness, women, youth violence, postcolonial perspectives, racism, and Holocaust are described by Webb (2001).

Because students generally lack the background knowledge to define social norms, you will need to provide students with readings or artifacts about the historical or cultural worlds portrayed in texts. For example, in studying *Pride and Prejudice* (Austen, 2009) you can provide students with information about the class hierarchy and the roles for women in early 19th-Century England. You also need to help them learn to use that information to define norms constituted by these class differences that in turn influence the meaning of characters' practices. For example, because

Elizabeth Bennet's family is simply middle class, they differ from the upper-class families represented by Darcy's family. As a result, the women in the Bennet family must focus on finding husbands to ensure their financial future—something that does not concern the females in wealthier families, who will simply inherit wealth. Elizabeth's friend Charlotte and sister Lydia are desperate to be married, entering into marriages Elizabeth perceives to be less than desirable. It is therefore the norm for middle-class women to define their agendas primarily in terms of finding husbands—something that is not a priority for Elizabeth, much to the concern of her mother. (Whaley and Dodge's [1993] *Weaving in the Women: Transforming the High School Curriculum* is a resource for secondary teachers interested in women's literature.)

Once students identify a problem or issue, you can help them contextualize or frame that issue in terms of the larger institutional, cultural, psychological, or economic forces. Formulating reasons for issues leads students to explore competing explanations and different perspectives on that issue and to identify gaps or tensions between competing perspectives (Myers & Eberfors, 2010). In doing so, students broaden their perceptions of an issue through "stepping outside one's usual modes of perception and comprehension using new frames to understand experience" (Lewison et al., 2008, p. 8). Analyzing institutional forces shaping urban neighborhoods shifts the focus away from analyzing social practices as solely a matter of individuals' actions to also examining social practices as driven by larger economic, political, cultural, and historical institutional systems.

One major challenge, however, in fostering *critical engagement* is that students may have difficulty recognizing how these systems, as largely invisible forces, operate in and shape their everyday lives. Students are often not aware of how the systems of schooling, government, justice, military, religion, the family, business, etc., structure and inform even their own roles and beliefs. For example, students could study how the military system operates as a system controlled by hierarchical rules and roles. Understanding the military as a system offers students knowledge they can apply to interpreting military characters' traits, beliefs, and goals in a novel about war, for example, *Catch-22* (Heller, 1961), which parodies the military system. In responding to *Catch-22*, students can then apply this knowledge to understanding how Heller is parodying the military as a system.

Students are more likely to be engaged in critical analysis of systems when they can relate the influence of these systems to their own daily lives and concerns—recognizing that this issue really matters to them (Flower, 2008; Kinloch, 2009). For example, when students perceive how foreclosure rates in their neighborhoods influence their neighbor's everyday lives, students may be more engaged in considering the influence of larger systems on foreclosures. Recognizing that foreclosures are adversely affecting their neighborhood lives will then mean that they may want to address this issue.

This raises the question of what instructional methods contribute to students adopting a critical engagement stance related to critiquing larger, global systems, particularly for students who may not be accustomed to engaging in critical analysis.

Inferring How Values Influence Characters' Perspectives

Students can also be taught to reflect on how characters' values influence their perspectives (Thein, Beach & Parks, 2007). To interpret the influence of characters' cultural values on their perspectives, students may first start by listing their own beliefs and values. They may note that they value friendship, career/work, family, appearance, having fun, power, fairness, social acceptance, independence, etc. They can then rank their top and bottom four values and compare them to those of their peers (Johannessen, Kahn, & Walter, 2009).

After considering their own values, students can rank the most versus least important values of characters. For example, in Alice Walker's (1973) story, *Everyday Use*, Dee, a graduate student who has developed a strong interest in African-American history and culture, and her boyfriend, come for a brief visit to her mother, Mama. In contrast to the assertive, worldly, college-educated Dee, Dee's sister, Maggie, still lives at home and subscribes to Mama's values. While they are visiting, Dee asks Mama if she can have an old butter churn and a quilt, an item she considers to a valuable part of her heritage. Her mother is reluctant to give up the quilt, which she wants to give to Maggie for her own "everyday use." Dee is applying a more academic perspective of the outsider anthropologist/ethnographer, who would treat a butter churn and quilt as cultural artifacts rather than items for "everyday use," as Maggie, who could sew her own quilts, would perceive them.

Students may then rank Dee's, Mama's, and Maggie's values (Johannessen et al., 2009). For example, students might notice that Mama and Maggie value their family ties over Dee's academic agendas, while Dee values her academic agendas over her family ties. Students can then use these value rankings to explain characters' actions—for example, the fact that Mama keeps the quilt for Maggie because she values the fact that Maggie has remained with her while Dee has entered into another

world. There's no "correct" ranking in this activity, and no easy interpretation for this story—the ranking is designed more to foster discussion of how students' values shape their perceptions of the characters.

Students could analyze characters' discourses as legal, economic, political, psychological, religious, and cultural ways of knowing and thinking
constituting characters' actions. To do so, they could identify instances of
characters double-voicing (Bakhtin, 1981) of certain discourses—for
example, the discourses of "old money" versus "new money" in *The Great
Gatsby* (Fitzgerald, 1991), or discourses of race, class, and religion in *To Kill
a Mockingbird* (for an example of students' blogging about these discourses
in *To Kill a Mockingbird*, see the website). Once students identify these
different discourses, they can then reflect on how those discourses shape
characters' actions. For example, while Gatsby voices the importance of
accumulating his own wealth—a "new money" discourse—Tom voices
the value of "old money" and inherited wealth. And, while Atticus Finch
voices the legal and moral discourse of civil rights in defending his client at
the trial, many townspeople voice a discourse of separate-but-equal rights.

Students can then discuss how these discourses position characters as
having different kinds of power. While the discourse "new money"
resonates with characters tied to the boom world of the 1920s, the fact
that Gatsby acquired this money illegally through liquor smuggling
means that it doesn't necessarily enhance his status in the eyes of the "old
money" characters.

FOSTERING CRITICAL ENGAGEMENT ABOUT ISSUES OR THEMES IN STUDENTS' LIVES

One approach to fostering critical engagement involves having students
explore issues or themes related to certain aspects of their lives that
concern them. Addressing such issues may enhance their engagement
in critical analysis. These units can combine literary texts portraying
these issues or themes with lived-world experiences. As described in
Chapter 4, Ms. Oberg's 9th grade students were engaged in her place-
based unit on urban neighborhoods as portrayed in *Days of Rondo*
(Fairbanks, 1990) and *The House on Mango Street* (Cisneros, 1991), and
with the "oral history" project and interviews of neighbors, asking questions such as "What are the best parts of your neighborhood and why?
What needs improvement in your neighborhood and why? How have
you impacted your neighborhood and how has your neighborhood
impacted you? How has your neighborhood changed over time?"
Students also created interview questions relating to their neighbors'

social lives, educations, economic forces, occupations, avocations, skills, passions, political roles, ethnic/cultural identities, and personal lives.

In this unit, students were motivated by what we define as critical engagement with the local as portrayed in literature and their own lives. In responding to *Days of Rondo*, students identified with the unique, particular qualities of an African-American neighborhood located in the largely white Minnesota world, as well as resistance to how that neighborhood was destroyed by the construction of an interstate highway—a construction project into which Rondo neighbors had no input. And, by engaging in the local, they also experienced instances in which the local was limited or constrained by the fact that it is local (Pennycook, 2010). For example, in responding to the alternative perspectives of neighbors in *The House on Mango Street*, students experienced how different cultural norms regarding gender, class, and race influenced and limited the characters, leading Esperanza to perceive both the strengths and parochial limitations of her neighborhood. And, in descriptions of their own neighborhoods, students recognized how crime or poverty could shape opportunities in their own lives.

ACTIVITY: IDENTIFYING ISSUES IN TEXTS

Identify an issue that concerns you. Then, reflect on and/or share reasons why you are concerned about this issue and how you believe it should be addressed. Then, find a story, play, novel, or poem that addresses this issue. How do the characters and/or author frame or address this issue? Compare your own with the characters' and/or author's way of framing or addressing this issue.

CRITICAL ENGAGEMENTS IN LITERARY WORLDS AS SIMULATIONS

In responding to literary portrayals of social worlds, students also experience simulation of everyday life in a manner that provides some understanding of its complexities. Literary versions of social worlds are not replications, but abstractions and generalizations that simplify and select those certain details most relevant for creating models of social interactions. In contrast to expository essays, readers experience firsthand the simulations through uses of sensory images that evoke readers' imaginative construction of experience, leading to the emotional experience of empathy for characters' experiences. And, experiencing these simulations provides the reader with social knowledge about how to cope with interpersonal interactions and conflicts.

While works of literature can be seen themselves as a kind of virtual world simulation, the Literary Worlds project (LiteraryWorlds.org) that houses the *Teaching to Exceed* virtual cases you've already been using along with this book, also provides secondary students with engagement in critical inquiry in a wide range of literary works, from Anglo-Saxon poetry and Shakespeare plays, to 18th-Century novels, to commonly taught modern works such as *Lord of the Flies* (Golding, 1999), *The Great Gatsby* (Fitzgerald, 1991), *Of Mice and Men* (Steinbeck, 1982), and *Things Fall Apart* (Achebe, 2009). In these worlds English language arts students role-play as literary characters, extending and altering character conduct in purposeful ways. In the process of these role plays, students use new technological tools to engage in the literacy practices of *framing events, constructing and enacting identities*, and *relating to and collaborating with others*. You and your students are invited to use Literary Worlds in your classes— our discussion of these worlds suggests a wide range of engaged, literacy practice approaches that language arts teachers can bring to literature instruction, with or without specific technological support.

For example, in teaching a 9th grade class of "loud, belligerent, unmotivated, funny young men and a smattering of shy girls," Cara Arver "hoped to use students' interest in technology to inspire them to delve into the literature that we were reading." Teaching *Lord of the Flies*, she found that descriptions in the novel of "vivid features such as ethereal beaches, steamy jungles, and a broad mountaintop" helped her "envision a diversity of 'rooms' for the virtual environment" she created using enCore.

Avatars or virtual characters were created so that, with the right user-name and password, her students could "wake up" in the world. Once there the students were able to further develop the characters, creating "their own names and descriptions; they were all English schoolboys, ranging from five to thirteen years old." Cara explained that:

To further organize our entry into the virtual world, I divided the class into five groups of three or four students: Hut Builders, Firebuilders, Hunters, Littleuns, and Food/Fruit Finders. I grouped the students with at least one member who would act as leader. Together they created a description of their meeting place, relevant and appropriate to their assigned character. This encouraged students to think about the island, its appearance and their roles. The group interactions fostered both independence and group cooperation. (Arver, 2011, pp. 18–19)

She reported:

The virtual world opened up new ways to work together as a class and a team. Students communicated without being nervous or intimidated by face-to-face contact, and those who are reserved may break out of their normal boundaries and interact differently. Inevitably, students drew connections between their lives and those of the characters they read about. (p. 21)

As the students became participants in creating the virtual-reality environment, they role-played and discussed the events of the novel.

Cara specifically designed activities in the *Lord of the Flies* world to connect to several different Common Core State Standards. She said she was able to:

Link the vocabulary exercise to the Language standards, and the writing/conversation assignments would work well with the Reading and Writing standards. At the very minimum, to be able to interact successfully within the virtual world, the students would have to read this complex text, and complex texts are strongly encouraged in the CCSS. It would be difficult for them to fake their way through a conversation as a boy on the island without having the background knowledge of the story and the characters . . . My last Common Core assignment for the virtual world was a short writing assignment addressing argumentative text, which links up with the Writing Standard W.11–12.1, "Write arguments to support claims in an analysis of substantive topics or texts, using valid reasoning and relevant and sufficient evidence" (p. 45). The students were to write, in character, about who they believed is truly responsible for the deaths of either Piggy or Simon. (p. 22)

Writing argumentative pieces in character, students engaged in literacy practices of *critiquing and representing issues*, and *formulating effective arguments*.

The virtual worlds engaged these and other literacy practices as response to a variety of literary texts. Drawing on performance approaches to teaching Shakespeare, secondary teachers Joe Haughey and Jen Barns designed virtual worlds for *A Midsummer Night's Dream* and *The Tempest*. A performance approach emphasizes that to understand a work of drama it is not enough to only read the script. Students must *relate to and collaborate with others* as characters, *constructing and enacting identities*. The worlds Joe and Jen created were actually designed as role-playing games where students as characters had specific and interactive goals. Joe explained that:

Midsummer Madness is an interactive, multi-player game, in which participants take on a role from the play *A Midsummer Night's Dream*, and together with other students, explore Shakespeare's magical Athenian world. Through their immersion in the virtual world, participants become familiar with Shakespeare's characters, settings, objects, and themes, and develop a stronger understanding of the elements of Shakespeare's drama. But, even more importantly, through their "play," they create their own unique variation of the drama, a loose translation of Shakespeare's story, created by the student/character's novel interplay, a performance that has never been played before nor will ever be played again. Though the product of their "play" will resemble Shakespeare's story, the performance they create is also entirely their own, much as actors make a stage performance their own. Thus, the true value of the virtual world stems from this playful interaction— immersion in the virtual world inevitably leads to participants' more profound engagement with the actual play. (Haughey & Barns, 2011, p. 29)

This process of a performance response to literature offers precisely the kind of literacy practice that can help students engage with and understand complex texts such as Shakespeare. Rather than an archaic language fixed or frozen on the page, Shakespeare becomes what he was for performers in his own day: an opportunity to *relate to and collaborate with others* by creatively *constructing their own texts* and actions.

A particularly powerful example of a literary virtual world learning experience for *synthesizing and connecting texts*, *critiquing and representing issues*, and *formulating effective arguments on issues* is the virtual world for *Of Mice and Men* (Steinbeck, 1982), created by former high school teacher Gretchen Voskuil, which focused on migrant labor, human rights, and union organizing. Gretchen said that:

The topic of migrant farm labor is not only central to *Of Mice and Men* but an important focus of Steinbeck's work, especially *In Dubious Battle* as well as *Grapes of Wrath*. Somehow the topic of 1930s migrant labor is often missed in contemporary classroom analysis of *Of Mice and Men*. In the 21st Century, migrant labor remains a compelling issue, though all too often invisible in our curriculum. (Voskuil & Dykema, 2011, p. 40)

To connect Steinbeck to the present, Gretchen developed a fascinating virtual world that brought together *Of Mice and Men* with an important Chicano text, by Tomas Rivera's (2007) *And The Earth Did Not Devour Him*, a short novel divided into 14 vignettes addressing Mexican-American migrant labor. Gretchen pointed out that:

The text is bilingual, which may appeal to teachers with Spanish-speaking ELL students . . . Rivera's blunt honesty about migrant labor conditions (the lack of water, nourishment, acceptable shelter, and safety) holds the attention and sympathy of young adult readers. Pairing a Mexican-American text with Steinbeck is especially appropriate given Steinbeck's great appreciation of Mexico. (p. 41)

To prepare for this virtual world and help them *relate to others,* students wrote about a time when they felt that their rights were violated, or about what they thought of as the most basic human rights. Students also considered working conditions and *enacted identities* by writing letters in characters' voices. Gretchen suggested:

Lenny could write a letter to Slim regarding the harassment he receives from Curley, or the unnamed child in the chapter titled . . . [in] *And the Earth Did Not Devour Him* could write a letter to a faraway uncle about his father's heat stroke. (p. 41)

Gretchen had students do Internet research on unionization of migrant workers and brought to bear a wide variety of informational and visual materials to help students *develop connections* and *formulate arguments.* She explained that PBS's program "On the Border" "detailed various aspects of migrant labor, such as its early history, Cesar Chavez's involvement in the movement, the current state of migratory labor, and children of migrant workers." Her students also looked at photographer Dorothea Lange's collection "Migrant Farm Families" (Figure 7.1).

Figure 7.1 Migrant Farm Families

National Archives and Records Administration. Original caption: On Arizona Highway 87, south of Chandler, Maricopa County, Arizana. Children in a democracy. A migratory family living in a trailer in an open field. No sanitation, no water. They came from Amarillo, Texas. Pulled bolls near Amarillo, picked cotton near Roswell, New Mexico, and in Arizona. Plan to return to Amarillo at close of cotton picking season for work on WPA (Dorothea Lange).

Gretchen's students viewed films addressing the unionization process. She recommends *"The Fight in the Fields* (1997), which tells the story of the life of Cesar Chavez as related to the United Farm Workers Union and *Salt of the Earth* (1954), a groundbreaking film about striking Mexican American mine workers with a powerful feminist perspective which was banned and blacklisted during the McCarthy period (now in the public domain and available on YouTube)." Other possibilities include *Harlan County, USA* (Kopple, 1976) (winner of the Academy award for Best Documentary in 1976) or *Matewan* (Sayles, 1987) (a film depicting union organizing in the 1920s).

To more deeply understand these works and the issues they raise, Gretchen drew upon participatory literacy practices, where students *framed events, constructed and enacted identities,* and *related to and collaborated with others.* Students were assigned to play roles from the two literary works as well as characters including "Union Organizers," "Union Dissenters," and "the Boss." The role-play experience began in a virtual space called the "Field":

Described as "hot and dusty" and causing workers a terrible thirst, the Field is an ideal place to begin because it provides the conditions that fuel much of the conflict. Workers from the Steinbeck and Rivera texts may complain about these conditions; union organizers can quietly gather support by suggesting meetings elsewhere in the world.

The virtual world contained a number of spaces including a "Country Store":

The Country Store is where workers meet at the end of a long day as well as on weekends. In this room, they can purchase whiskey, coca-cola, ice cream bars, and beer. And as a public place, The Country Store seems to be the most likely venue for discussions between union organizers and workers. It is there that they can approach all workers—whether from Steinbeck or Rivera's text—about further discussions about the union. It is also where union dissenters might spy on conversations and threaten workers that speak to union organizers. It provides an authentic representation of the complications one encounters when organizing, as all roles have to weigh their moves carefully, only speaking to the right people at the right times. (pp. 43–44)

This role play raised many questions for student participants as they engaged in the literacy practices of *synthesizing and connecting texts, critiquing and representing issues,* and *formulating effective arguments.* Gretchen explained that:

I recommend that students process their virtual world experience as a whole-class or small-group. They can consider questions such as:

- What did you expect to do with your role in this activity? Did your prediction come true? Why or why not?
- If you were a worker, what did you decide to do regarding unionization, and why?
- In this activity, what contributed to—or discouraged—the unionization process?
- As a character, what might you do differently next time, if given the opportunity?
- What might make this virtual world experience more valuable for you? Why?
- Given on-going local and national debates about unions and collective bargaining, discussions can be further enriched with contemporary news events, YouTube clips of contemporary public demonstrations, visiting speakers, and students can discuss parallels between the virtual world experience and contemporary union struggles. (p. 45)

Engaged literacy practices are crucial for understanding complex cultural situations. Chinua Achebe's (2009) novel *Things Fall Apart* relates a version of the encounter between colonizing Europeans and indigenous people that took place around the globe and shaped much of world history in the last 500 years. Though histories of this encounter are usually told by the victorious side, this work is fascinating because it is written from the point of view of the Ibo people in Eastern Nigeria during their domination by the British empire when their world "falls apart." Writing in an African-inflected English, Achebe creates a kind of ethnographic novel that introduces the rich culture of the Ibo through the experience of a community we come to know as individuals. A worldwide bestseller and popular classroom text, the novel brings forward a vital perspective on colonialism.

Even though the language of the text is not difficult, understanding the cultural differences of the Ibo and their perspective on the British can be challenging for students. A role-play virtual world that allows students to simulate a complex cultural interaction and utilize a wide range of literacy practices is the Village of Umuofia, which was designed by Webb to support the teaching of *Things Fall Apart*. Using usernames and passwords, students enter into the Village of Umuofia and "wake up" as a wide range of African Ibo villagers, British missionaries, and colonial administrators in a visual space based on an extensive archive of authentic black-and-white photographs taken by an anthropologist near the time and place that the novel is set. The novel sets the stage for immersion in an historic and polarized social world, where students from classrooms around the world have been able through role play and simulation to *construct and enact identities, relate to and collaborate with others, critique issues,* and *formulate effective arguments* (Figure 7.2).

The virtual village is filled with images, characters from the novel, and recordings of traditional West African music. Given the lack of information contemporary students have about traditional Africa, perhaps it is not surprising that students visiting the Village of Umuofia have commented:

I have never seen anything like it before. The most important thing for me was seeing the pictures of huts, walking sticks, and tools. I was amazed at the quality of craftsmanship and the amount of time these people must put into carving them. Also the website did a good job reinforcing how characters communicated with each other and how they came to their

Figure 7.2 African Dressed as British Colonizer

G. I. Jones Photographic Archive of Southeastern Nigerian Art and Culture administered by the Museum of Anthropology at Cambridge University.

decisions. This activity helped me to place myself in a villager's shoes and try to think like they did. I got to kind of experience first hand what they went through. I enjoyed my on-line experience in the Village of Umuofia. It really made you feel as if you were in the book and living as your character. (Webb, 2011c, p. 64)

A literary virtual world can be considered a map, and as such can be read as a form of analysis and interpretation of the source text. Black-and-white photographs decorate the interface of each room in the Village of Umuofia and exist in different rooms as "objects" that can be opened and viewed. Given the unfamiliarity and the cultural, historical, and geographic remoteness of setting of *Things Fall Apart*, this mapping of the text and the gallery of images constitutes a compelling and persuasive *framing* of the novel that students can *critique*.

Before taking on the roles of characters from the novel, students engage in a "First Visit," an overnight assignment to become familiar with the virtual world, to write about, and analyze the images they found there. In this assignment the world functions as a virtual museum gallery. Visits to the gallery can be made individually or in groups. Logging in from different computers, perhaps from home, students can plan to meet each other in the virtual space at a particular time and move from room to room together viewing the historical photographs, which decorate the walls. When viewing the Village in groups, students can talk with each other about the images they see, developing their interpretations *collaboratively*, and a transcript of their comments is sent to the students and to their teacher. Class conversations after students have undertaken the First Visit have led to many observations, questions, and new understandings about the novel. As students study and respond to the images they encounter in the Village of Umuofia, students are highly self-conscious about their perspectives and the cultural distance between themselves and the Africans portrayed.

There are 39 possible characters taken from the novel that students can role-play in the village. As they assume, *construct and enact these identities*, they both attempt to remain true to the novel and also extend and evolve the events and dialogue using their own imaginations. Since there are 13 rooms in the virtual Village of Umuofia, at any one time there could be 13 different conversations between characters. Students who are in a room together at a given time will have the same transcript for that portion of their visit. At the end of the role play, transcripts are sent to the student and their teacher.

During normal play, students' role-playing characters can come and go from the rooms. The teacher usually role-plays a unique character, the Village Crier, who can speak so as to be heard in every room, and announce events that the villagers and the British characters discuss. The Village Crier can also "lock doors" so that students cannot move between rooms, and can magically transport groups of characters to different rooms, such as placing all the British and British-sympathizing characters in the same room, all the African traditional characters in the same room, all the characters in the same room, all the characters spread in small groups throughout the village, and so on.

The interactive dialogue students employ in the Village of Umuofia illustrates their knowledge of individual characters and their relationships with others. As students continue to "speak" as their characters, they explore character motivation and further *construct and enact their identities*, both as individuals and as members of different cultural groups—Ibo and British. While students typically engage in complex conversations, even short comments can express substantial social knowledge. For example, in one role play the student playing Ekwefi (the main character Okonkwo's second wife) commented that "Okonkwo is sadly prone to anger." This comment illustrates not only knowledge of Okonkwo's personality, but the word "sadly" shows that the student understood the affection between Ekwefi and Okonkwo, that such behavior is wrong in the context of the novel, especially during Peace Week. Further, students demonstrated that they understood that the tone—factual, not outraged—suggests that such behavior is common, if not entirely acceptable, in the Ibo world of Achebe's novel. We can see that *enacting an identity* is a literacy practice that develops a sensitive and complex understanding.

In participating in the post-colonial worlds of Achebe's *Things Fall Apart*, students adopt the cultural perspectives operating in the social world of Africa that serve to challenge their Euro-American discourses and cultural models.

In the virtual world students not only perform personally different viewpoints, but they also enact cultural conflicts in complex, multiple, and interrelated social worlds. In one transcript a student performing as Mr. Smith, the Christian missionary, said that "The bible says that polygamy is a sin. Maybe if Okonkwo had one wife he would not feel so stressed . . . He is breaking God's law!" The student role-playing as this character compared cultures and made a judgment based on an awareness of a differing belief system. Enacting the identity of the rigid fundamentalist missionary, the student was also in a position to *critique* that value system.

These virtual worlds offer a richer experience when students write and discuss what they are learning during, or soon after, the activity, *synthesizing and connecting the text* and the virtual experience and *critiquing issues*. One valuable approach is for students to analyze at least a portion of the transcript of their role play. Questions they might consider include:

- How was our experience similar to and also different from the source text?
- Why did certain characters act the way they did during our experience in the virtual world?
- How has the virtual reality changed or enhanced my understanding of the source text and the historical events on which it is based?

These examples of a literature pedagogy based in literacy practices and 21st-Century technology illustrate the Common Core State Standards addressed. Teaching with virtual worlds is likely new to many teachers, something they themselves probably did not experience in school. Knowledge of how best to manage virtual world experiences and weave them effectively into existing curriculum and instruction requires repeated experimentation. Increasing familiarity with the technology reduces problems and generates new strategies. Experience observing and assessing student learning in virtual worlds leads to clearer and better integration of literacy practices. Moreover, understanding what is possible with specific kinds of online virtual activities can stimulate English language arts teachers to develop many different kinds of engaged, simulation activities that don't necessarily involve using computers or innovative technology.

CASE STUDY: MR. VIRTUAL'S HALLWAY (CRITICAL RESPONSES)

In this chapter, we've described ways to foster your students' critical responses to literature and the media, focusing particularly on how to use the LiteraryWorlds.org site to engage students in critical responses within simulated literary worlds.

This case study involves you in Mr. Virtual's 12th grade World Literature course, in which he engages students in virtual learning thanks to a substantial grant that brought computers into his classroom. His students' attendance and performance on both in-class and state-standardized assessments are high, and your methods teacher suggests you observe him in action. After perusing various Literary Worlds on the LiteraryWorlds.org site with Mr. Virtual's students, you will choose one to explore and discuss its representations, interpretations, and potential uses in the classroom.

Please find two or three peers, and go the the LiteraryWorlds.org site and then to the *Teaching to Succeed* link for this case study for Chapter 7; your group will then go back to one of the Literary Worlds to discuss using that Literary World in the classroom.

CHAPTER 8

Argumentative, Informational, and Explanatory Writing

CHAPTER OVERVIEW

Advantages and Disadvantages of the Common Core Approach to Teaching Writing

Framing Writing Events: Devising Effective Writing Prompts

Gathering Information for Writing

Using Informal Writing to Learn: Developing Material and Ideas

Teaching Argumentative Writing

Steps Involved in Argumentative Writing

Explanatory Writing

Informational Writing

Case Study: Ms. In-Need-of-Persuasion's Hallway (Argumentative Writing)

> "Writing is not only a skill, but a way of being and acting in the world in a particular time and place in relation to others" (Anis Bawarshi, 2003, p. 123).

In this chapter, we describe methods for teaching argumentative, informational, and explanatory reading and writing—three forms that serve as the basis of the Common Core State Standards informational reading and writing standards. In doing so, we posit the need to go beyond an approach to teaching writing that focuses on teaching the formal structures to a literacy practice perspective where meaningful curriculum and critically engaging classroom activities and events provide the context for thoughtful writing, as Anis Bawarshi (2003) notes in the introductory quote, as "way[s] of being and acting in the world in a particular time and place in relation to others."

ADVANTAGES AND DISADVANTAGES OF THE COMMON CORE APPROACH TO TEACHING WRITING

As previously noted, the Common Core State Standards adopt a formalist focus on teaching writing, a focus that has both advantages and disadvantages.

Advantages

The Common Core writing standards are organized around certain forms or modes of writing: argumentative, explanatory, informational, and (as discussed in Chapter 5) narrative. One advantage of conceptualizing the writing curriculum in this way is that, as a teacher, you can focus on specific literacy practices involved in reading and writing these different forms. As illustrated in Chapter 5, you can have students analyze features relevant to these different forms so that they can then employ those features in their own writing. For example, in teaching argumentative writing, students can analyze writers' use of claims and supporting evidence to craft their own arguments

Another advantage of emphasizing argumentative, explanatory, and informational as different forms is that students may thus gain a clearer sense of the rhetorical purpose and organization of their writing. In the past, one generic form of essay was typically taught in English classes—the five-paragraph form. Recognizing argumentative, explanatory, and informational modes can lead to more detailed and complex approaches to writing.

Instruction on the expository essay has often been tied to specific standardized writing tests, including those required by No Child Left Behind legislation. This is certainly a narrow way to think about "writing ability," since there is such a range of different kinds of writing that students can and should master. As a result of concern about testing, much of secondary writing instruction in recent years has been shaped and limited in preparing students for tests (Applebee & Langer, 2006; Hillocks, 2002). Given the focus on generating an essay based on the five-paragraph-theme template, teachers have employed a formalist approach that emphasizes mastery of the conventions of the five-paragraph essay as opposed to emphasizing development of ideas and structures that correspond with purposes.

Rather than preparing students for writing at the college level, teaching students to plug ideas into pre-made forms or training them in a simplistic test-preparation format creates a disconnect between secondary and post-secondary writing instruction. Interviews with both college and 6–12 writing teachers found that the college writing teachers were critical of their students' lack of experience with composing processes associated with developing ideas (Fanetti, Bushrow, & DeWeese, 2010). In preparation for the high-stakes expository essay exam, 6–12 teachers have focused on students simply creating a single draft and then editing that draft. As one college instructor noted, "Process is not draft, revise, revise, revise. That is not the writing process. It is not pre-writing or revise" (Fanetti et al., 2010, p. 81).

Disadvantages

On the other hand, there are some disadvantages to adopting a primarily formalist approach to teaching writing. An emphasis on forms or modes can readily turn into teaching cookie-cutter templates, as has been the case with teaching the five-paragraph theme. A cookie-cutter approach is not something that the framers of the Common Core State Standards would support, but we see it as a risk of the standards.

Another disadvantage is that it is often difficult to distinguish these *forms* in published texts because their *functions* overlap. For example, narrative, explanatory, or informational writing could readily serve as an argument; while argumentative writing contains narrative, explanations, or information to support argumentative claims. In terms of organizing your curriculum around meaningful units with relevant writing assignments, it may be more valuable to focus first on content and ideas, and on the function and purpose for the writing, rather than on simply engaging in a set of writing modes disconnected from a richly developed curricular context.

Focusing on teaching forms or modes of writing may also limit recognition of writing as an interactive social activity mediated by use of language, genres, and discourses defining roles, purposes, and audiences. Writing is never done in a vacuum; it is always shaped by the event or context in which students are writing, the purposes for their writing, and audiences to whom they are communicating. As Marilyn Cooper (2010) noted:

Writers are never separate from the rhetorical situation in which they write. They do not study the situation as something apart from them and then create in a vacuum a text that will change the situation; instead, they fully engage in the situation and respond to it. (p. 27)

A formalist approach may also limit students' engagement in writing about certain topics or issues. Students are, for good reason, more engaged by a topic or issue they care about than by learning an argumentative or explanatory form. And this is as it should be. An emphasis on forms or modes puts to use a familiar metaphor, the cart before the horse.

ACTIVITY: RECALLING PAST WRITING ASSIGNMENTS

Recall some previous writing assignments from your college or secondary school classes. What was it about those assignments that engaged you or did not engage you? Was it the topic or issue you addressed or the type of writing that was meaningful to you?

All of this suggests that in teaching writing your goal should be to create engaging events or rhetorical contexts that position students as engaged with topics or issues that are important to them within the contexts of particular events. In this chapter, we first discuss ways of *framing events* through writing prompts, gathering information, and use of informal writing to develop materials and ideas (@ = General methods for teaching writing).

FRAMING WRITING EVENTS: DEVISING EFFECTIVE WRITING PROMPTS

Writing assignments create a context that positions students as certain kinds of writers engaged in specific rhetorical actions. Students therefore need to know how to understand a writing assignment so that they situate or invent themselves in ways that are consistent with the prompt (Bawarshi, 2003).

When you formulate your writing prompts you will be creating a context for writing, and drawing on the literacy practice of *framing events* in terms of goals, plans, roles, norms, and beliefs. Your prompt will provide your students with directions for drawing on their background knowledge to invent and construct their ideas.

Use of Genres to Frame Events

To help students frame the writing event in terms of goals, plans, roles, norms, and beliefs, you can provide them with a particular genre that constitutes the use of particular goals, plans, roles, norms, and beliefs. As noted in Chapter 2, students employ certain genres as ways of defining their social practices related to defining their goals, plans, roles, norms, and beliefs. For example, in formulating arguments, students may employ the genre of the editorial, letter, essay, manifesto, legal brief, etc. Notice how many specific genres there might be for "argumentative writing," and how those genres can be tied to real world activities and events. For example, 7th grade students collaboratively constructed a letter to be read at their local school board arguing against closing their school (Sheehy, 2003). While students orally shared different, competing arguments to develop ideas for their letter/statement, use of the letter genre served to unify their writing around a single message for their audience—members of the school board (Sheehy, 2003). Knowledge of the letter genre therefore helped focus students' attention on conveying their position to their audience in the most effective way. There are many other similar genres these students might have used to make their arguments. For instance, the genre of the manifesto focuses on voicing one's critique of an existing situation, and setting forward an agenda and vision for change that needs to take place. The genre of the petition addresses a specific change that needs to take place and is typically accompanied by a list of signatures.

Goals/Plans

The writing assignments you craft will provide your students with a sense of goals or purposes for their writing. Providing students with a sense of purpose goes beyond asking them to simply write about a topic or issue; instead it asks them to consider how their writing may convince their audience to believe or do something related to that topic or issue. Your assignment can also help students envision an audience that differs from you, the teacher. For example, if students are writing about the issue of the lack of public spaces in a small town for adolescents to congregate, your assignment might ask them to write a letter to the town council making recommendations for setting up such public spaces.

Roles/Beliefs

In your assignments, you may also define roles or persona students may adopt in their writing depending on their beliefs or stances on a topic or issue. Such roles or personas are often implied or constituted when a specific writing genre is chosen. For example, in one form of explanatory writing—the science report—students learn to adopt the role and stance of a scientist by using a passive voice—"analysis of the data . . ." as opposed to "I analyzed the data"—and use of a scientific discourse that places value on the scientific method.

Norms/Criteria

In your prompt, you may also want to define the norms or criteria constituting effective use of literacy practices in students' writing—criteria we describe in more detail in Chapter 12. For example, in writing a biographical profile of a favorite relative, students can be assessed on their use of specific descriptions of that relative, accuracy and depth of information about the relative, validity of any generalizations or judgments about the relative, and use of interview data to support those generalizations or judgments.

GATHERING INFORMATION FOR WRITING

The quality of effective writing depends on students' ability to cite relevant, valid, current, and credible information as evidence to support their claims or explanations. To help students conduct effective search strategies for acquiring information, you can provide them with instruction on formulating keyword topics, use of search engines and library databases, analysis of sources, and validity of information. In conducting online searches, students experience a number of difficulties. They will often first turn to search engines like Google, Yahoo Search, or Ask/Teoma, which produce a lot of results, but which may not be relevant or scholarly. Students may also initially go to Wikipedia, which also provides a lot of useful information, but should not be students' final, definitive source given that not all information on the site is accurate. With help from media center staff, you can steer students to library sites such as InfoTrac Junior Edition, Academic Search Premier, Gale Group, CQ Researcher, or General Reference Center Gold. Advanced students can use Google Scholar and Book searches, as well as many of the electronic scholarly databases. And, as we noted in Chapter 5, students also need to have some specific questions that provide them with a purpose for conducting searches, as opposed to unsystematically browsing for anything that comes up on the screen. With a clear purpose in mind, students can specify search terms that lead to relevant results. And, in cases when students don't find relevant results, they can reflect on problems with their original search terms and formulate alternative terms. This type of revision requires metacognitive awareness of the direction of their search. As Julie Coiro (2003) notes, "It's not just point and click. It's point, read, think, click" (Coiro, 2003, p. 459).

Students also need to know how to cite references using the Modern Language Association (MLA) (2009) style guidelines typically used in literature or the arts and the American Psychological Association (APA) (2009) style typically used in social sciences. Students can develop their skills with these style guidelines by using free tools such as StudentABC Citation Creation, Citation Builder, CiteULike, Connotea, Citation Machine, or Zotero.

USING INFORMAL WRITING TO LEARN: DEVELOPING MATERIAL AND IDEAS

In acquiring information and formulating ideas, students can also employ informal writing tools to generate, develop, connect, rethink, and share information and ideas (Elbow, 1973). In using writing to learn, students need to initially adopt a tentative stance by taking up "passing theories" (Kent, 1993) or hypothetical hunches about a topic that they can then test by seeking out supporting or conflicting evidence. For example, a high school student, Jill, was writing about a high school hybrid composition class in which students conducted some of their work online in a library or study space and some of their time in face-to-face interactions in class. To explore positive versus negative aspects of hybrid classes, Jill listed some possible "passing theories" based on her own experience taking a hybrid class the previous semester—the fact that she had more time to work on her own on her writing as opposed to having to be in class every day and that she learned to take responsibility for writing autonomously, a skill she knew she would need for college. She also listed possible limitations of a hybrid class: that some students have difficulty working on their own and may not devote enough outside time to the class. Knowing that these were just tentative hypotheses, Jill decided to interview some of her peers who also took the class to gain further information to determine the validity of her hypotheses. She therefore used her listing as a means of generating material for her analysis and report.

TEACHING ARGUMENTATIVE WRITING

We now turn to describing methods for meeting the standard "write arguments to support a substantive claim with clear reasons and relevant and sufficient evidence" (@ = Teaching argumentative writing) (Newell, Beach, Smith, & VanDerHeide, 2011).

The Challenges of Teaching Argumentative Writing

Teaching argumentative writing is challenging. Students often have difficulty writing argumentative essays. On writing assessments, only 18 percent of 8th graders' and 31 percent of 12th graders' essays in the 2002 NAEP assessment were rated as "skillful"—they could generate a thesis and supporting reasons but did not consider counterarguments (Persky, Daane, & Jin, 2003). One reason for this is that students are more likely to be assigned summary or worksheet writing than argumentative writing (Applebee & Langer, 2006); one survey found that teachers assigned argumentative writing only once a semester (Kiuhara, Graham, & Hawken, 2009).

Most students in your class will also have limited experience reading argumentative texts and may therefore have difficulty identifying differences between claims, reasons/evidence, and warrants; and may not understand that different genres—editorials, reports, sermons, essays, letters, etc.—can function as arguments (Chambliss & Murphy, 2002). Moreover, students are often unfamiliar with the conventions of written argument related to the ability to formulate claims supported by credible evidence.

Students may be accustomed to engaging in verbal arguments that consist of voicing their opinions about, for example, whether their football team is superior to their rival school's team. They are also accustomed to TV or radio talk shows in which participants voice their opinions about current issues. However, these verbal arguments differ from written arguments employed in an academic context in which it is assumed that claims are supported by reasons and evidence, and counterarguments are considered and refuted.

Students also have difficulty writing argumentatively when they don't know the topic well. Thus the kind of thematic instruction advocated elsewhere in this book—instruction that includes significant cultural study, literary works, visual texts, research, and nonfiction—is important to helping students, over the course of a rich unit or full semester or year, develop in-depth knowledge and thinking about a complex, controversial subject. This kind of knowledge will go far toward helping students create meaningful arguments, not only about the topic at hand, but on other topics in the future.

As an alternative to viewing arguments as competitive debates, students can be encouraged to perceive argument as scholars do, as "collaborative reasoning" (Johnson & Johnson, 2009) designed to address problems. Adopting a "collaborative reasoning" stance entails students' willingness to bracket out disagreements in order to seek common ground and develop solutions.

Arguing to Learn

It is important not only that students learn to argue in a productive, collaborative manner, but also that they see arguing itself as a way of learning. In *learning to argue*, the goal is for students to acquire the literacy practices involved in convincing others of the validity of their positions. In *arguing to learn*, the goal no longer involves convincing an audience, but rather gaining an enhanced understanding of a topic or issue (Andriessen, 2006). In arguing to learn, students engage in dialogic interactions with peers where they explore and challenge each other's beliefs and positions without necessarily being concerned about their audience's uptake. Effective arguing to learn requires the ability to empathize with and respect others' positions even though they may not agree with those positions. Teachers can model and foster this kind of collaborative classroom environment.

STEPS INVOLVED IN ARGUMENTATIVE WRITING

There are a number of steps involved in teaching argumentative writing.

Identifying Issues and Stances on Issues

As previously noted, one challenge you will face is students' perception that argumentative writing is simply completing an assignment as opposed to being engaged with the idea of arguing to address problems with the status quo. Immersion in meaningful curriculum is a key to changing this perception.

Students can identify issues by noting problems or tensions associated with status quo social practices they are learning about as they study literature and other texts. In engaging in this work they may notice that something's "just not right" about the local, national, or international issues they are learning about. Students can identify these problems or tensions by asking "how come?" or "why is this the case that . . .?" as a means of "disrupting the commonplace" (Lewison et al., 2008, p. 7).

Students can then read different material on the issue at hand, and take notes on, list, and map or create graphs of the competing arguments in this material and the reasons/evidence for those arguments. Students could also work in small groups, collaboratively assessing the arguments in the texts, and comparing their own analyses. Students can also find information about certain issues on various online sites or games (@ = Sites/games on issues).

Conducting Rhetorical Analysis of Nonfiction, Informational Texts

To help students learn to critically read texts and develop material for their arguments, you can provide them with engaging original documents or texts, including videos, that adopt arguments or positions on an event or issue. For example, in having her students study the Virginia Tech shooting, Lisa Beckelhimer (2010) had her students read a range of different texts that rhetorically framed and actually shaped events in different ways from sites such as the American Rhetoric website (http://www.americanrhetoric.com) and the National Archives (http://www.archives.gov). For example, students read a Wikipedia entry and a Virginia Tech Massacre.com site that described it as a "massacre" as well as showing videos of the shootings and the shooter.

Such analysis requires what Mary Lamb (2010) describes as "rhetorical reading" that, consistent with the literacy practice of framing events, involves going beyond inferring *what* an author is saying to considering *how* they are saying it by inferring an author's motives and ethos involved in positioning themselves within certain historical or cultural contexts. Students can focus on the *how* through describing the literacy practices or rhetorical strategies employed using online "sticky note" annotations. Lamb (2010) asks students to summarize the text using the following outline:

a.   Sentence 1: Name of author, genre, and title of work, date in parentheses; a rhetorically active verb (such as *claims, argues, asserts, defines, explores*, or *suggests*); and a "that" clause containing the major assertion, main idea, or thesis statement in the work.

b.   Sentence 2: An explanation of how the author develops and supports the thesis (i.e., evidence), usually in chronological order.

c.   Sentence 3: A statement of the author's apparent purpose, followed by an "in order to" phrase.

d.   Sentence 4: A description of the intended audience and/or the relationship the author establishes with the audience. (p. 47)

Once they have identified the claims, reasons, and evidence, students then need to assess the validity of the argument by defining the warrant or premise linking the claim to the reasons or evidence. (Warrants are the inferences or assumptions deriving from cultural or personal experiences that are taken for granted by the writer, and sometimes by the argument, and they connect—explicitly or implicitly—the argumentative claim and its support.) Warrants are essential to achieving positive uptake in convincing audiences to accept a claim. Because warrants are based on lived-world knowledge, people use them to support or refute claims. It may be useful to describe them as "gap-filling" (Ennis, 1995) in that they fill the gap between the claim and the reason/evidence.

To help students understand the concept of warrants, you can begin with if-then syllogism statements about familiar phenomena. For example, a student may note that it is going to rain since it is cloudy out. Underlying this statement is the warrant that, when it is cloudy outside, then it is going to rain. The warrant can be challenged with evidence of instances of students experiencing cloudy days but having no rain, hence the claim that it is going to rain since it is cloudy out is not valid. Or, an environmental organization may argue that, if we develop more clean energy alternatives, then we will be less dependent on foreign oil. Underlying this if-then claim is the warrant that using more clean energy alternatives lowers foreign oil use. This warrant can certainly be challenged—while we may use more clean-energy alternatives, that does not necessarily mean that we will reduce oil use.

The strengths of these claims and warrants, whether they are convincing, therefore depends on the believability and validity of the evidence. Students can assess the evidence based on the criteria of whether that evidence is:

- *Credible*—as being consistent with accepted, scientific knowledge about a topic or issue or from an authoritative source. If students cite sources that are not credible, then their evidence will not be taken seriously.
- *Sufficient*—as providing enough evidence so that audiences are convinced of the validity of their claims. If students provide only one, limited bit of evidence, then audiences may not be convinced in terms of the quality of the evidence.
- *Accurate*—as providing evidence that is accurate and verifiable as well as sources being cited and properly quoted. (Rex, Thomas, & Engel, 2010, p. 59)

(For an example of applying critical reading to a Coca-Cola™ promotion campaign, see the website.)

Analyzing Rhetorical Appeals: Logos, Pathos, and Ethos

In addition to analyzing the logical relationships between claims, reasons/evidence, and warrants, students need to analyze the use of rhetorical appeals to audiences in terms of what Aristotle defined as logos, pathos, and ethos.

In employing rhetorical appeals, students need to consider their audiences' roles, status, power, knowledge, needs, and interests, so that they can provide relevant, appropriate knowledge. For example, for audiences with extensive knowledge on a topic, they need not provide certain background knowledge needed for audiences with less background knowledge. They also need to consider their own relationship to their audiences—whether they are writing for familiar versus unfamiliar audiences. To help students consider audiences, you can have them write the same arguments for different audiences; for example, writing to a school administrator versus a relative or friend (Carbone & Orellana, 2010). Students can then reflect on differences in their language use across different audiences—the fact that they may use more informal language, and different genres, in writing for a relative or friend while using more formal language and genres in writing for an administrator.

Students can also be taught ways to gain their audience's identification with their stance or belief about a topic or issue, by employing logos, pathos, and ethos (Burke, 1969). To gain an audience's identification, writers or advertisers draw on experiences related to a topic, product, or issue. For example, in arguing for the need for improved bus services, a student may describe the experience of being stuck in rush-hour traffic— an experience with which audiences may identify that would then lead them to perceive the need for alternative transportation using the bus.

Logos refers to the use of language employed to appeal to an audience. In examining how language is employed, students may also consider how specific words may be used in deceptive ways. For example, the Coca-Cola® Livepositively website (http://www.livepositively.com) describes high-fructose corn syrup as "made from corn, a natural grain product. The high fructose corn syrup used in our products contains no artificial or synthetic ingredients or color additives." The use of the word "natural" to describe corn is valid, but when used to imply that high-fructose corn syrup itself is "natural" it is misleading. In examining these uses of language, students may consider how and why they may be appealing. The word "natural" has a certain appeal, as contrasted to "artificial" or "unnatural."

Writers also employ *pathos* as emotional appeals to their audiences— emotions related to establishing a positive connection with an audience. One basic emotional appeal is the idea that the writer cares about their audience and the problem, so that the audience should then identify with the writer's agenda or stance as a solution to the problem. For example, the Livepositively website describes the relationship between Coca-Cola® and its consumers as an assumed emotional bond:

Each time someone enjoys one of our products, they invite us into their lives. With that privilege comes the responsibility to make a positive difference. The products, programs and policies we support help make it easier for people to enjoy refreshing and hydrating products, to be physically active, to make informed choices and to strike a balance that contributes to active, healthy living.

Coca-Cola® is employing an emotional appeal to gain their audience's identification as a company that not only provides people with "refreshing and hydrating products" but also helps people "make informed choices" and contributes to their health.

Ethos refers to how writers construct their role or persona so that they are perceived to be knowledgeable, credible sources of information. For example, in arguing for enhancing disabilities services in her school, the fact that a student herself has a certain disability and is limited by the lack of services in her school adds to the credibility of her ethos or persona—her audience will believe her when she cites examples of the lack of disabilities services.

Online/Paper Role Play

As described in Chapter 1, you can use online role plays on a blog or discussion forum, as did Liz Boeser, to foster her students' argumentative writing (if your students have no computer access, they can exchange paper writing as memos to others in a classroom) (Beach & Doerr-Stevens, 2009; Doerr-Stevens et al., 2011). As previously described, her students adopted the roles of administrators (principals, superintendent, technology people), teachers, students, librarians, lawyers, counselors, coaches, parents, businesspeople, computer hackers, etc. to argue for the need to unblock sites to provide access to needed material for their work. The online role play may conclude with the issue being decided by a governing board, council, organization, or group of voters.

You can also have students engage in online role plays about issues portrayed in literature. In teaching *The Adventures of Huckleberry Finn*, Elizabeth Barniskis (2011) engaged students in an online role play on a Ning, addressing the question of whether the novel should be taught in a fictional high school in which parents had raised questions about its appropriateness. Students created topics such as whether parents should decide on what books should be taught in the English curriculum. For

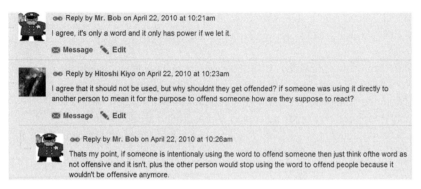

Figure 8.1 Online Discussion of the Use of the N-Word in *Huckleberry Finn*

example, in Figure 8.1, two students in different roles discussed whether the use of the "n-word" in the novel is grounds for banning its inclusion in the classroom. Mr. Bob, a law enforcement person, did not object to the use of the n-word in the novel, while Hitoshi Kiyo raised the possibility that people could still be offended by uses of the word.

Students then stepped out of their roles and debriefed/reflected on their experiences in the role play, noting which roles were perceived to be effective given the quality of their arguments, how roles built alliances with each other, and reasons for the final decision related to the arguments formulated in the role play.

Students then analyzed these arguments and self-assessed their own posts/memos using a rubric (@ = Online role-play rubric). Using the online/paper role play as "prewriting" material, and the in-class argument rubric as a guide, students began writing drafts of their own essays. As noted in Chapter 1, because students were writing their papers for an actual audience and purpose, they were motivated to develop effective arguments.

EXPLANATORY WRITING

Explanatory writing is similar to argumentative writing in that students need to be able to organize and develop their ideas in a logical manner about a topic, issue, or text. To cite the 9th–10th grade Common Core Standards, they need to:

A. Introduce a topic and organize information under broader concepts and categories to make clear the connections and distinctions between key ideas appropriate to the purpose; include formatting (e.g., headings) and graphics (e.g., figures, tables) when useful to clarify ideas.

B. Develop a complex topic through well-chosen, relevant, and sufficient facts, concrete details, quotations, extended definitions, or other information and examples.

Logical Processes in Explanatory Writing

One key skill in explanatory writing is providing logical explanations or reasons for certain actions, events, or phenomena. In their literature classes, students are frequently asked to explain why a character did certain things. In their social studies classes, they are asked to identify causes for certain events or reasons for the success or failure of certain policies. In their science classes, they are asked, having conducted an experiment, to note reasons based on their findings for their results (@ = Teaching explanatory writing).

As with argumentative writing, students need to determine the logical relationship between their opinions or positions and their reasons and evidence based on the assumptions or warrants linking the two. For example, to support the thesis that Elizabeth Bennet in *Pride and Prejudice* is a strong female character, a student may cite the evidence that she is consistently critical of her sisters marrying men primarily for economic reasons.

Students define these warrants or assumptions by drawing on their lived-world and literary knowledge. Therefore, it is important that students learn to recognize differences between the norms operating in their own lived-world contexts and the norms operating in a text world. To appreciate Elizabeth's strengths, they need to recognize that, in contrast to their own contemporary world, in the world of *Pride and Prejudice* (Austen, 2009) women had limited status in terms of selecting martial partners and were totally dependent on their husbands for financial support.

Students can use diagrams to visually portray the relationship between their claims and evidence and how their warrants or assumptions link those claims and evidence. For example:

Claim: Elizabeth is a strong, independent female character.
Evidence: Elizabeth rejects the idea that she needs to marry any man who wants to marry her.
Warrant: In the early 19th Century, women expressed their independence by not having to marry any man who wanted to marry them.

INFORMATIONAL WRITING

In informational writing it is important that students know how to provide sufficient, relevant, and valid information based on audience needs. Therefore, you will need to teach students to adopt the perspective of their audience in determining what constitutes sufficient, relevant, valid information. You can do this by asking students to write directions for how to perform a task—for example, how to play a simple, online game. Then, with the writer watching, the audience performs the task, noting whether certain information was or was not helpful (@ = Teaching informational writing).

Students also need to reflect on variations in their potential audience's prior knowledge so that they can determine when to provide more or less information. Then, they can consider their audience's needs and interests by using questions they expect their audiences to be asking as subheadings, for example, "How can I purchase my tickets online?"

Writing in Social Studies and Science

The Common Core writing standards for social studies and science focus on the importance of engaging in inquiry-based, constructivist social studies and science instruction. While we assume that you're not teaching social studies or science, you are certainly teaching students how to write in ways that can carry over to these disciplines. As you do so, you are helping students learn how to adopt inquiry-based stances associated with posing questions and reading/writing to address those questions.

In working at the middle school level, and planning with your social studies and science colleagues, you can also devise an interdisciplinary curriculum that revolves around topics and issues about which your students can read and write in your language arts class, and study in their social studies and science classes. As described in Chapter 4, students in Rebecca's 9th grade English class read about their urban neighborhoods in literature while they were conducting analyses of Minneapolis neighborhoods in their social studies class.

In science classes, students are continually arguing to learn through sharing their observations and findings with each other. For example, students are familiar with many chemical reactions in their everyday lives that they are not likely to recognize as chemical reactions. Raising related questions that students wonder about (such as "What makes fireworks different colors?" or "Why do people cry when they peel onions?") might interest them in learning about chemical reactions in a way that seeing "Chapter 3: Chemical Reactions" in a textbook might not. These questions, along with original, student-generated questions, foster motivation to explore. As students progress in school, content-based questions (such as "How can two materials have the same chemical composition and molecular mass but have very different properties?") might motivate students more than announcing "Today we begin studying isomers" (Krajcik & Sutherland, 2010, p. 456).

Writing Mini-Ethnographies as Explanatory/ Informational Writing

As we noted in Chapter 5, you and/or your students can conduct ethnographic research to examine social practices in events or sites (Heath & Street, 2008; Sunstein & Chiseri-Strater, 2007). This research can also be a part of writing in English language arts or in social studies related to explaining phenomena or providing information about an event or site.

Ethnographers are primarily interested in understanding social events or interactions as shaped by unique cultural norms or expectations. For example, in studying a rock concert event as a subculture, you might examine the particular roles, norms, and beliefs unique to that social context. Rather than attempting to study an overall subculture, you typically want to focus on specific events as the primary unit of analysis. For example, students could study a classroom event such as a discussion, drama activity, or video production (Bloome et al., 2005). The primary focus of your analysis in events is determining the who, what, where, and when, with a particular focus on what is happening in an event (Heath & Street, 2008). Such analysis is less interested in why things happen in terms of explaining, passing judgments, or assuming that certain things should happen in certain ways. Students should therefore be taught to try to bracket out their preconceptions about what should happen to focus on what is actually happening.

To illustrate students' mini-ethnographies, we cite some examples of students' writing completed in Scott Wertsch's and Linda Mork's 12th grade English classes at Champlin Park High School, Champlin, Minnesota—Jessica Carlson and Blair Gjevre's study of an auto body repair shop, Jennifer Gorman's study of a university sorority house, Phillip Holzchuch and Sarah Loosbrock's study of a Boy Scout troop, and Alicia Lanars's study of rehearsals for a middle school production of *Beauty and the Beast*.

It is also important for students to make explicit what could be stereotyped preconceptions of the people or sites they are studying. For example, in studying the sorority, Jennifer noted that she "tried to wipe away my preconceived opinions, but the opening scene of *Legally Blonde* kept running through my head: platinum blonde girls, pink rooms, and little lap dogs dominated my thoughts" (Gorman, 2010, p. 1). And, in studying the Boy Scouts, Phillip and Sarah recognized the need to challenge the stereotypes that "they are rigid in their tradition, somewhat nerdy, very insistent, and extremely good at tying knots" (Carlson & Gjevre, 2010, p. 2).

It is also useful for students to have a culture broker who can provide them with insider perspectives of a culture. For Jessica and Blair, Jessica's father, who worked in the body shop, provided them with a tour of the different sections of the body shop. For Jen, the sorority president provided her with information about the practices, roles, and norms operating in the sorority. For Phillip and Sarah, the oldest member of the troop provided them with information about the troop.

You can teach your students to use field notes to record descriptions and observations of particular social practices, labeling these notes based on time, date, and topics. Field notes capture concrete observations or "verbal snapshots" of behaviors, objects, talk, settings, etc., in an event or site. To introduce students to using field notes, they could observe a local fast food restaurant, taking dual-entry field notes. On the left side of their page they could record specific aspects of the décor, people, conversations, ordering rituals, language, etc. Then, on the right side of the page, for each of their observations, either during their observations or at a later time, they can reflect on the social or cultural patterns they notice.

Capturing the specific details of an event or site serves to convey the cultural norms or attitudes operating in that event or site. For example, Jessica and Blair described the fact that certain sections of the body shop were very messy and smelly, suggesting that the appearance of those sections did not concern the owners.

In addition to descriptive field notes, students can also write "conceptual memos" (Heath & Street, 2008, p. 79) that include reflections on and ideas about the data being collected. They can then use these memos as well as further questions—for example, "What surprised me? What intrigued me? What disturbed me?" (Sunstein & Chiseri-Strater, 2007, p. 106)—to begin the writing process.

Students can also create maps to portray the locations and dimensions of different physical aspects of a site. For example, Jessica and Blair drew a map of the different sections of the body shop related to the functions of these different sections. Phillip and Sarah drew maps of the church basement in which the Scout troop met to document the size of their meeting room and a gym, along with another map showing where the different members sat.

Your students can also use interviews to acquire information about participants' perceptions of an event or site (Zemliansky, 2008). Students can interview participants about their perceptions of key moments or incidents in their lives related to their involvement in social worlds. In doing so, it is often useful to have them represent turning points or shifts in their perceptions related to their identity construction (Gubrium & Holstein, 2003). Jen interviewed some different members of the sorority to garner their perceptions of their experiences. One member noted that, contrary to her expectations, she found that other members had a variety of different interests and personalities. She also interviewed a male "sweetheart"—someone who helps members establish relationships with members of his fraternity—about his role and relationship and the fact that he could have no relationship with any member and that he enjoyed the attention he received as a male member.

Phillip and Sarah interviewed different members of the Scout troop to determine their perceptions of the practices operating in their meeting. They learned from the Scout leader that he lets the boys control the meeting to teach them leadership skills. From an interview with a member, they learned that what motivates members is the goal of becoming an Eagle Scout.

In analyzing data in the form of notes or interview transcripts, your students can then attempt to locate patterns in the data that can lead to some generalizations about the social practices operating in an event or site. In a study of four males who work at the body shop, Jessica and Blair documented consistent instances of what they characterized as a gendered masculine world—pictures of nude women in the bathroom, lack of consideration of sanitary conditions, competition between the males, and an instance in which one male easily fixed the windshield wipers of Jessica's car, with the comment, "Well, what do you expect from a teenage girl?" This led them to infer that the body shop "is a man's domain. They talk 'man talk,' and their environment is not a place for women." Alicia noted that, in their rehearsals, the middle school students consistently supported each other—when one student had difficulty singing a certain note, another student coached him so that he then could sing that note.

Students may also reflect on how, through conducting their research, they may have changed their preconceptions about a group or site. In her study of the sorority, Jen learned that her preconception about the sorority as being simply a social club was inconsistent with the ways in which members assumed responsibilities for supporting each other as "an enduring family." Alicia noted that her assumptions that middle school students would not be good actors turned out to be wrong.

Through conducting these mini-ethnographies, students acquired the ability to employ detailed descriptions of cultural sites that let them engage in critical analysis of how cultural norms shape people's social practices.

CASE STUDY: MS. IN-NEED-OF-PERSUASION'S HALLWAY (ARGUMENTATIVE WRITING)

So far in this chapter, we've described different strategies for teaching argumentative writing in ways that provide students with some engaging purpose and audience.

This case study will call on your creativity, energy, and knowledge of literacy practices. You are observing Ms. In-Need-of-Persuasion's lifeless classroom, in which students are obviously disengaged. You learn why right away: in teaching a unit on argumentative writing to her 11th grade composition students, she asked them to write a persuasive essay on whether or not the Electoral College should be changed. However, she discovered that the students' writing is largely perfunctory because they have little interest or engagement in completing the assignment. Today, she is passing back students' work and, as she goes on about the flaws she saw in their writing, you can't help but think how this teacher may have approached the unit differently. You will work with your peers to brainstorm ideas for how you'll persuade Ms. In-Need-of-Persuasion to plan an argumentative writing unit that will engage her students in literacy practices. For inspiration, though, you'll first watch and then discuss a video clip in which Sarah Hechlik, practicing high school teacher, discusses an argumentative writing unit that is part of her Advanced Composition course.

Please find two or three peers and go to the LiteraryWorlds.org site and then go to the *Teaching to Succeed* link to find this case study for Chapter 8.

CHAPTER 9

Digital/Media Literacy

CHAPTER OVERVIEW

Digital and Media Literacy Competencies

Employing Digital Literacy Practices

Using Video-Game Playing to Engage Students in Learning

Integrating Uses of Digital Tools: Blogging about Literature

Critical Analysis of Media

Case Study: Ms. In-Network's Hallway (Digital Literacy)

One of the important developments in teaching English language arts is the increased focus on helping students use digital tools to communicate and produce their ideas, as well as teaching students to critically analyze media.

The Common Core State Standards do make some important references to digital and media literacies associated with communication of ideas. For example, the 6–12 reading standard, "synthesize and apply information presented in diverse ways (e.g., through words, images, graphs, and video) in print and digital sources in order to answer questions, solve problems, or compare modes of presentation"; the 6–12 writing standard, "use technology, including the Internet, to produce, publish, and interact with others about writing"; and the 6–12 speaking/listening standard, "make strategic use of digital media and visual displays of data to express information and enhance understanding" perceive reading, writing, and speaking as using media/digital tools to access and share information (for more specific references to media/digital literacies in the Common Core State Standards, http://www.frankwbaker.com/media_core.htm).

While we consider these references significant, we believe that in the 21st Century standards for digital and media literacy should have a central priority in language arts instruction, and should, while including communication, also address uses of digital/media to *build social relationships and connections*, and address learning to *critically analyze* the media and Internet resources. This lack of emphasis on media/digital literacies in the Common Core State Standards stands in contrast with the UK, Canada, Australia, and New Zealand, all of whom have well-developed media literacy curricula and assessments. As English language arts teachers, if we fail to adequately prepare our students to read and write using digital tools, to deeply understand and utilize the resources of the Internet and new and emerging media tools, we have failed to prepare them for college, for the workplace, and for the world in which they currently live.

DIGITAL AND MEDIA LITERACY COMPETENCIES

An important first step in planning curriculum and instruction that authentically incorporates digital and media literacies in a manner that meets and exceeds the Common Core State Standards is to consider the digital media knowledge and skills that you want your students to attain. Renee Hobbs's (2010) (http://www.knightcomm.org/digital-and-media-literacy) list of digital and media literacies competencies is particularly useful:

- *Access.* Finding and using media and technology tools skillfully and sharing appropriate and relevant information with others.
- *Analyze and evaluate.* Comprehending messages and using critical thinking to analyze message quality, veracity, credibility, and point of view, while considering potential effects or consequences of messages.
- *Create.* Composing or generating content using creativity and confidence in self-expression, with awareness of purpose, audience, and composition techniques.
- *Reflect.* Applying social responsibility and ethical principles to one's own identity and lived experience, communication behavior, and conduct.
- *Act.* Working individually and collaboratively to share knowledge and solve problems in the family, the workplace and the community, and participating as a member of a community at local, regional, national and international levels. (p. 19)

It's important to notice that these competencies suggest that your instruction related to digital and media literacies should go beyond simply helping students access and analyze digital or media texts, and instead ought to move students toward actively creating texts and multimodal resources in a responsible, ethical manner that involves civic participation to address social problems.

Creating and Participating in "Learning Commons"

Increasing uses of these involves redesigning classrooms or school media centers into "learning commons" (Loertscher, 2011) based on the idea of students constructing and sharing knowledge through accessing and producing digital content. The concept of a "learning commons" is evident in the increase in hybrid classes that combine face-to-face time in class with time in media centers organized around providing students with online resources (Loertscher, Koechlin, & Zwaan, 2008; Loertscher & Marcoux, 2010). Effective participation in "learning commons" involves the use of the competencies noted above; for example, the ability to access and share relevant knowledge.

To promote the need to create a "learning commons" redesign of schooling, you can also draw on the *National Education Technology Plan 2010: Learning Powered by Technology* (United States Department of Education, 2010) (http://www.ed.gov/technology/netp-2010). This report recommends that "all learners will have engaging and empowering learning experiences both in and out of school that prepare them to be active, creative, knowledgeable, and ethical participants in our globally networked society" (p. 9).

A primary focus of this report is the need for teams of teachers and librarians to collaboratively engage in "connected teaching" to create a "learning commons" to provide students with 24/7 access to digital tools and data (Loertscher, 2011). Consistent with the idea of face-to-face team teaching prevalent in middle school, this involves your use of "connected teaching" to foster sharing of knowledge and information between students, educators, experts, organizations, and parents. For example, you may use your class website, wiki, or blog to invite people to contribute their own perspectives on issues you are studying in your classroom. In doing so, you are positioning students, educators, experts, organizations, and parents as co-learners who can contribute their expertise and ideas to a shared "learning commons."

EMPLOYING DIGITAL LITERACY PRACTICES

There are a wide variety of digital literacy practices involved in meeting the competencies outlined above. In this section we detail several key practices that you may wish to consider (@ = Using digital communication tools).

Accessing, Acquiring, and Organizing Information

As we noted in Chapters 5 and 8, an important digital literacy practice for students to learn is how to readily access and assess online information. Understanding how to use search engines effectively, and how to access the "deep web" of digital archives of literature, news, and scholarly writing are basic to English language arts instruction. News feeds (RSS) are a rich tool for developing expertise and focusing research (Rozema & Webb, 2008). Equally important is learning to capture, store, and organize that information. You may want to teach your students to use digital note-taking tools such as Zoho Notebook, Evernote, Notetaker, Diigo, FreeMind, Trailfire, Keynote, WebNotes, or Journler both to take notes and to copy and paste those notes into drafts of writing.

Students can also use social bookmarking and annotation tools such as Diigo or Evernote to share bookmarks, annotations, and information with their peers. As a teacher, you can use Diigo to set up an educator account. This kind of account allows you to add your students to private class "groups" (www.diigo.com/education) that you can create for sharing bookmarks of websites relevant to topics or issues of interest to your class. Once you add your students to a group, Diigo can send emails to your students alerting them when you have added new bookmarked sites. Students that you have added to a group can also add annotations to any site or blog post to share either with you, with the entire group, or with smaller subgroups. In Diigo, annotations are made by highlighting a section of a text and then adding a "sticky note" that pops up when others click on a "sticky note" icon.

Hyperlinking

Another important digital literacy practice that is important for adolescents in your English language class to learn is hyperlinking, or creating links between digital texts. For example, if students were writing autobiographical essays, hyperlinking could help the students to construct digital texts that include links between aspects of their own lives and historical events, places, and popular culture topics. Hyperlinking can be used to teach close reading and interpretation of texts (as discussed in Chapter 5). As you teach your students to use hyperlinks, you'll find that they learn other key literacy practices. For instance, hyperlinking requires students to carefully read online texts with an eye toward audience and purpose so that they can select links that will lead to information consistent with their purposes.

Networking

Another important literacy practice with particular importance related to digital and media literacy is networking—put simply, learning to make connections within and across social worlds (Figure 9.1). Although networking is something that people, of course, engage in in face-to-face settings, digital media have changed the nature and the magnitude of networking, making it a literacy practice well worth integrating into your instructional repertoire.

Connectivist learning theory suggests that knowledge itself now exists in the online network as opposed to simply in people's heads or in isolated texts or locations (Siemons, 2008). Moreover, people now define their roles and relationships in terms of participation in collaborative or collective networks, as evidenced by the popularity of Facebook. As an English language arts teacher, you can help your students to learn key

Figure 9.1 Networking

networking literacy practices by engaging them in an activity like sharing their writing with their peers or larger audiences using a class blog, wiki, or social networking site such as Facebook, Moodle, Ning, Twitter, or Google+. Sharing their writing in such forums can help students learn to write in a dialogic manner; in other words, students will learn that writing on networking sites functions much like a public essay, editorial commentary, or speech, given the possibility that it will be read and commented on by others. Our students need to learn how to use social networking tools and web publishing appropriately, and safely—another responsibility for the English language arts classroom. We discuss an example of one teacher's work with such dialogic writing later in this chapter.

It is also important for students to learn how to take on a critical stance toward social networking. To help students take on such a stance, you could engage students in a project in which they examine their own uses of social networking. For instance they could study how they create new friendships or maintain current friendships through social networking sites, comparing these practices with face-to-face interactions or texting. Students might notice, for example, that face-to-face interactions provide more information about emotional connections through non-verbal cues, while online interactions provide venues for gaining instant information about peers' everyday activities or plans.

Collaboration

Related to networking is the literacy practice of collaboration. Again, although people collaborate in a variety of ways in their everyday lives, digital collaboration tools have substantially changed the nature of collaboration. For instance, in collaborating on this book from three different cities, we as authors frequently met via Skype, while simultaneously writing and editing via Google Docs, which allowed each of us to write on the same document at the same time. Just 20 years ago we may have relied on many hard-copy drafts of the manuscript sent back and forth numerous times via U.S. mail. Class blogs, wikis, or Google Docs are just a few of the digital collaboration tools that are easily accessible for use in your classroom.

You can create wikis using free wiki platforms such as PBworks (http://pbworks.com), Wikispaces (http://www.wikispaces.com), or Wetpaint (http://www.wetpaint.com). Wikis can serve as useful spaces for students and teachers to collaboratively build study guides to share information about a particular text, author, or topic. For example, in teaching a novel, you can organize a wiki based on categories such as characters, setting, key events, themes, information about the author, reviews, critical analysis, etc. Future classes can then add further information to the wiki so that, over time, students will have access to a collaboratively constructed repository of information about a text, author, or topic. Outstanding projects from previous classes can serve as models for future students, helping to set high expectations for student work.

Wikis are also useful spaces for students to collaboratively share information with other students, including in other schools or other parts of the world. For instance, middle school students in New York shared essays on the similarities and differences in their lives with students in Amman, Jordan (Maltese & Naughter, 2010). Similarly, 8th graders from two different communities shared their responses to young adult novels in a wiki space. These responses led them to discuss their identities as adolescent females—discussions they drew upon to create a zine on these gender-construction issues (Schillinger, 2011).

Another way to engage students in practices of digital collaboration is to ask them to revise or add their own entries to Wikipedia, for example, creating an entry about their school or town. Such a project might help students learn not only how to collaboratively construct knowledge, but also the importance of a critical stance toward the knowledge that is available in such spaces. For instance, students might find misinformation about their school on a pre-existing Wikipedia site that they can work to correct.

Finally, as we did in writing this book, students can use tools like Google Docs for collaboratively writing texts. Programs like Google Docs allow students to collaborate at any time or place as long as they have access to a computer or tablet.

Multimodal Communication, Critique, and Production

Implicit in much of your instruction that incorporates digital and media literacies will be the practice of multimodality, or the use of multiple text modes for communication and—as the Minnesota media/digital literacy standards remind us—for critiquing and producing texts that represent issues in various social worlds. By engaging your students in practices of multimodality, you will be helping students learn that certain combinations of modes can be useful for engaging particular audiences in particular issues. In other words, a central concept in multimodality is the idea that *how* meaning is conveyed matters. By combining different elements of print, images, videos, and sound/music students will learn to creatively and effectively capture the attention of the specific audiences they hope to reach.

One example of multimodal communication that you or your students might employ in the English language arts classroom is a "vlog," or a talking-head video that serves as a blog post. Using a vlog, you or your students can record your thoughts on a webcam for viewing by other members of the class. This activity might be used as part of a larger multimodal project or perhaps as an initial group-process activity in the beginning of the school year for students to introduce themselves. Vlogs can also be used as part of a free-reading program as a means for students to share their reactions and recommendations about books.

In order to record blogs in your classroom, you will need access to an internal or attached webcam. Then you can use either iMovie or Windows Movie Maker to record the video. Once a vlog post is recorded, clicking on "Share" will compress and save the file to the desktop. Finally, the vlog can be stored on a school server, YouTube, or a free video storage site.

Another tool that students might use in creating multimodal productions is digital comic software or VoiceThread. For example, students can use Comic Life (http://plasq.com/comiclife) to create their adaptations of stories that involve visual representations of characters and settings, which can then be converted into QuickTime video files for posting on the web.

Students can also create VoiceThread (http://voicethread.com) slideshows in which they add audio or written comments to their slides or video clips. For example, students could construct autobiographical digital storytelling portrayals of growing up in certain neighborhoods or hometowns in which they consider how phenomena such as race, class, gender, or age differences in their communities have been represented in the media. To find images, students can search for Creative Commons images on Flickr that can be automatically imported into VoiceThread. Students can also import video clips into VoiceThread. Students can then add audio or written annotations to these images or clips. And, they can also have peers or parents add their own annotations. Once they have completed their VoiceThread, their URL links can be added to a class website, blog, or wiki.

Students can also use iMovie or Windows Movie Maker to create digital responses to literature or digital poetry/storytelling that combine images or video with language, audio, or music. In teaching your students to do this kind of work, you can help them understand the unique copyright issues involved in multimodal construction. For instance, although students need to provide proper attribution when they use original texts, if their purpose is to rework, remix, or revise for the purpose of critiquing or parodying material, this "transformative" use of material falls under the "fair use" of such texts (for a description of idea of the "transformational" fair use of digital media related to the fair use code, Aufderheide & Jaszi, 2011; see also http://www.centerforsocialmedia.org/resources/publications/fair_use_in_online_video/).

Another important aspect of multimodality is audio. Newer digital tools such as podcasts provide dynamic means for incorporating audio modes into the English language arts classroom. Students can create podcasts to record commentaries about texts, lectures, field trips, or school and community events. Such podcasts might also include interviews with participants. For example, as part of a family history project, students could interview their grandparents about their past experiences. They could also create radio talk shows or spoken-word performances. Students can record podcasts using GarageBand (on Macs) or Audacity (http://audacity.sourceforge.net/) (on Macs and PCs). For example, students in Robert Rozema's college literature class created a podcast based on their reading of the futuristic novel *Feed* (Anderson, 2002) in which one student spoke as the main character, Titus, summarizing events in the novel, while other students quoted passages from the novel amidst background music (Rozema & Webb, 2008).

USING VIDEO-GAME PLAYING TO ENGAGE STUDENTS IN LEARNING

One third of adolescent gamers play games daily and one fifth play games three to five days a week (Lenhart, Kahne, Middaugh, Macgill, Evans, & Vitak, 2008). None of this necessarily means that you need to bring games into the classrooms. What it does suggest is the value of creating game-like activities that actively involve students, such as the online role-play activity described in Chapter 1.

In playing games, students experience instant "just in time" feedback and data about how they are progressing, as well as the fact that they have clearly defined criteria for what constitutes success (Gee, 2007). Games also immediately involve students in participating in activity even prior to their acquiring conceptual knowledge or rules related to engaging in that activity (McGonigal, 2011). And, players often learn to play collaboratively as well as becoming fans of a game. Also, in adopting the roles of avatars, they are acquiring alternative perspectives about the world. For example, players of *The Sims* game adopt the perspective of a poor, single parent, leading to creating a graphic novel about that experience (McHenry, 2011).

Using Games in the Classroom

In selecting games for use in the classroom, you may want to explore some of the free, online, interactive games that may be consistent with the themes or issues you are addressing in your classroom. In an English methods course, preservice teachers each sampled a number of different games based on the degree to which playing the game with their students and peers fostered critical inquiry in engaging, multimodal ways (Sardone & Devlin-Scherer, 2011) (@ = Games for use in ELA).

The preservice teachers noted how these games could be incorporated into their teaching. For example, they noted that the game *Darfur is Dying* could be used as part of a larger unit on issues of poverty and human rights. Video games often include disturbing images and sequences regarding war and supposed "enemies." Since these games are such a popular part of youth culture it is important to help young people learn to think critically about them. Many sequences from games can be found on YouTube and can be used to critically examine representations of violence, gender, and racial others.

Students can also create their own video games. For example, 7th graders created their own video games over a three-month period using the software program Game Maker (http://www.yoyogames.com/gamemaker) based on their responses to *A Wrinkle in Time* (L'Engle, 1962; Oldaker, 2010). Drawing from scenes and characters from the book, the students wrote narrative plans for creating different levels for their game. For each level, they had players coping with a conflict in a certain situation involving multiple complications. In creating their games using Game Maker, the students recognized that some of their original written plans had to be modified during the creation process. Students then wrote narratives describing what they learned in creating their games.

INTEGRATING USES OF DIGITAL TOOLS: BLOGGING ABOUT LITERATURE

In this section we have outlined several key literacy practices that integrate digital and media literacy, as well as a number of brief examples of how you might incorporate such practices into your classroom. We want to point out, however, that these practices need not be taught in isolation, and in fact are most powerfully taught when integrated with one another and with traditional elements of the language arts curricula covered in the Common Core. For instance, Thein, Oldakowski, and

Sloan (2010) documented one teacher, DeAnn's, experiences using blogs to teach her students tools for critical inquiry into both their own lived social worlds and the worlds of a commonly taught literary text, *To Kill a Mockingbird* (Lee, 1960).

DeAnn asked each student to create a blog in which they wrote about the practices, roles, norms, and beliefs operating in one of their lived social worlds. In these blogs students considered how they and others were positioned and what kinds of tensions, issues, or dilemmas were relevant in the world in question. Constructing the blogs and writing entries for the blogs engaged students in digital networking, as they wrote for an authentic audience. Responding to their peers' blogs engaged students in practices of digital collaboration and dialogue. Ultimately, DeAnn found that students' work on the blogging project led them to a better, more critical understanding of how social worlds functioned within the text world of *To Kill a Mockingbird*. This classroom example illustrates how integration of digital and media literacy practices is not only useful in and of itself, but can also aid teachers in more effectively meeting the more traditional aspects of the reading and writing Common Core State Standards.

CRITICAL ANALYSIS OF MEDIA

In the previous section we outlined key digital and media literacy practices that will be important for you to address in your English language arts classroom. In this section we move beyond acquiring and engaging in these practices to focus on the importance of teaching critical analysis of media as a key component of digital and media literacy competency (@ = Critical media literacy resources and organizations).

As we have suggested earlier in the chapter, adolescents make extensive use of the media in their day-to-day lives. For instance, many adolescents spend a great deal of time each day viewing YouTube videos, playing video games, and listening to music. Additionally, in 2010 North American adolescents averaged 4 hours and 39 minutes daily of television viewing (Eurodata TV, 2011), often while multitasking with other media. While adolescents are clearly extensive users of the media, they do not always respond critically to the media (Beach, 2007; Hammer & Kellner, 2009). They often do not have experience in challenging stereotypical media representations of race, class, or gender; for example, how television or magazine advertising perpetuates normative notions of femininity to sell beauty products. And, while adolescents may have a great deal of experience in consuming the media, they may have had little opportunity to produce their own media—production that enhances their understanding of media (Dockter et al., 2010). All of this points to the importance of teaching adolescents to engage in thoughtful critique of the media, both through critical analysis and through production of media.

Engaging in critical media literacy presupposes the following five principles, leading to posing related questions for each of these principles (Thoman, 2006):

- All media messages are "constructed." Who created this message?
- Media messages are constructed using a creative language with its own rules. What creative techniques are used to attract my attention? How is it put together?
- Different people experience the same media message differently. How might different people understand this message differently from me?
- Media have embedded values and points of view. What lifestyles, values and points of view are represented in, or omitted from, this message?
- Media are organized to gain profit and/or power. Why was this message sent? (p. 24)

For example, students can apply these questions to analyze oil and coal companies' ads claiming that, given the need to preserve the environment, they are then committed to finding new alternative sources of energy, including "clean coal." However, these messages are constructed by the very fossil fuel industry that is now linked to climate change leading to environmental damage. Students can analyze language such as "clean coal" as an example of creative techniques designed to divert attention from the concept of "dirty coal." They can also contrast their own interpretations with people who are skeptical about the human causes of climate change. And, they can determine that these ads omit references to how fossil fuel use is impacting climate change, as well as the fact that oil and coal need to present a positive image to justify the fact that they continue to reap high profits.

Critiquing Images and Video

One place to begin in teaching your students to engage in meaningful critique of media is to ask students to examine images from Flickr, Picasa, or Google Images or video clips from YouTube, TeacherTube, Vimeo, Hulu, or CurrentTV (to show YouTube videos in schools, you can use VuSafe [http://m86vusafe.com], which eliminates inappropriate material). In teaching students to view these images critically, you can ask students to employ Visual Thinking Strategies (Housen, 2007) by posing questions such as:

- What's going on in this image?
- What emotions do you associate with this image?
- What in the image made you think X?
- What are you seeing that suggests X?
- What is missing or left out of this picture?

After you work through holistic questions like these, you can begin to teach students to analyze use of techniques in the construction of images and video—for instance, film shots, angles, editing, design, color, music, and sound that engage or position viewers in certain ways. Relevant questions to pose in this work include:

- What is near to you, far away, and in between?
- What colors are used and how do you respond to those colors?

Other appropriate questions include those created by Delainia Haug for her photography class that was part of the DigMe program at Roosevelt High School in Minneapolis. Haug asked students to respond to photography through the following prompts:

- What do you see? Start with the literal. List only tangible things—not ideas, feelings or conclusions. (For example, you can see a smile, but you cannot see happiness.)
- Make three supported inferences from the photo. (I think _____ because I see _____.)
- Do some analysis and make predictions. If you were in the photo, what would you be thinking, hoping and wondering? If you asked a person in the photo a question, what would they answer? Support your analysis with photographic evidence and background knowledge.
- What does the photo tell you about the time and place, and these people?
- What is missing from the photo? What do you think has been cropped out of the image? What questions do you have about what's outside the frame? (Beach et al., 2009, p. 110)

Students can also use tools such as Google Annotations or VideoANT (http://ant.umn.edu) to add text annotations to specific scenes or techniques in videos (Beach, 2009). In using VideoANT, for instance, students import a YouTube video URL into VideoANT, view the video in a screen on the left side, and then stop the video to write annotations in a sidebar on the right.

ACTIVITY: CRITIQUING IDEOLOGICAL ASSUMPTIONS IN MEDIA TEXTS

One goal of critical media literacy education involves unpacking and critiquing media text representations of cultural norms and roles constituted by what seem to be natural, commonsense ideological assumptions. For example, ads for Halloween costumes reify gender roles in which costumes for males feature action hero costumes that focus on physical action, while costumes for females focus on physical appearance consistent with traditional notions of femininity.

Select a media text—a television series, film, advertisement, magazine, website, or music lyrics—and identify certain consistent patterns in the images or language. Then, infer the underlying value assumptions regarding representations of cultural norms or roles, for example, constituting race, class, gender, or age differences. Also, note what is missing in these representations that provide more complex, alternative perspectives of a certain phenomenon.

Analyzing and Constructing Film Adaptations

Analyzing and constructing film adaptations is a powerful way for students to examine how different modes can convey different meaning related to the same content. For many years, English language arts teachers have asked students to analyze film adaptations of texts they are reading in order to examine differences in their experiences with film versus print versions. This is a useful instructional technique, especially when students are asked to notice the affordances and limitations of the various tools that are employed in print and film modes. For instance, you may want to help students examine ways that film versions employ visual imagery, music, and camera shots to construct the meaning of events from a text while print texts ask the reader to create his or her own imagined version of events guided by descriptive passages and particular uses of language. You may also want to ask your students to contrast three different types of adaptations—"the loose, the faithful, and the literal" (Giannetti, 2007, p. 406). In loose adaptations, a director constructs her own original story based roughly on a text, while in faithful or literal adaptations a director attempts to replicate the text as closely as possible. Considering a variety of versions of film adaptations can help students notice that loose adaptations are more successful because they are more likely to exploit the strength of film techniques. Students can also create their own video adaptations of texts they read, working as teams to first create scripts and storyboard versions that serve as starting points for filming those scenes.

Critiquing Advertising

After you have engaged your students in critique of images, you can move on to helping them examine how advertising takes up images, signs, and symbols to convey persuasive messages. Rhetorical analysis can be employed to help students examine the social and cultural meaning and appeal of signs and codes in advertisements. For example, you might ask your students to examine advertisements related to weight-loss or diet programs and tools. Through careful study of the before and after images in these advertisements, students might notice the presupposed value of slimness as culturally desirable and as linked to certain kinds of femininity and even social-class-specific dispositions. By contrast, you could point out that in the late 1890s being obese was perceived to be culturally positive as a class marker. Some questions that you might find useful in engaging students in a rhetorical analysis of advertisements are:

- Who is the intended or target audience?
- What signs, markers, images, language, and social practices imply that audience?
- How is the audience linked to use of the product?
- What are the underlying value assumptions (having white teeth enhances your popularity; casino gambling is enjoyable)?

Critiquing Film and Television Genres

Given the amount of time adolescents spend watching television, it is certainly important that they learn tools for critiquing popular film and television genres. One way to engage students in this sort of critique is to begin to unpack the ideological assumptions underlying narratives or storylines in film and TV genres such as detective, mystery, science fiction, horror, romance, soap opera, musical, comedy, and reality TV. Here you might employ literacy practices related to framing events in terms of prototypical roles, goals, plans, norms, and beliefs (Beach, 2007). For example, in leading students through an analysis of narratives in the genre of the crime drama, you could pose questions about:

- *Roles*: who engages in and solves the crime?
- *Goals*: what is the detective's purpose?
- *Plans*: what means or tools does the detective use to solve the crime?
- *Norms*: what are the norms constituting appropriate actions?
- *Beliefs*: what are the underlying value assumptions related to the above?

By considering these questions, students may infer that, in some cases, crime dramas assume that crime is largely a function of minority people in urban settings who are prone to violent actions, requiring tough deterrents in the form of law enforcement. This portrayal of urban settings fails to examine many of the other factors—poverty, lack of employment, poor services, etc., that may lead to crime.

Critiquing News and Documentaries

Another area of television and film that warrants critical attention is news and documentary. It is important for students to develop a critical awareness of the construction of both television and print news in order for them to develop responsible civic engagement in current events. For instance, you might engage students in an examination of the journalistic quality of television and print news related to depth of reporting, use of evidence, and issues of bias or objectivity (Figure 9.2). Students can also study the financial challenges facing traditional print journalism now that they have lost a lot of their advertising revenue, coupled with the fact that people acquire news from online outlets for free.

You can also have students examine the journalistic quality of local TV news related to informing audiences about important topics and issues in their community. To do so, you could ask students to keep a log of a local TV news broadcast to determine the topics and length in number of seconds devoted to coverage of different stories. In their analysis, students may notice that many stories provide only superficial coverage of events or issues with little or no contextual information. You could also ask students to investigate the ownership of news outlets and consider how that ownership may shape the news content.

You might also ask your students to study bias and objectivity in documentaries. For instance you could ask them to examine the degree to which editing, voiceover commentary, or selection of material may or may not capture the reality of a topic, event, or issue. Extreme examples of lack of objectivity, such as propaganda films like *Triumph of the Will* (Riefenstahl, 1935) that glorified Hitler and the Nazi Party, can provide a useful starting place for this work. They may then view some of

Figure 9.2 You Write What You're Told

Used with permission from Micah Ian Wright.

Frederick Wiseman's "cinéma vérité" documentaries about schools, hospitals, towns, government/welfare agency sites, prisons, stores, parks, etc. that have little or no editing or voiceovers.

Critiquing Social and Cultural Hierarchies in Media Representations

In all of your instruction on media critique, you can include analysis of representations of social and cultural hierarchies pertaining to gender, race, class, age, context (urban, suburban, rural), schooling, leisure activities, and dispositions. Questions that are useful for this kind of analysis include:

- How are various groups of people represented?
- Where do these representations come from?
- Who produces these representations?
- What might be the goal of producing these representations?
- How is complexity limited by these representations?
- What is missing in these representations?

For example, representations of masculinity often portray males as having to be "tough" in terms of being competitive, assertive, and physical (see *Tough Guise*, http://tinyurl.com/ye99q6h) while representations of femininity portray women as having to be physically attractive, thin, and compliant (see *Killing Us Softly 3*, http://tinyurl.com/d37y5h). For example, female athletes are often portrayed just as much in terms of their appearance as they are in terms of their athletic prowess (see *Playing Unfair: The Media Image of the Female Athlete*, http://www.mediaed.org/cgi-bin/commerce.cgi?preadd=action&key=208). Another interesting example is representations of teachers in Hollywood films. One analysis of teachers' methods of instruction in six films found that, while the teachers moved from a more teacher-centered to a more student-centered approach, the films portrayed their changes as due to their own individual motivation rather than resulting from changes in the schooling system itself. Likewise this analysis suggested that such representation of teachers fails to portray how larger institutional forces can limit student achievement (Kelly & Caughlan, 2011).

Media Ethnographies

In critically analyzing media texts, students also need to recognize that different audiences ascribe different meanings for the same texts given differences in audiences' needs, purposes, or stances. As suggested by the discussion of ethnographic research in Chapter 8, students can study how audiences or participants as fans construct meaning in television viewing, Internet chat rooms, blogs, online fan club activities (soap opera/*Star Trek*), responses to magazines/e-zines, participation in media events (sports broadcasts, rock concerts), playing video games, or surfing the web. For example, students could study game players' social participation in their game playing or fan sites for fans of *Star Trek* (http://www.startrek.com/startrek/view/index.html or http://www.trekweb.com), *Star Wars* (http://www.starwars.com), *Harry Potter* (http://fanfiction.mugglenet.com), *Lost* (http://abc.go.com/primetime/lost/index), or *Twilight* (http://community.livejournal.com/twilight_fandom), as well as how their peers may define their identities through participation in these sites. For example, middle school students may study how an online virtual site invites tween females to enjoy the experience of "fashion, fun, friendship" by creating their own avatars and talking or shopping with other tweens on the Barbiegirl (http://www.barbie.com) site.

Through critiquing and producing media texts, your students are learning to actively resist the underlying ideologies of consumerism inherent in commercial media, resistance that leads them to perceive the media, as well as digital communication, as tools for exploring alternative values shaping their lives.

CASE STUDY: MS. IN-NETWORK'S HALLWAY (DIGITAL LITERACY)

In this chapter, we've discussed ways of using digital tools for communicating with others—tools such as cell phones that students frequently use outside of school. The challenge for you is how to consider using these tools to foster learning within school.

In this case study, while observing teachers at this middle school, you will find yourself an active member in addressing crisis, as a shooting has taken place at the neighboring high school, and middle school students, faculty, and staff must cope. In particular, you will observe how one teacher, Ms. In-Network, addresses the traumatic events of the day, as well as how her students deal with the day. Interestingly, she engages the students in free-writing about the day's events and their emotions. After class, Ms. In-Network suggests meeting after school to read through students' responses and plan a follow-up lesson or unit that addresses either or all of the following issues: domestic violence, violence and trauma in schools, and suicide. After reading students' papers with other intern teachers, you realize that many students wrote about being able to communicate at times of crisis. Many were thankful for their phones today. You and Ms. In-Network see this as a perfect opportunity to tackle the issues that came up today from a digital/media literacy framework; you'll make more specific plans with your peers.

Please go the LiteraryWorlds.org site and the *Teaching to Succeed* link to find this case study for Chapter 9.

CHAPTER 10

Speaking and Listening

CHAPTER OVERVIEW

The Common Core State Speaking/Listening Standards

Single Public Presentations

Alternatives to Classroom Public Speeches

One-to-One Social Interactions: Active Listening and Support

Studying Oral Communication as Shaped by Social Genres

Fostering Dialogic Interactions in Class Discussions

Case Study: Ms. Discussion Meltdown's Hallway

Small-Group Discussions or Literature Circles

Online Group Discussions

Reflecting on Your Discussion Facilitation

Case Study: Sarah Hechlik's Hallway (Literature Circles)

This chapter addresses speaking and listening standards related to making oral presentations and engaging in discussions. It describes activities for critical analysis of language practices involved in effective oral presentations and discussions. It reframes assumptions about oral language use in the Common Core State Standards by describing the use of oral language for engaging in the social practices of *constructing identities, building relationships, empathizing with others' perspectives, collaborating with others, formulating plans, problem-solving,* and *achieving consensus.* It includes examples of teachers creating plans for use of group process strategies and small-group/book club discussions to foster collaborative responses to texts. And, it describes the uses of podcasting tools for recording presentations and Skype inter-views for broadcasting to audiences. It also discusses making accommoda-tions for learning-disabled, blind, or deaf students using text-to-speech and speech-to-text software tools, as well as strategies for assisting English Language Learners through oral presentation/translation activities.

THE COMMON CORE STATE SPEAKING/ LISTENING STANDARDS

The Common Core State Standards speaking/listening standards go beyond traditional speech instruction that typically involve students giving public speeches. These standards include the standard "present information, evidence, and reasoning in a clear and well-structured way appropriate to purpose and audience." Achieving this standard entails more than the ability to give public speeches. Moreover, the standards recognize that there are a range of other literacy practices involved in oral interactions with others. To cite the standards (Common Core State Standards, 2010), this includes the ability to:

- Participate effectively in a range of interactions (one-on-one and in groups), exchanging information to advance a discussion and to build on the input of others.
- Integrate and evaluate information from multiple oral, visual, or multimodal sources in order to answer questions, solve problems, or build knowledge.
- Evaluate the speaker's point of view, reasoning, and use of evidence and rhetoric.
- Present information, evidence, and reasoning in a clear and well-structured way appropriate to purpose and audience.
- Make strategic use of digital media and visual displays of data to express information and enhance understanding.
- Adapt speech to a variety of contexts and communicative tasks, demon-strating a command of formal English when indicated or appropriate.

SINGLE PUBLIC PRESENTATIONS

One focus of the speaking/listening standards is the single public presen-tation associated with the familiar public speech (@ = Public speeches). The ability to effectively deliver public speeches is an essential literacy practice. Students need to know how to clearly present their ideas to an audience in an organized, engaging manner. They also need to know how to sequence their ideas in a logical way so that the audience can easily follow their reasoning. And, as noted in the standards, they need to "adapt speech to a variety of context and communicative tasks" (Common Core State Standards, 2010, p. 44), by determining the nature of their audiences' knowledge, needs, interests, attitudes, and expectations.

In having students prepare for public speeches, it is essential that they select topics about which they have a strong interest so that they have some purpose for giving their speeches. As with every other skill in this book, we advocate weaving instruction into a thematic curriculum focused on students gaining knowledge of important and meaningful content that fosters student choice and includes literacy practice events. This approach is more effective than simply breaking your curriculum up into isolated units related to literature, writing, media, speaking, and so forth. This kind of curriculum can give students a sense of purpose and provide inspiration for finding real audiences for their speaking.

Students need to know how to "make strategic use of digital media and visual displays of data to express information and enhance understanding" (Common Core State Standards, 2010, p. 44). For example, in using presentation tools such as PowerPoint, Keynote, or Prezi, students need to know how to provide information on their slides that supports their oral presentation.

One problem with many presentations supported by digital tools, including teacher lectures with PowerPoint, is that presenters put too much information on their slides and then simply read that information to their audiences. To create more effective presentations, students need to know how to limit the amount of information they provide so that they are using their slides as summary prompts for conveying their ideas. They also need to know how to incorporate images or video clips as illustrative, visual means of conveying their ideas as opposed to relying only on language.

Criteria for Evaluating Public Speeches

To assist students in making their speeches, it is useful to provide them with clearly defined criteria or rubrics for their self-assessment, as well as peer and/or teacher assessment. These criteria may include:

- *Use of voice and non-verbal cues.* Students employ variations in voice and pitch, as well as pauses, to convey their ideas. They also use non-verbal cues such as eye contact or gestures to build a relationship with their audience.

- *Adoption of a persona and stance.* Students adopt the persona of a believable, knowledgeable spokesperson with a clearly defined stance on a topic or issue.
- *Gaining audience identification.* Students seek audience identification through referencing their audience's knowledge, beliefs, or interests in a topic or issue.
- *Logical organization of ideas.* Students organize and present their ideas in a logical order, forecasting their overall structure and providing a summary conclusion.
- *Use of illustrative examples.* Students provide illustrative examples of their ideas based on consideration of their audience's prior knowledge, interests, and beliefs.
- *Use of visual/digital presentation tools.* In using presentation tools (PowerPoint, Keynote, Prezi, etc.), students use language and/or images in a manner that supports versus substitutes for their presentation.

ALTERNATIVES TO CLASSROOM PUBLIC SPEECHES

The traditional classroom public speech can be intimidating for some students. And, having each student make a presentation can consume a considerable amount of class time. Plus, it is more meaningful to students when they speak to real audiences about the knowledge/expertise they are developing in your class. Here are some alternatives to these large-group, classroom presentations (@ = Alternatives to public speeches).

Podcast or Vodcast Presentations

You can ask students to create podcasts or video presentations for sharing with the class, with other students in the school, or with community members. For example, they could record a vodcast (video-podcast) recorded through their computer's webcam using iMovie or Windows Movie Maker. To do this, students simply need to click on the "Record" button to record themselves. When they are done recording, they can click "Share" to compress and save the file to the desktop. You might also ask students to use vodcasts to share autobiographical narratives, their positions on certain images, or book/media recommendations. Or, rather than engaging in face-to-face presentations, students could import the PowerPoint or Keynote presentations to Google Presentations, SlideShare, or VoiceThread and then add audio voiceovers to their presentations.

Interactive Poster-Presentations

You can also ask your students to prepare poster-presentations using printouts from their PowerPoint or Keynote presentations for face-to-face interactions with their peers. Or they could address a younger audience to educate them about a topic they are learning about in your class. They could also create digital poster presentations by putting their presentations online.

Spoken-Word Presentations

Students could create and record their podcasts of spoken-word presentations as described in Chapter 6 to perform poems, rap lyrics, or essays (for examples, http://tinyurl.com/3n6p875). Engaging in these spoken-word presentations involves students employing their voice, pitch, pauses, and non-verbal cues and gestures to convey certain meanings. Presenting in different classes, at student assemblies, meetings of teachers, professional conferences, community organizations, churches, and various public settings can all be excellent opportunities to engage your students in a consideration of appropriate speaking genres for addressing specific audiences. You may be surprised by the goodwill that can be generated for your teaching and your students by their making successful presentations.

ONE-TO-ONE SOCIAL INTERACTIONS: ACTIVE LISTENING AND SUPPORT

Another important aspect of addressing the speaking/listening standards involves one-to-one oral interactions between yourself and students (@ = One-to-one social interactions). For example, you may be conferencing with a student about an issue she is coping with or providing them with feedback about their work. In these one-to-one interactions, you can help students address challenges in their schooling and their lives, and you can model ways of engaging in productive, supportive conversations.

In these conferences, it is important to let students participate in setting the agenda for the conference so that they feel comfortable sharing their thoughts and feelings. You can do so by letting them begin the conference by asking, them, for example, "what's on your mind?"

It is also important to engage in active listening so that you can discern their thoughts and feelings. Restating or playing back students' words can help them understand what they are communicating. In some cases, students may have difficulty formulating their thoughts and feelings, for example, the fact that they are having difficulty in making friends in a class. By restating what they are saying—"You seem to be saying that you're having difficulty making friends"—you're assisting students in clarifying their thoughts and feelings, as well as giving them a sense of your ability to empathize with their difficulties. Robyn Campbell (2011) argues that "The first step for teaching listening in the classroom is for teachers to evaluate their own listening skills" (p. 67).

STUDYING ORAL COMMUNICATION AS SHAPED BY SOCIAL GENRES

In speaking and listening in everyday social interaction, people employ a range of different social genres—interviewing, making a sales pitch, debating, bargaining, lodging a complaint, proposing marriage, negotiating an agreement, lecturing, etc. These social genres serve to organize or structure social practices in some consistent, codified manner as "forms of life, ways of being, frames for social action" (Bazerman, 1994, p. 79). They also "make it possible to act with others over time in more or less, but never entirely, predictable ways, individually, collectively, and institutionally (Russell, 2009, p. 43) (@ = Social genres).

People know how to act in certain events based on those genres they perceive constituting an event. An utterance will be identified as a "joke" more readily in a stand-up comedy routine than in a religious sermon. Conversely, participants signal to one another the relevant context of activity—how others should frame their language use in an event through manipulation of generic features: telling a string of jokes in a "sermon" or preaching by a comedian may transform participants' interpretation of the social situation (Lefstein & Snell, 2011, p. 44).

Students also learn to reflect on their effectiveness in employing social genres or speech acts by determining whether they have achieved their intended "uptake." If a wait person knows how to effectively prompt a customer to place their order—saying, for example, "Are you ready to order?" and the customer orders—then this initiation speech act has a positive "uptake." However, if customers have difficulties knowing how to order or aren't ready to order, then the "uptake" is more problematic.

To help students understand how uses of social genres shape their oral communication, you can have them reflect on ways they or characters in a novel or play use social genres and speech acts. For example, they could discuss what they do to perform the social genres of greeting someone, arguing, making a sales pitch, posing questions/interrogating, giving feedback, creating a plan, reciting a poem or rap, pleading one's case, gossiping, sympathizing, etc.—genres that serve to build certain kinds of relationships or identities in social contexts.

For example, in reflecting on their participation in the world of their sports team, students could note how players, parents, and/or coaches use various social genres of giving motivational pep talks, providing positive feedback, debriefing plays, sending in plays, advising players, modeling ways of thinking about techniques, responding to interview questions, supporting peers, etc. They can also reflect on instances when players, parents, and/or coaches are overly critical of players or fail to provide pep talks or positive feedback, and how not employing certain genres may adversely influence a team's success. They could then role-play different instances of using specific types of social genres. For example, they can assume the roles of waitresses/waiters and customers and engage in different scenarios that include breakdowns or successes in employing certain speech acts within genres.

FOSTERING DIALOGIC INTERACTIONS IN CLASS DISCUSSIONS

One of your primary jobs as an English teacher involves leading discussions. In doing so, one of your goals should be to foster dialogic interactions between students. Unfortunately, teacher-led discussions often involve more monologic, authoritative interactions which serve to limit alternative meanings (Bakhtin, 1981). Such teacher-led discussions often involve use of the Initiate-Respond-Evaluate (I-R-E) teaching—a questioning genre that limits students voicing different perspectives or interacting with each other. In this ritual-like I-R-E pattern, the teacher poses a question, a student answers, and the teacher evaluates their answer, as in "Jill, what was the setting for *The Crucible*?", Jill: "Salem, Massachusetts," Teacher: "Very good, Jill." In using the I-R-E pattern, the teacher maintains total control of the discussion. And, when the focus always returns to the teacher, there is little interaction between students, interaction essential for dialogic discussions.

Unfortunately the use of the I-R-E pattern and closed questions (questions with just one correct answer) predominate in classroom discussions, with few instances of students responding to each other. One study of hundreds of classrooms found that three or more students only interact with each other an average of 1.7 minutes per every

60 minutes of class time (Applebee, Langer, Nystrand, & Gamoran, 2003). The lack of student interaction with each other has to do with the use of closed questions. Of the questions posed in the study, only 19 percent of teachers' questions were authentic, open questions—questions with no predetermined answers. And, only 31 percent of the questions involved follow-up questions in which teachers asked students to elaborate on or extend their responses. Such follow-up questions are indicative of teachers actually listening to and acknowledging students' original thoughts.

In contrast, in dialogic interactions, teachers allow students the space to explore alternative meanings with each other by following up or piggybacking on each other's ideas. They may also "double-voice" others' language or discourses in ways that challenge or resist monologic, limited meanings by bringing in multiple, competing voices or stances (Bakhtin, 1981). Unfortunately, teachers often limit discussions to only their voice or certain accepted student voices (Applebee et al., 2003). Given this compelling research, it is important that you take the time to carefully develop—and write down—clearly worded, authentic, open questions before a discussion begins.

Dialogic interactions occur when students are encouraged to mimic, parody, or, what Bakhtin (1981) describes as "reaccenting" and "ventriloquation" of others' languages and discourses. To foster dialogic interaction in her middle school classes, Karen Brooks (2011) encouraged her students to engage in "reaccenting" texts through uses of intertextual links to popular culture texts. For example, in reading *Romeo and Juliet*, students in her class used a talk show format for the Capulets and Montagues to voice their attacks on each other, and create text message scripts for characters' interacting with each other. Brooks explained that a novel like *Twilight* by Stephenie Meyer:

Can be analyzed alongside the film, fan sites and fiction on the web, YouTube interviews by the author, previous vampire narratives (Stoker's *Dracula*), TV series (*Buffy the Vampire Slayer, Vampire Diaries, True Blood*), associated images and music; while discourses around romance, social mores, parent/child relationships, peer expectations, Otherness, faith, ethical codes, consumer culture and marketing can also be explored. (p. 75)

Leading discussions involves using a number of techniques for facilitating interactions between students (@ = Leading large-group discussions).

Discussion Starters

It is often the case that it is difficult to initially engage students in discussions. Some students may not have thought much about the topic or text being discussed. Or, students are reticent to share their ideas, particularly in a large group setting. You can begin by organizing desks so all students can see each other. Rather than begin the discussion with posing questions, you can employ some of the following discussion strategies techniques.

Students could engage in some informal free-writes to help them spontaneously generate some thoughts about a topic or text. You might then ask them to share what they wrote and have other students react to their peers' ideas. You can also provide students with a prompt for their free-writes related to the topic or issue being discussed. Writing can also be used during a discussion ("Let's everyone write about the response student X just made") or at the end of a discussion ("What are the most important things you learned from our discussion today?").

Students could list different questions on a whiteboard that intrigue them related to the topic, issue, or text under discussion. They could then organize these questions into categories or rank-order the questions, leading up to determining which questions they most want to address in the discussion. Or, based on your reading of students' writings about a text, you could select some provocative student quotations to read anonymously to the class for their reactions.

You can also launch a discussion around a case-study scenario similar to those we're using with this book to foster your own reflections and discussions. An essential component of case-study scenarios is to raise doubt in students' minds related to their beliefs about a certain topic or issue—doubts that lead them to collaboratively consider alternative ways to cope with a topic or issue (McCann, Johannessen, Kahn, & Flanagan, 2006). For example, in our work with online role plays employed in Liz Boeser's class (Doerr-Stevens et al., 2011), one case study based on an actual situation had to do with administrators in a neighboring high school accessing students' Facebook pages to verify when students were reported to be drinking in violation with the state's athletic code. This case study raises doubts about administrators' rights related to student privacy. In another case-study scenario, "Lost at Sea," a ship was sinking and passengers were on a lifeboat, but the lifeboat was overweight, so the passengers needed to toss certain items overboard—food, blankets, water, first aid, etc., necessary for survival (McCann et al., 2006, p. 44–47). In considering this scenario, students then need to determine which items the passengers should throw overboard to survive.

You can also encourage more student participation by having them employ "backchannel" instant-message tools such as TodaysMeet (http://todaysmeet.com) or Chatzy (http://www.chatzy.com) during a discussion, which are projected on a screen or whiteboard. Students can also share tweets using a class Twitter or topic hashtags; use microblogging tools such as Tumblr or synchronous chat tools such as Google Talk (http://www.google.com/talk/), iChat, or chat forums within Nicenet, Moodle, or Ning; or use the discussion pages of a wiki. These tools serve to encourage those students who are reticent to orally share their thoughts to participate. As one student noted, "When we have class discussions, I don't really feel the need to speak up or anything . . . When you type something down, it's a lot easier to say what I feel" (Gabriel, 2011, p. 1). And, another student noted, "It's made me see my peers as more intelligent, seeing their thought process and begin to understand them on a deeper level" (Gabriel, 2011, p. 2).

Inviting Student Participation

As discussion leader it is important that you clearly remember who has participated and who has not, and find ways to invite *all* students into the discussion. Some students go through school, day after day, and never speak in class—and are never invited to speak. Be sure that everyone in your class is included in your discussions. Sometimes you can say simply, "Let's hear from someone who hasn't yet spoken." Some students may need specific invitations to participate, and such invitations can be issued in ways that are not intimidating: "Jose, I'd love to hear what you think about this topic."

In starting a discussion, it is important to begin with initial engagement, reactions, descriptions, or autobiographical narrative responses to a topic, issue, or text, as opposed to high-level abstraction or interpretation questions such as "What did you think about this book?" or "What is this poem saying about the world?" Beginning with these responses allows students to inductively build up their ideas to later make more abstract, interpretive inferences. It is also important to recognize that, while you may have previously discussed a topic, issue, or text multiple times, your students are just coming to that topic, issue, or text for the first time.

Fostering Interactions between Students

All of this suggests that as the primary facilitator of discussions you will want to shift the focus from yourself, as the central initiator and evaluator of all interactions, to your students, as people interacting around important issues. You will therefore need to develop strategies teaching students to build on each other's comments or conversational turns so that they are collaboratively developing their ideas about specific topics in some depth. Developing ideas in depth leads to extended stretches of turns focused on the same topic, as opposed to jumping from topic to topic. Encouraging extended stretches involves avoiding evaluating each student's contribution using the I–R–E pattern with comments such as "Good answer." Instead, you can ask students to respond to each other with questions such as "What do others of you think about Brittany's idea?" And, consistent with the listening standards, you can encourage students to listen to each other's contributions by having them restate previous students' contributions before they share their own ideas.

You can also encourage students to pose their own open-ended questions of each other or themselves. To do so, you can model question-asking strategies that students internalize in order to engage in their own self-questions or questions to each other, using, for example, the Critical Response Protocol (CRP) questions described in Chapter 7.

When you repeat your questions you teach students that they don't need to listen the first time. And, rephrasing your questions is likely to lead to confusion. It is also important to know that when you repeat student comments you may think that you are showing support for your students and demonstrating your active listening, but what is more likely happening is that you may be training your students not to listen to each other, but to listen to you. If a student didn't hear or understand your question or a question or comment of a peer, ask a different student to share it with the class.

Students are more likely to respond to each other when they frame their positions as hunches or hypotheses as tentative "passing theories" (Kent, 1993) as opposed to definitive statement. For example, a student may state, "I'm wondering why the main character is always so reluctant to speak out," a statement that invites others to mutually explore ways of addressing that hunch or hypothesis.

You can also spark discussions by administering opinion surveys about the topics or issues under discussion in the beginning of, or during, a discussion using online survey tools such as SurveyMonkey or Poll Everywhere. For example, if you are discussing portrayals of war litera-ture, you can make the statement "There is no such thing as a just war" and have students indicate whether they agree or disagree on a scale of "1" (agree) to "6" (disagree). You can then project the results on a screen and have students discuss reasons for these results.

To help students learn some practices and norms for engaging in effective discussions, you can ask them to observe each other and note instances of effective versus less effective discussion practices and norms. In her middle school classroom, Anne Richardson (2010) asked her students to identify practices and norms for "accountable talk" by having members of the class engage in a "fishbowl" observation of four to six students engaged in a discussion. From their observation, the students identified six basic "rules of conduct" associated with "accountable talk":

1. One person speaks at a time.
2. Use a one-foot voice (a voice that can be heard only from a foot away or less).
3. Stay on topic.
4. Listen actively to each other.
5. Keep eyes on the speaker.
6. Make connections to the previous speaker's ideas before moving on to another idea. (p. 85)

To focus the other students' observations, she asked them to consider the following questions:

- How did you know that the participants were prepared for the discussion?
- What method did the participants use to get started?
- Did you notice any examples of eye contact or active listening during the discussion?
- Did you notice the use of accountable talk language?
- Which of the six key reading strategies did you notice being used in the discussion? (p. 86)

Using Narratives in Discussions

It is also useful to have students share narratives in discussions about their everyday experiences evoked by a topic, issue, or text. In doing so, students can connect these experiences to topics, issues, and texts. For example, in responding to a novel or story, students may recall experiences related to the events in a novel or story. It's important that students elaborate on their narratives rather than simply summarize a related event. Elaborating on a related narrative event can help students develop their perspectives or beliefs associated with that event. For example, students were reading a story about a breakdown in a friendship. Students then share their experiences of learning that their good friends may not always support them in challenging situations. They then cycled what they learned from the lived-world experiences about friendship breakdowns to interpret the story. We do caution, however, that you ensure that your students understand that their lived-world experiences are not necessarily equivalent to the experiences portrayed in the text. This is particularly important when students read multicultural texts about characters with whom they may share little in common.

In an analysis of the use of narratives in discussions about the Holocaust, Mary Juzwik (2009) found that the teacher, Jane, employed narratives to enhance discussions in four different ways involving different rhetorical purposes: referential, interpersonal, expressive, and ethical. In discussing the Holocaust, Jane and her students employed narratives in *referential* ways to describe Holocaust victims and survivors' experiences for the purpose of enhancing understanding of historical events. They engaged in *interpersonal* sharing of related experiences. And, she and her students were aware of how they structured or developed their narratives in *expressive* ways to engage their audiences. Finally, they used narratives in both positive and troubling *ethical* ways, in some cases to portray Jewish people in essentialized or subordinate positions. Using narratives for these different rhetorical purposes enhanced the quality of the discussions, suggesting the need to encourage students to share narratives in their discussions.

ACTIVITY: ANALYZING CLASSROOM DISCUSSIONS

Observe some large-group classroom discussions, taking notes of specific instances of student talk and teacher use of facilitation techniques. Compare differences between these discussions in the level of student participation related to differences in the teacher's use of facilitation techniques and activities. Determine reasons why use of certain techniques served to foster student engagement and interaction. Then, reflect on how you might employ these techniques to foster facilitation of your own classroom discussions.

CASE STUDY: MS. DISCUSSION MELTDOWN'S HALLWAY

These, then, are some techniques you can use to facilitate large-group discussions. However, in some cases, you may encounter breakdowns in discussions when students do not respect each other's contributions.

In this first case study, you will find yourself observing a class in which a discussion has gotten out of control, as students personally attack one another during a discussion of John Steinbeck's *The Pearl* (2002). You will work with your peers to assess the situation. In particular, you'll review the "Discussion Starters" and "Fostering Interactions between Students" sections of Chapter 10, as you devise a discussion plan for use in Ms. Discussion Meltdown's classroom. Not only is your goal to engage the students in critical thinking regarding personal interaction, but you will also devise a discussion plan that you believe illustrates your content.

Please find two or three peers and go to the LiteraryWorlds.org site and the *Teaching to Succeed* links to locate this case study for Chapter 10.

SMALL-GROUP DISCUSSIONS OR LITERATURE CIRCLES

One alternative to large-group discussions is the use of small-group or book club discussions, with ideal group sizes of three to five students. In small-group discussions, students can pose their own questions to each other, often resulting in more development of topics than in large-group discussions (Hulan, 2010) (@ = Small-group discussions or literature circles).

To assist students in working effectively in small groups, you can model ways of posing questions and assuming the roles of facilitator, note-taker, summarizer, devil's advocate/challenger, etc. (Daniels & Steineke, 2004). You can also have students share summaries of their discussions with the large group, reporting that fosters some accountability to completing their tasks in their groups.

In having students engage in book club discussions, it's important that students have some say as to the books they read and discuss, so that they seek ownership and engagement. And, students need to collaboratively build on each other's responses so that they move beyond their own individual responses to generate new composite interpretations that transcend their own individual responses.

It is important that when you engage students in small-group literature circles or book club discussions you do not have any set expectations for the nature of their discussions. Teachers often choose literature circles for teaching texts that aren't otherwise approved for use in their school—typically multicultural and political texts. However, as Thein, Guise, and Sloan (2011) found, without teacher guidance students often struggle to take up the critical invitations that such books encourage. Moreover, critical discussion of political and multicultural texts requires careful and consistent teacher scaffolding that student-directed small groups typically cannot accommodate.

ONLINE GROUP DISCUSSIONS

Students are increasingly engaging in large- and small-group discussions in online asynchronous and synchronous chat sites found on Moodle, Desire2Learn, Nicenet, Blackboard/Collaborate, WebCT/Vista, Angel, Tapped In, or Ning platforms. Some of these platforms, for example, Tappedin.org, as does the *Teaching to Exceed Virtual School* site in LiteraryWorlds.org, provide you with transcripts of student discussions sent via email. Students can also engage in videoconferencing using tools such as iChat or Skype video so that students can perceive each other physically simultaneously on a screen. And, as noted in Chapter 9, students can also share digital annotations with each other using Diigo as a form of online discussion (@ = Online group discussions).

To foster their students' online discussion of *Brave New World* and *Lord of the Flies* over the summer, Constance Ruzich and Joanne Canan (2010) asked them to select a partner and determine how they would interact online for at least 30 minutes with that partner—through IM'ing, texting, chat, or email about the books. The students were asked to prepare three discussion questions for their partner and two responses. The students then created a transcript of their discussions in which they highlighted their contributions. For example, two students responded to *Brave New World* in the following chat:

Nestle33: what did you guys think about the process of "conditioning society" as nadia said
MCwawa: well, i think every society has conditioning. theirs was much more controlled
StarTrekkie: i think it happens today
MCwawa: i think Huxley was critisizing our own society and how we're meant to believe things
StarTrekkie: all we are told is that we should work hard to go to college
StarTrekkie: and then get a job
StarTrekkie: and make money
MCwawa: no theres so much more than that
MCwawa: you just dont even realize
Nestle33: there might be but it isn't like you can't go against it
StarTrekkie: if we were to say "money is dumb" we wouldn't survive
Nestle33: like if you noticed in the novel they would repeat something from there conditioning without even noticing
(p. 64)

The students' transcripts were then evaluated in terms of the quality of their questions, reactions, length of discussion, and quality of interpretations.

One advantage of these online discussions is that students who are intimidated by the non-verbal aspects of sharing thoughts in face-to-face discussions are often more comfortable sharing their thoughts in online discussions.

In using online discussions, you also need to choose between real-time synchronous chat versus asynchronous chat. While synchronous discussions are more spontaneous, having to write out their responses in an asynchronous chat also means that students are more likely to reflect on others' written responses prior to reacting to those responses.

Students can also engage in online discussion after school hours, so that they are not limited to discussion during classroom hours. And, students also have a written transcript record of a discussion for use in their further writing.

You can also set up online cross-cultural discussions in which students communicate with other students in different cultures using sites such as ePals (http://www.epals.com), Youth Voices (http://youthvoices.net), and TakingITGlobal (http://www.tigweb.org). You and other teachers might ask students across schools to respond to the same or a similar text, event, or experience and then compare their responses in terms of similarities and differences in their cultural backgrounds and perspectives. For example, in a chat exchange on the PICCLE Forum (http://piccle.ed.psu.edu/moodle), American and Swedish students compared their responses to characters' actions in a short story in terms of how people in each of their cultures might act, as well as how their beliefs and values influence their actions and identities (Myers & Eberfors, 2010).

As with small-group discussions, it is important to provide students in online discussions with some direction and purpose for their discussions, as well as norms regarding online netiquette—for example, that students should avoid personal attacks or flaming. You can also provide students with some criteria for what constitutes productive discussions and for how you will be evaluating their contributions, with some illustrative examples from discussion transcripts for specific criteria. Rozema and Webb (2008) also extensively discuss how to lead online discussions and the value of such discussions as archives of student learning.

One further advantage of online discussions in contrast to face-to-face discussions is that you can use the written transcript record of their contributions to assess students' contributions. You can assign points to students for contributing posts and additional points for commenting or elaborating on others' posts, as well as providing insightful posts. You can then also note changes in the number of comments/amount of elaboration over time, giving positive feedback for increased participation over time.

When students are responding to literature, you can assess them on their use of a variety of different types of literary responses. For example, students may employ not only summary/descriptive or engagement responses, but also intertextual (text-to-text; text-to-world; text-to-self), interpretation, critical analysis, and aesthetic judgment responses. You can also assess students on their uses of various social practices that serve to enhance the group's social harmony or cohesion—practices such as responding positively to, validating, or building on others' ideas in ways that provide group members with a sense of accomplishment (Bowers-Campbell, 2011).

REFLECTING ON YOUR DISCUSSION FACILITATION

To develop your ability to facilitate discussions, as part of microteaching discussion practice in your methods courses and/or your practicum or student teaching, you can use various techniques to reflect on your use of facilitation strategies (@ = Reflecting on discussion facilitation).

You can create audio or video recordings of your facilitation, or use written transcripts from online discussions. You can then reflect on your facilitation in these video recordings using video annotation tools such as VoiceThread (http://voicethread.com) or VideoANT (http://ant. umn.edu), referred to in the last chapter, to make specific annotations about your facilitation techniques and the results or uptake in terms of the quality of student participation or engagement. For example, you may note the results of posing open versus closed questions related to the degree to which students developed their ideas. You can also determine the extent to which different students collaboratively developed their thoughts on the same topics as opposed to jumping around superficially from topic to topic. To determine students' development of topics, for each topic, you can count the number of turns (change in speakers), reflecting the fact that different students are interacting with each other to develop a topic (Beach & Yussen, 2011).

You can also have your peers respond to your audio or video recordings to obtain their feedback and perceptions of your facilitation strategies either in face-to-face interactions or through online annotations. For example, teachers in one study were giving feedback to each other's

five-minute video clips of their teaching using VoiceThread (http://
voicethread.com) (Heintz, Borsheim, Caughlan, Juzwik, & Sherry,
2010). Teachers were asked to pose questions about their own clips; their
peers then reviewed the clips, responded to these questions, and made
other comments and posed other questions. For example, peers made the
following responses to a discussion led by Matt on *Lord of the Flies*, in
which he began the discussion with the question, "What is social
Darwinism?":

Alexis: "I noticed your question, 'What is social Darwinism,' and you're getting
kids to think about what that means, I think your question was too
difficult. And, I didn't see you ask many probing questions, so it seemed
the conversation sort of lulled, until one student brought up some textual
support, and then you saw several students participate."

June: "I think you demonstrate the importance of enthusiasm, like the way a
student asked you a question and you responded, 'I don't know!' Just the
way you said it seemed to engage many of the students who didn't talk.
And even though it's a bit theatrical, I think that's needed every now and
then."

Matt: "In the beginning, all the students were asking me questions, so part
of doing that was to turn it back to them. I got the impression that not
many of them have had much experience in that sort of discussion."

Maggie: "I saw that too, how they seemed to look at you, but then I also
thought, well maybe they were just trying to get their points, since you
were grading them based on their participation. And that's how
participation points can sometimes get in the way." (Arver, 2011, p. 23)

From sharing their feedback, Matt and his peers recognized the
need to both provide structure as well as providing a safe space for
students to participate. They also realized that teachers' beliefs about
teachers' roles in discussions had a strong influence on how they facili-
tated discussions. And, they learned that, while they had different,
conflicting perspectives about effective discussions, such conflicts were
important to share in formulating their beliefs about facilitating
discussions.

Changes in Facilitation of Discussions Over Time

Learning to facilitate effective discussions takes practice over an extended
period of time. You may also want to reflect on changes in your facilitation of discussions over time to determine the effects of altering your
questioning or use of pre-discussion activities. For example, in one

action-research project, teachers analyzed changes in 45 whole-class discussion videos over time (Wells, 2011). By comparing the early with later discussions, they found that they were asking more open-ended questions and fewer closed questions or evaluations of students' responses (use of the I-R-E pattern), resulting in students voicing more alternative opinions and more frequently initiating discussions.

At the same time, while the teachers still retained control of the discussions, there was also a shift in the teacher's stance from being the primary expert on a topic or issue to adopting a more inquiry-based, dialogic stance in which both teacher and student were collaboratively constructing knowledge. This suggests that it is important not only to alter your facilitation techniques, but also not to assume that you are the primary source of all knowledge, as opposed to acknowledging your students as contributing their knowledge.

CASE STUDY: SARAH HECHLIK'S HALLWAY (LITERATURE CIRCLES)

In this chapter, we discussed the value of engaging students in various types of discussions—for example, use of literature circles. The challenge in doing so is that you may need to justify your use of literature circles in your school and to your students, who may wonder, "What's the value of participating in literature circles?"

In this second case study for this chapter, you'll visit practicing high school teacher Sarah Hechlik's classroom. You'll watch and listen to her as she discusses both the challenges she encounters when planning, facilitating, and assessing literature circles, as well as the specific manner in which she does so. You'll then discuss Sarah's methods, as well as your own experiences and beliefs about literature circles.

With these ideas in mind, you'll engage in your final task: to present for about 15 minutes on literature circles at the English department's next professional development session, per your new principal's request. Keeping in mind that your audience may be sensitive to a new teacher presenting teaching methods at a meeting, you decide to take on a facilitator role in teaching these teachers about literature circles. You will navigate this task in more detail with your peers.

Please find two or three peers and go to the LiteraryWorlds.org site and then to the *Teaching to Succeed* link to find this case study for Chapter 10.

CHAPTER 11

Language, Grammar, and Usage

CHAPTER OVERVIEW

Issues with Direct Instruction of Traditional School Grammar

How Does Language Variation Work?

Language as Social Practices

Engaging Students in the Study of Language Variation as Social Practice

Conducting Ethnographies of Language Use

Case Study: Majorie Addressing the Needs of Her ELLs

Case Study: Ms. Variation's Hallway

For many people English teachers are associated with "proper" grammar, spelling, mechanics—and a lot of red ink. It is a primary job of the English teacher to teach students to speak and write in Standard English, isn't it? The answer to this question isn't a simple one and neither are the Common Core State Standards related to language, grammar, and usage. In this chapter we discuss current theory and research on language variation, vernacular dialects, and English language learning, with the goal of making sense of this complex issue. At the same time, we consider what the Common Core State Standards ask of English teachers with regard to the teaching of language, grammar, and usage, highlighting ways that you can both meet and exceed these standards as you acknowledge and build upon students' language and literacy practices.

ISSUES WITH DIRECT INSTRUCTION OF TRADITIONAL SCHOOL GRAMMAR

Direct instruction of traditional school grammar, naming parts of speech, grammar exercises and worksheets, and extensive correction of student errors of grammar and usage have, for decades, been extensively studied as ways to improve student writing. The results of this research are absolutely clear. George Hillocks (1984), senior professor at the University of Chicago, after examining over 500 studies of the teaching of composition, puts it this way:

The study of traditional school grammar (i.e., the definition of parts of speech, the parsing of sentences, etc.) has no effect on raising the quality of student writing. Every other focus of instruction examined in this review is stronger. Taught in certain ways, grammar and mechanics instruction has a deleterious effect on student writing. In some cases a heavy emphasis on mechanics and usage (e.g., marking every error) results in significant losses in overall quality. School boards, administrators, and teachers who impose the systematic study of traditional school grammar on their students over lengthy periods of time in the name of teaching writing do them a gross disservice that should not be tolerated by anyone concerned with the effective teaching of good writing. Teachers concerned with teaching standard usage and typographical conventions should teach them in the context of real writing problems. (p. 160)

Writing years ago, Hillocks finds research proving the most effective mode of instruction to be:

"Environmental" because it brings teacher, student, and materials more nearly into balance, and, in effect, takes advantage of all resources of the classroom. In this mode, the instructor plans and uses activities that result in high levels of student interaction concerning particular problems parallel to those they encounter in certain kinds of writing, such as generating criteria and examples to develop extended definitions of concepts or generating arguable assertions from appropriate data and predicting and countering opposing arguments. In contrast to the presentational mode, this mode places priority on high levels of student involvement. In contrast to the natural process mode, the environmental mode places priority on structured problem-solving activities, with clear objectives, planned to enable students to deal with similar problems in composing. On pretest-to-posttest measures, the environmental mode is over four times more

effective than the traditional presentational mode and three times more
effective than the natural process mode. (p. 160)

Although Hillocks was writing before scholars and researchers had
developed the language of "literacy practices" that we use in this book,
we quote his conclusions at length because it is clear that his extensive
review of the research on teaching writing rejects direct grammatical
instruction and supports the inquiry-based, literacy practices approach
we advocate in every chapter.

At first glance, the Common Core State Standards only describe a
traditional approach to language, grammar, and usage. For instance, the
anchor standards for language state that students should "demonstrate
command of the conventions of standard English grammar and usage
when writing or speaking." Indeed this emphasis on knowledge and
command of Standard English is found throughout the language standards across grade levels. However, in their section on key points in the
English language arts standards, the writers explain that "the standards
recognize that students must be able to use formal English in their writing
and speaking but that they must also be able to make informed, skillful
choices among the many ways to express themselves through language."
This caveat can be seen in standards that state that students should "apply
knowledge of language to understand how language functions in different
contexts, to make effective choices for meaning or style, and to comprehend more fully when reading or listening." In other words, while the
standards certainly place a high value on Standard English, they also
importantly suggest that students must be able to understand and use
language variation within the English language as well as other languages
that students might speak in their homes and communities across different
social and academic contexts. We believe that one of the most important
and effective areas of inquiry to support student mastery of the language
standards of the Common Core State Standards is the study of language
itself, particularly its variation and diversity.

HOW DOES LANGUAGE VARIATION WORK?

In order to teach your students how language functions in different
contexts, you will first need to consider how language varies and changes.
In order to consider this phenomenon, let us take the example of English
as it is spoken in the United States. Most Americans recognize that
English speakers in the United States speak differently in various regions.
Americans also know that English-speaking adolescents in the United

States use different words, turns of phrase, and even sentence construction in 2012 than they did in 1970. How do these differences happen and what do they suggest about Standard English?

People often imagine that there is one correct, formal, or standard form of any language that anyone can acquire through education. Variations on the standard form of a language—for instance, African American Vernacular English or Chicano English—are then considered to be informal, colloquial, or even improper or incorrect. Research has found that Americans who see themselves as speaking Standard English— typically white, middle-class people—tend to hold negative views of people who speak vernacular Englishes (Blake & Cutler, 2003; Perry & Delpit, 1998). Likewise, research suggests that teachers often have lower expectations for students who speak in vernacular forms of English (Cazden, 2001; Ferguson, 1998). However, these common beliefs about how language works and about the value of vernacular dialects have been widely debunked by linguists and literacy scholars. For instance, Godley, Sweetland, Wheeler, Minnici, and Carpenter (2006) explain that:

Scientific research on language demonstrates that standard dialects are not linguistically better by any objective measures; they are socially preferred simply because they are the language varieties used by those who are most powerful and affluent in a society. In addition, although schools often refer to Standard English as if it were a single dialect, there are numerous regional standard dialects in the United States and around the world, as well as significant structural differences between written and spoken Standard Englishes. (p. 30)

While we may assume that this means white, middle-class people, this ignores the reality that, by 2030, the majority of students in American schools will be students of color. This massive demographic shift towards a more diverse American population means that the idea of Standard English as the norm associated with a white, middle-class majority needs to be challenged.

In his seminal book, James Gee (1996) persuasively argued that even people who see themselves as Standard English speakers rarely, if ever, speak standard English. Instead, all English speakers (and speakers of any language) speak a range of informal variations of English that vary in their faithfulness to Standard English across different social contexts. For example, you almost certainly speak a different variation of English in your classroom as a teacher than you do at home with your friends or family. And, even in your most formal teaching moments, an audio recording of your speech would quickly convince you that you do not speak perfect Standard English in this context. Ultimately Standard English—like the standard form of any living language—is an abstract ideal or model for writing, but not something the people actually speak (Lippi-Green, 1997). Moreover, the rules and norms related to usage vary across contexts with regard to Standard English. In other words, even Standard English is not "standard" (Wolfram, Adger, & Christian, 1999).

Gee also notes that people vary in their use of formal versus informal language depending on how they frame the social contexts in which they are participating. In giving a formal talk about the representation of women in Hollywood films, a teacher, Sarah, may note that "formal content analysis of Hollywood films indicates that female characters are generally portrayed in limited, often subservient ways." In talking with her peers, Sarah may note, "there's not a lot of strong women in Hollywood films." These differences in use of formal versus informal language reflect the ways in which the meaning and use of language vary according to differences in social and cultural contexts constituted by different discourses. In her formal language use, Sarah is drawing on a discourse of media/feminist analysis associated with her identity in an academic context. In talking with her friends, she is simply assuming her identity as friend sharing her thoughts (@ = Critical discourse analysis).

ACTIVITY

One topic for applying critical discourse analysis involves how discourses are evoked or double-voiced in media texts. Find some online or print magazine advertisements. Analyze the use of language in these advertisements in terms of discourses of race, class, gender, and age. For example, many "beauty ads" appeal to a gender discourse of idealized perfection that positions audiences as always being imperfect or lacking in some way, for example, not having a "perfect smile" or "shiny hair."

Students can also analyze the discourses adopted on television shows—detective/crime, sitcoms, news, soap operas, reality TV, etc. For example, you can analyze how characters in detective/crime shows adopt discourses of law and order/control as ways of coping with deviant behavior. Or, you could analyze how news programs portray urban worlds in terms of negative discourses of crime, poverty, and decay.

LANGUAGE AS SOCIAL PRACTICES

If standard forms of language are something that no one really speaks, then how do languages actually function? Pennycook (2010) asks us to see language differently. Rather than understanding languages as systems that are used more or less formally or accurately in various contexts, he suggests that social contexts themselves drive language use and construction. In other words, Pennycook understands language as a social practice; he states that "languages are activities, not systems." Language as social practices emphasizes the idea that we use language to achieve social goals associated with our literacy practices framework—for example, to construct identities or collaborate/build relationships.

The concept of language as a codified system of grammar rules underlies much of the focus of the Common Core language standards as well as much of traditional grammar instruction. What much of traditional grammar rules ignore is that language use varies according to social contexts, with its own unique norms.

What is important about Pennycook's theory is that it suggests that languages develop and are constructed through their use as part of "bundles" of social practices. This is far different from imagining that use of a language *system* in a social context changes or even distorts that system. For example, the advent of social networking and Facebook has brought about a functional shift in the use of the term "friend" and has led to the establishment of the term "unfriend." The construction and use of these terms, as well as other languages and discourses surrounding digital social networking, developed within bundles of social practices related to participation in social media. In other words, we use these terms because they are a necessary part of digital social networking. Moreover, the terms "friend" and "unfriend"—as they are used as part of social media literacy practices—are not distortions of Standard English, but are socially driven variations. Similarly, abbreviations such as "lol" and "btw," which have developed and increased in use in association with text messaging, are not simply informal, incorrect, or even careless means of communication. Instead, they are logical, useful variations that developed as part of the social practice of texting (@ = Theories of social language use).

If All Language is Part of Social Practice, Then Why Teach Standard English?

Even as we argue that Standard English is, to some extent, a myth, we also want to be clear that students need to learn about the concept of Standard English, what it looks like, and its gatekeeping role in allowing some people access to power while denying it to others. Lisa Delpit (2006) has written about Standard English as part of "codes of power" that we should not deny any of our students from accessing and understanding. She stated:

To act as if power does not exist is to ensure the power status quo remains
the same. To imply to children . . . that it doesn't matter how you talk or
how you write is to ensure their ultimate failure. I prefer to be honest with
my students. I tell them that their language and cultural style is unique and
wonderful but that there is a political power game that is also being played,
and if they want to be in on that game there are certain games they too
must play. (pp. 39–40)

To be clear, Delpit is not suggesting that language variation somehow be
eliminated (something that we've argued is an impossibility), or that all
students be taught to give up their home languages or variations in favor
of Standard English. Instead, Delpit is arguing that students be taught
how to code-switch, and to learn to effectively use Standard English—
perhaps as one of several equally valuable variations or languages in their
linguistic repertoire—in order to gain access to power structures and to
ultimately change the status quo.

Recent work by Kirkland (2010) provides a useful extension on
Delpit's ideas. Kirkland argues that the English language might more
accurately be thought of as Englishes, because of the intense plurality of
its variations. He also argues that, although it is useful to teach all students
Standard English, teachers ought to also acknowledge the ways that other
Englishes (and variations of languages other than English) provide access
to particular kinds of social power or status. For instance, Jones (2006)
found that the working-class girls in her study used a regional variation
or discourse "to shout back at a mainstream society that judged them
harshly" (p. 122). Shouting back took on many forms for the women in
this community, including (among other performances) literally *shouting*
at authority figures such as police. Jones explained that "The girls in this
study *needed* these practices for survival, just as their mothers, fathers, and
grandparents have needed similar tactics and strategies" (p. 123). In other
words, the young working-class girls in Jones's study would have had
difficulty accessing power in their own community had they approached
daily life through Standard English. Jones stresses the importance of
ethnographic inquiry into communities in which we teach so that we can
better understand the purposes and value behind the discourses and
linguistic variations our students use. With this kind of community
knowledge, teachers are better equipped to talk explicitly about how
differences in language provide access to different kinds of power.

The scholarship discussed in this section is consistent with an understanding of language as social practice. Each language variation can be
understood as part of a bundle of social practices related to the maintenance
of particular power structures, norms, and beliefs. Learning how Standard

English and other variations of English and other languages work as social practices can help students to both access and transform that status quo.

ACTIVITY: REFLECTING ON VARIATION IN LANGUAGE USE

Consider the variation in your own language use even within your role as an English teacher. Working with a partner, audio-record yourself role-playing three different scenarios. In each scenario you should attempt to describe your goals for the year in one of your classes, or your teaching philosophy. In the first scenario, imagine that you are talking with a student; in the second, with your principal; and in the third, with a parent. Transcribe each of your role-play discussions and analyze the transcripts for patterns in your language. What kinds of differences and similarities do you find in your word choice, grammar/usage, affect, and tone? What information do you include or omit in each scenario? To what extent is your language consistent with Standard English in each scenario? What other social practices is your language use linked to in each scenario? What kinds of social access might you gain through your use of language variation in each scenario?

ENGAGING STUDENTS IN THE STUDY OF LANGUAGE VARIATION AS SOCIAL PRACTICE

There are number of ways that you can engage your students in studying how their language variation is a social practice.

Framing Language Variation

A first step in helping students understand language variation is to *frame* different varieties of English and other languages within the larger scope of history, politics, and grammar. Given the prevailing belief that Standard English is the best and most important language variation to learn in school (Zuidema, 2005), you might begin this work through activities that help students understand that Standard English is not a static system that is somehow indicative of intellectual or moral superiority, but instead that it is a continually shifting, abstract model that should be understood as a tool that provides certain kinds of social access (Flynn, 2011). Goodman (2011) suggests that a close examination of language in Shakespeare's plays can illustrate for students the dynamic, fluid nature of the English language. She points out how Shakespeare's use of functional shifts in words—for instance, using a word commonly used as a noun as a verb—led to functional shifts in those words in everyday use. Similarly, Zuidema (2005) suggests that teachers might show students the same poem written in Old English, Middle English, and Modern English as a means of demonstrating the useful and necessary evolution of the English language. She explains that:

Some words or phrases become linguistic fads; others fall into disuse or "misuse." Rules of taste change, and the pronunciations, uses, conjugations, and spellings of words are altered over time to adjust to new contexts, speakers, purposes, and audiences. We call this adaptability "survival of the fittest" when we discuss other kinds of evolution; it is evidence of the resilience of language and not a matter for concern. (p. 672)

Zuidema also posits that students might better understand the flexibility of English if teachers more explicitly teach key linguistic concepts. For example, she argues that most people confuse grammar, or "internal patterns that a given language naturally follows" and usage, which is really rules of taste. Such confusion causes people to see the English language as far more "rule" laden than it is in reality. Zuidema explains that "Most people believe that observing the rules of taste is the same as knowing the rules of a language" (p. 688). A rule of taste or usage might be using the word "ain't" or ending a sentence in a preposition. Neither of these forms of usage impede understanding and are therefore not grammatically incorrect from a linguistic standpoint. Instead, this sort of usage is frowned upon in certain contexts based strictly on taste.

Once students begin to see that English is not static you can engage them in activities that "de-center" Standard English (White, 2011). For example, White (2011) asked his students to translate a section of Tupac Shakur's "Just Me Against the World"—which is written in a variation of African American Vernacular English—into Standard English. He explained, "Though each passage—the original and its translation—says the same thing (each has the same literal message), the original, non-Standard English passage inevitably holds far more emotional and rhetorical power regardless of audience . . . via different translations of the same texts, my students experienced firsthand how meaning can be lost when we insist on a rigid form of English for making meaning." (p.46)

You can also help your students to de-center Standard English by guiding them through activities that shed light on linguistic prejudice. Wilson (2001) suggests that students can learn how particular regional, racial, cultural, and generational variations of English—as well as variations on languages such as Spanish—become stigmatized by examining how people who use particular variations are portrayed in popular culture and in the media. She suggests that students "tape-record sitcoms in which certain dialects are used to delineate particular character types and how those linguistic features suggest character, level of education, degree of intelligence, etc." (p. 34). She also recommends that students "record evidence of language prejudice in cartoons, newspaper or magazine articles, or editorials" (p. 34).

Finally, you can help your students *frame* language variation by asking them to examine their own uses of language within the larger context of language variation. For instance, Hagemann (2001) suggests engaging students in a role-playing activity in which they describe a car accident to their parents, a friend, and an insurance agent. In her own work with such an activity she found that, "depending on the audience, [students] chose different words, added/deleted particular details, used a different tone, etc." (p. 78). Hagemann argued that this sort of role-playing activity illustrates for students that we all use different variations of language all the time to suit different purposes and to perform various aspects of our identities. Similarly, Flynn (2011) detailed a unit in which a teacher asked students to brainstorm a list of dialects of language variations that they hear and speak in their everyday lives—for instance, "dinner table," "church," and "military," as well as those that are most overtly racial, cultural, or regional. Students in this classroom also studied Gary Soto's (1997) play *Novio Boy* with the goal of examining how and for what purposes characters in the novel chose to speak particular variations of English and Spanish. Overall, students in this study learned that no one language, dialect, or variation is correct, but instead that all dialects and variations of any language can be appropriate and useful depending on audience and purpose. For further consideration of how language categories of race are shaped by meanings we assign to those categories, please visit the wiki website for Chapter 11 and read first year teacher, Kim Kosach's, description of different meanings of race in her work in an urban high school (@ = Studying language variation).

Constructing and Enacting Identities through Language Variation

Once you have helped your students to *frame* languages and variations in social, political, and grammatical relation to one another, you can begin to lead them through activities that both help them understand how their *identities are constructed* through their uses of language as social practice and challenge them to rethink their status quo uses of language as they impact their ability to access particular kinds of power. This kind of instruction is particularly important for students who are English language learners (ELLs) and for students who speak stigmatized dialects of English—who some scholars refer to as Standard English Language Learners (Hollie, 2001; LeMoine, 1998).

In order to help students understand how their identities are constructed through language use, you first need to acknowledge and value students' home languages. Hollie (2001) offers several useful suggestions for valuing students' home languages that are supported by the Linguistic Affirmation Program (LAP), which is "a comprehensive nonstandard language awareness program designed to serve the language needs of African American, Mexican American, Hawaiian American, and Native American students who are not proficient in Standard American English (SAE)" (p. 54). Perhaps most importantly, Hollie suggests that teachers allow for students to use home languages whenever possible in the classroom "as an acknowledgement of their culture and history" (p. 57). Hollie also recommends that teachers acknowledge students' cultures and histories by using culturally relevant literature. For instance, teachers that Hollie worked with used literature in which authors use African American Vernacular English such as works by Julius Lester and Virginia Hamilton. Studying such literature moves beyond acknowledgment of students' linguistic backgrounds toward providing students with a means of exploring connections between language practices and identity construction. Hollie explained that "these works give the students the opportunity to see the language in the text versus simply hearing it all the time. Then they are able to make comparisons and contrasts with the language they read and the language they speak, as well as with Standard American English" (p. 58). Finally, Hollie recommends that teachers engage students in activities with a significant amount of physical movement such as role play and readers' theater, which allow for expressions of identity and diversity in language use.

Medina and Campano's (2006) study of linguistically diverse students engaging in drama and role-play activities corroborates Hollie's recommendation. In their study students used role-play scenarios to critically examine the treatment of linguistically diverse students by teachers and administrators in one school. They also detail a unit in which students read a bilingual text (*My Diary from Here to There*); kept their own character journals in either English, Spanish, or both; and then engaged in dramatic dialogues based on their journals. After examining these drama activities Medina and Campano surmised that "drama affords a generative nexus between the students' own identities and more expansive understandings of school-based literacy practices" (p. 333). Further, they concluded that "texts and selves work together in a productive dialectic that creates a dynamic, in-between space where students explore characters' fictional lives but also their own actual lives and identities in schools. In the process, the students mine their cultural experiences to arrive at more complete and incisive understandings of how they are positioned by others, including educators, administrators, and policy makers" (pp. 339–340).

Relating to and Collaborating with Others in Exploring Languages, Dialects, and Discourses

As students begin to understand how their identities are constructed and positioned in relation to the languages and dialects they use, you will want to engage students in activities that encourage them to *collaborate with and relate to others* in order to explore multiple perspectives on social practices related to language use. A productive place to begin is through dialogic, student-centered discussions of language variation. For instance, Godley and Minnici (2008) found that by engaging in dialogic discussions of language variation, the primarily African American students in their study were able to identify nuances and variation in the use of African American Vernacular English across various neighborhoods in their city. Because students were encouraged to express conflicting ideas—even ideas that challenged their teacher—their collaborative work in these discussions led them to understandings of language variation and identity that went beyond their teacher's initial goals. Godley and Minnici explained that, "With this discussion, students moved from the curriculum's framing of language variation on a national scale to language variation on a much more local scale . . . The students' depiction of their linguistic identities, therefore, emphasized distinct identities within an African American community rather than a linguistic identity constructed primarily in opposition to White identities" (p. 336). What is important to notice here is that, through students' collaborative, dialogic discussion in this classroom, they began to see how language is used as a social practice that identifies one as being a member of a particular community with particular beliefs and values (@ = Studying language variation).

Language diversity and variation not only are topics for English in North America, but, indeed, are issues around the world (Figure 11.1). Linda Christensen (2009) has created a curriculum on language and power that examines the "colonial roots of linguistic genocide and analyzed how schools continue to perpetuate the myths of inferiority or invisibility of some languages" (p. 209). She explains that "over half of the world's languages have become extinct in the last 500 years." To help her high school students understand how and why some languages have

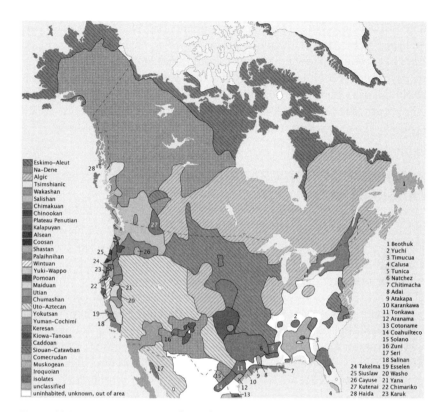

Figure 11.1 Native Languages of North America

power and others don't, Christensen holds a "linguistic tea party." She has created a set of carefully described roles based on the stories of real people in the present and in history that includes Hector Pieterson, a student from South Africa forced to learn Afrikaans; Damien O'Donovan, an Irishman whose friend was beaten to death by the British Army for speaking Irish; Gloria Anzuldua, a Mexican American writer hit when a child by a teacher for speaking Spanish; Lois-Ann Yamanaka, a native Hawaiian; Ngugi wa Thiong'o, a Kenyan novelist who stops writing in English and instead writes in his native Kikuyu; Molly Craig, an Aboriginal from Australia; Bud Lane, a Native American from Oregon and one of the last speakers of Coastal Athabaskan; and others (pp. 218–225). At the "tea party" Christensen provides her students with a list of questions, such as "Find someone who was forced to speak another language. Who is this person? How did this affect the person?" or "Find someone who started or joined an organization to preserve his or her language. Who is this person? Why did the individual decide to take this action?" After the tea party, students first write about questions such as, "What do the people who are forced to change their language have in common? How do they feel about their language?" They engage in additional research, reading essays and stories, and watching a film about Native American boarding schools (*In the White Man's Image*). They study the Soweto Uprising, write poetry and short pieces, create symbolic drawings, and study the language restoration movement.

CONDUCTING ETHNOGRAPHIES OF LANGUAGE USE

There are many other collaborative activities that you might consider engaging your students in with the goal of helping them relate to others and gain multiple perspectives on the social practice of language variation. For instance, groups of students could conduct language ethnographies in which they inquire into the roles, relationships, norms, beliefs, and social practices in a given community (Beach & Myers, 2001), while simultaneously examining oral and written language use in the community. Through a project like this one, students can begin to understand how language is driven by and constructed in concert with other social practices in particular social worlds. Possible social worlds for inquiry might include online gaming communities, neighborhoods, religious or cultural organizations, or even family worlds (@ = Conducting ethnographies of language use).

In her study of a sorority described in Chapter 8, Jennifer identified how certain words assumed certain meanings unique to the sorority. For example, the "townie" room was a place for members who did not live in the house to spend the night. She also described language use shared at an informational meeting, for example, language associated with their service learning fund drives, or awards related to contribution to the sorority, as well as categories associated with being in the sorority "family": "Big sister," "Little sister," "Grandma," and "Great-grandma."

Students may also study how use of certain kinds of language serves as social bonding within a group or event. In their analysis of the Boy Scout troop meetings, Phillip and Sarah noted that the members had a strong sense of "camaraderie" in that they "all feel completely free to speak openly and ask any question they may have" (Holzchuch & Loosbrock, 2010, p. 7). They noted that the members frequently teased each other in a good-hearted manner to foster this camaraderie. And, they observed how the use of language serves to reify cultural norms operating in a certain site. In another example, from Chapter 8, Jessica

Carlson and Blair Gjevre (2010) found that the use of the language of "man talk" served to create the body shop culture as "a man's domain" that "is no place for women."

By conducting these ethnographies, students learned how language is used to establish shared knowledge and to define identities within groups or events.

Synthesizing and Connecting Across Languages and Dialects

Once you have guided your students through instruction that a) *frames* all language as inherently variable, b) helps them understand their own language use as an important social practice that *constructs their identities*, and c) encourages them to explore multiple perspectives on language use and *relate to others* through *collaborative* discussion and inquiry, your students will be ready to *synthesize* what they have learned and *make connections* that will lead them to the acquisition of new language varieties and dialects. You will find that having treated your students' various home languages and dialects as "resources" rather than "problems" (Ruiz, 1998) not only will serve to acknowledge students' identities as they are constructed through language, but will also serve to improve their knowledge and use of Standard English—a primary goal of the Common Core State Standards in English Language Arts. According to Cummins, Chow, and Schecter (2006), "One of the most consistent findings in the literature on bilingualism is that literacy skills in a student's first language (L1) and second language (L2) are strongly related. In other words, L1 and L2 literacy are interdependent or manifestations of a common underlying proficiency" (p. 299). Based on this research the authors suggest that investing time in helping your students understand their use of their first languages (or dialects) has the potential to improve their proficiency in a second language or dialect such as Standard English.

One way that a student's knowledge of his home language or dialect can be useful in making connections and building proficiency in Standard English is through comparison, or what some scholars refer to as "contrastive analysis" (Godley & Minnici, 2008; Wheeler & Swords, 2006). For instance, scholars have found that when students struggle to understand particular features of Standard English—a certain punctuation mark or a subtle distinction between words—they can be taught to better understand those features first, by having a teacher explicitly point them out so that they notice and pay attention to them, and second, by comparing those features to their current uses of language (Hagemann, 2001; Siegel,

1999). For example, you might focus on negation with students who speak variations of African American Vernacular English or Southern U.S. dialects. These variations of English often use "ain't" as a general negative indicator, while more standard variations tend to use "is not," "have not," "haven't," etc. Similarly, these variations often use double negation, for instance in a phrase such as "I don't know nothing about that." Standard variations would more likely use a phrase like "I don't know *anything* about that." Drawing attention to the specific differences in a feature like negation can help your students determine with which audiences particular linguistic choices will be most effective.

You can also ask your students to view documentaries about language use, such as *American Tongues* (Alvarez & Kolker, 1988), *The Story of English* (Cran, 1997), or *Do You Speak American?* (Cran, 2005), in order to study patterns and rules in varieties of English that they may use in their home lives versus variations of Standard English that will provide them with different kinds of social access (Zuidema, 2005). For instance, *Do You Speak American?* (Cran, 2005) takes viewers on a journey around the United States, providing a glimpse into the history and social purposes behind language use in various regions and among various people. After viewing the film, students could be asked to study different regional, generational, or racial/ethnic variations that were discussed, constructing a list of rules for each variation that includes a comparison with rules of Standard English (@ = Studying dialect differences).

It is critical that as you begin to ask students to learn conventions of Standard English, you are clear that you are not asking them to give up their home languages or related identities. As Hagemann (2001) reminds us, our goal as teachers should be "expanding" rather than "erasing" a student's linguistic repertoire (p. 78). With this goal in mind, it is useful to teach students the concept of "code-switching"—or using different languages, discourses, and variations in different contexts—as you encourage their proficiency in Standard English (Delpit, 2006). Students may initially resist the notion of code-switching, assuming that it implies being authentic or true to one's identity in one context and less than authentic in others. Examining literary texts in which characters explicitly discuss their own code-switching can help students see that identities are fluid and that code-switching is useful (Zuidema, 2005). Zuidema recommends *A Lesson Before Dying* (Gaines, 1993) or Chapter 12 of *To Kill a Mockingbird* (Lee, 1960) as possible texts for this work. Other research has also found *To Kill a Mockingbird* to be a useful text for examining code-switching (Godley & Minnici, 2008; Thein et al., 2010). In a study by Thein et al. (2010), students studied how Calpurnia, the African-American housekeeper who worked in the white, upper-middle class Finch household, not only used different language, demeanor, and dispositions, but also held different norms for the Finch children's behavior in the Finch home and in her own church community. You could engage your students in this type of literary activity by asking small groups of students to study various characters in a novel, examining first how a character's language use, affect, discourse, and identity are depicted across contexts in a novel, then looking for ways that that character is depicted as gaining access to certain kinds of power by way of adopting various identities through language use.

Constructing Multimodal Texts that Incorporate Language Variation

As students gain an understanding of code-switching and of the usefulness of particular languages and varieties for particular audiences and purposes, they will need practice with constructing and producing texts that incorporate language variation. A useful entry point into this type of work might be to ask students to write and perform skits that incorporate various dialects (Flynn, 2011). In Flynn's study students tried to construct lists of rules for each of the dialects they used. Another useful addition to this project would be asking students to explain why each dialect was appropriate (or inappropriate) for each character in the skit for gaining particular kinds of access or meeting particular goals.

You might also ask your students to construct texts that will help them solve authentic problems in their own community. For example, if budget cuts threatened to dissolve your school's music programs, you could ask students to construct texts that would persuasively communicate with three different audiences to argue for help in keeping the programs. For each audience you might ask students to consider both the mode and the language and variation that would be most appropriate and persuasive. For instance, in trying to gain ground with the school board, students might write a formal letter in Standard English that makes arguments based on reason. In seeking the support of their peers, they might send a text written with texting symbols and abbreviations and with language variation that is common among adolescents in their community. If the school included a number of Spanish-speaking students, the message might include a Spanish translation or Spanish phrases commonly used by students in the school.

The Common Core State Standards for language and usage broadly convey two key points. First, they ask that you help your students gain proficiency in Standard Academic English in both written and oral forms. Second, they ask that you ensure that your students understand the contextual nature of language and usage and that they are prepared to communicate appropriately and effectively across social contexts. In this chapter we have argued that both of these standards can be met and exceeded by guiding your students through literacy practices that help them understand language variation and the role of Standard English within that variation. Beyond meeting the CCSS, this approach will aid you in acknowledging the linguistic resources that all of your students bring to your classroom and it will provide you with tools for helping all of your students to understand the socially constructed, fluid nature of language and its ability to constrain or empower people.

CASE STUDY: MAJORIE ADDRESSING THE NEEDS OF HER ELLS

Majorie has a relatively high number of ELLs in her 9th grade classroom, some of whom are immigrants from Mexico and Central America. For many of these students, Spanish is their primary home language as well as the language they use in speaking with their peers.

While these students are relatively fluent in oral English, they often struggle with English vocabulary in their reading and writing. They often have difficulty understanding the cultural meanings of the uses of English language in reading and writing. And, while Majorie uses texts about topics familiar to her Latino students—for example, issues of immigration—her students still struggle with translating English in their reading. They therefore also struggle with shifting their oral Spanish language use to writing in English. In this case study, you'll make some recommendations for Majorie as to what she can do to help these students with their reading and writing.

Please find two or three peers and go to the LiteraryWorlds.org site and then to the *Teaching to Succeed* link to find this case study for Chapter 11.

CASE STUDY: MS. VARIATION'S HALLWAY

In this chapter, we have defined language variation as social practices that shape students' identities. We have also outlined some of the challenges you may face in teaching students from a range of linguistic backgrounds as well as strategies for helping students become adept at valuing their home languages, variations, and dialects, while simultaneously becoming familiar with variations of Standard English that carry social power. Your next challenge will be to imagine how you might construct instructional strategies and activities for a specific group of students.

This case study provides you with a glimpse into Ms. Variation's urban, 10th grade English classroom. With 35 students in this basic writing class, Ms. Variation has her work cut out for her. On top of the sheer number of struggling writers in this class, about half of the students are English Language Learners, while most of the other students are speakers of African American Vernacular English. After thinking through the challenges that Ms. Variation faces, you will be asked to consider how her students' home languages and variations can be harnessed toward effective and engaging writing instruction.

Please find two or three peers and go to the LiteraryWorlds.org site and the *Teaching to Succeed* link to engage in this case study for Chapter 11.

PART III

Evaluation, Assessment, and Reflection

CHAPTER 12

Evaluating and Assessing Students' Work

CHAPTER OVERVIEW

Relationships between Learning and Assessment

Formative Assessment

Using Criteria to Engage in Self-Assessing

Defining Criteria for Assessing Student Use of Literacy Practices

Varying Criteria According to Differences in Grade Level Using Learning Progressions or Trajectories

Employing Rubrics or Scales for Rating Students' Work

Case Study: Sarah Pancost's Hallway (Assessing Writing)

Summative Assessments

RELATIONSHIPS BETWEEN LEARNING AND ASSESSMENT

Assessment is a crucial part of teaching. Regular assessment not only provides data about student progress in achieving learning goals; it also provides you the teacher with crucial information about your own instruction, and about changes you need to make in focus, approach, pacing, and differentiation. Good teachers do not only rely on testing and formal assessment; they are at every moment observing and evaluating student progress, and constantly modifying instruction to support inclusion and success.

The approach of this book is to develop curriculum and instruction around critical-inquiry-based literacy practices—the need for thoughtful, sensitive, and ongoing assessment is as important to this approach as it is to any other. You may be wondering how well students are learning the literacy practices that you are teaching. And, you also may be curious about how to provide students with feedback to help them become more skillful and capable in the wide range of inquiry and literacy practices that constitute the English language arts.

In this chapter, we describe various ways to assess students' uses of literacy practices. As you do so, you are drawing on different ways of thinking about learning. Knowing about how students learn best improves your assessment skills. Just as a critical-inquiry-based literacy practices approach takes you and your students to more sophisticated, powerful, and effective forms of instruction, so this approach also takes you to richer, better contextualized, and more meaningful forms of assessment.

As we've argued, we perceive learning as a sociocultural process and we have emphasized active uses of literacy and social practices within certain contexts or communities of practice. We have also posited that learning as a social process is mediated by shared uses of tools—language, genres, narratives, images, digital communication, etc.—all of which shape and mediate social interactions.

Assessments based on this sociocultural approach should particularly attend to learning as it occurs in authentic contexts or communities, so that assessment occurs "alongside learning" (James, 2008, p. 31) providing ongoing, descriptive, supportive, formative feedback to students as they are engaged in various activities (Swaffield, 2008). What this means is that you are not just assessing students based on their one-time performances of isolated skills on a standardized test or as isolated individuals. You are assessing students' use of literacy practices over time, in meaningful contexts, and relative to how those practices effectively function in social ways, for example, how effectively students are collaborating with others to achieve certain goals.

FORMATIVE ASSESSMENT

One key aspect of evaluating students' growth is the use of ongoing, *formative assessment* that provides students with continuous feedback about their work (@ = Formative assessment). Formative assessment differs from summative assessment in that it focuses on student learning as students are engaged in an activity or project.

Formative assessment cannot occur in a vacuum—its effectiveness depends on students having a clear sense of purpose for what they are trying to accomplish as well as expectations and criteria for what constitutes effective accomplishment (Frey & Fisher, 2011). However, these purposes, expectations, and criteria are continually changing as students engage in their work. While a group of students may begin creating a digital video documentary about the issue of cliques in their school, they may have discovered that they really want to focus on how clique membership results in bullying. As they are working, you can help students reflect on their purposes, expectations, and criteria by giving them "feed-up," "feedback," and "feed-forward" formative assessment (Hattie & Timperley, 2007).

Feed-up

In giving the "feed-up" formative assessment, you are having students continually clarify their purposes and expectations for what they want to accomplish. Having students clarify their purposes and expectations helps them then self-assess whether they are accomplishing their purposes and expectations. To identify their purposes and expectations, students may ask themselves, "where am I/are we going?" or "what am I/we trying to accomplish?" (Frey & Fisher, 2011). Students creating the video documentary may mutually determine that they want to capture how students perceive the influence of cliques in their school on bullying. For their videos, they may then interview members aligned to different cliques. They may then reflect on who in their group is responsible for accomplishing certain tasks: scripting, finding interviewees, filming, editing, etc.

Feedback

In providing feedback, you and/or your students are asking "how am I doing?" or "where am I now?" related to the use of certain literacy practices (Frey & Fisher, 2011). For example, as students are working on their documentary, they may be continually asking themselves whether they are capturing the kinds of material that will convey their ideas about cliques in the school.

As we noted in Chapter 8, it's important to provide "reader-based" feedback that describes how you are processing the students' work in terms of how you are engaged, entranced, moved, involved, disturbed, struck by, intrigued, puzzled, overwhelmed, lost, besieged with, missing something, wanting more, anticipating events, or expecting support or evidence and not finding it (Elbow, 1998). Peter Elbow calls this approach providing students with "movies of the reader's mind," and he talks about "pointing," "summarizing," "telling," and "showing." This descriptive, "reader-based" feedback does not involve judgments. It involves describing how you perceive what they are doing in using literacy practices as well as how you as their audience are responding to what they are doing.

Then, from hearing or reading this descriptive feedback, students use that feedback to make their own judgments about what in their work is eliciting this feedback. For example, you tell them that in "reading your opinion about the negative effects of ethanol production, as a reader, I expected some more empirical evidence to support that opinion, but didn't find such evidence." Note that this differs from judging them in a negative way as "lacking supporting evidence" or telling them that they need to provide more evidence. The student then recognizes that they need to provide some supporting evidence for their opinion to address concerns of their reader. In the process, students are learning to make their own judgments based on your reader-based feedback. If, however, students have difficulty engaging in self-assessing, you may then need to talk with them about self-assessment and model your own self-assessing process for them.

In addition to providing descriptive feedback in oral or written comments, you can also use digital audio files recorded on GarageBand (Macs) or Audacity (Macs and Windows) that students can listen to as they are reviewing their work. Or, you can use free screencasting tools such as Jing (http://www.techsmith.com/jing), CamStudio (http://camstudio.org), or BB FlashBack (http://www.bbsoftware.co.uk/BBFlashBack_FreePlayer.aspx) to record voiceover comments of the students' writing on the screen. And, if you're responding to students' images or video, you can employ VoiceThread (http://voicethread.com) to record audio or written annotations, or VideoANT (http://ant.umn.edu) or Google Annotations to make written annotation comments to their videos (@ = Digital tools for giving feedback).

Defining Practices/Goal Relationships within Social Events or Contexts

In engaging in self-assessing, students need to define goals for achieving their use of literacy practices. By defining their goals, students then have some basis for assessing whether they are effectively employing literacy practices. In providing information about different countries, students know that their goal is to provide information relevant to making comparisons between countries in terms of the nature and availability of food.

Engaging in "feed-up" self-assessing involves defining one's goals related to choosing uses of certain literacy practices to achieve those goals. To help her college students identify goals and practices, Jody Shipka (2009) has them complete a "statement of goals and choices (SOGC)" for the written or multimodal texts they produce in response to the following questions:

1. What, specifically, is this piece trying to accomplish—above and beyond satisfying the basic requirements outlined in the task description? In other words, what work does, or might, this piece do? For whom? In what contexts?
2. What specific rhetorical, material, methodological, and technological choices did you make in service of accomplishing the goal(s) articulated above? Catalog, as well, choices that you might not have consciously made, those that were made for you when you opted to work with certain genres, materials, and technologies.
3. Why did you end up pursuing this plan as opposed to the others you came up with? How did the various choices listed above allow you to accomplish things that other sets or combinations of choices would not have?
4. Who and what played a role in accomplishing these goals? (p. W355)

This feedback involves fostering students' metacognitive reflection about what they are learning from engaging in a certain project, for example, recognizing that, while editing a video can be a tedious, time-consuming task, the quality of such editing can make a difference in the final product.

Feed-forward

In providing "feed-forward" formative assessment, you and/or students are reflecting on the future direction of their work by posing the question, "Where am I going next?" (Frey & Fisher, 2011). Students then reflect on how they can change or improve on their uses of literacy practices in the future, providing some direction for their future development. Students may determine that, in adopting roles in drama activities, they need to experiment more with adopting alternative language and perspectives consistent with their roles. Or, in revising their writing, they may determine that they need to adopt a different stance.

Teaching Peers to Give Feedback

Given the challenge of responding to your students' work, it may be difficult if not impossible to provide as much feedback to all of your students as you would like. You may therefore want to train students to provide one another with feedback. Without such training, peers typically provide vague, overly judgmental feedback; students need training in how to provide descriptive, reader-based feedback. They may also believe that their peers are not capable of giving feedback or they may be reluctant to provide feedback that might be perceived as judging their peers as people.

To teach your students about providing feedback to others, you can model giving reader-based feedback or fostering self-assessing and revisions, followed by students' practicing feedback and self-assessing in one-on-one conferences or small groups. You can also model effective conference techniques, for example, how as writers or producers of texts students need to be open to receiving feedback as opposed to being overly defensive.

ACTIVITY: GIVING READER-BASED PEER FEEDBACK

As you are drafting reports in your class, pair up with another student and provide each other with reader-based feedback. Describe how you as a reader are engaged or intrigued with, confused by, lost, needing more information, etc. in response to specific aspects of your partner's draft. Then, based on this feedback, your partner can self-assess their draft's limitations and describe how their revisions will address these limitations. (As an alternative, share your drafts online, and use a screencasting tool such as Jing to provide audio reader-based feedback to the online draft; you can use these screencasts to model peer feedback for your students.)

USING CRITERIA TO ENGAGE IN SELF-ASSESSING

To foster self-assessing you can provide students with criteria to help them assess their work. Self-assessing involves more than determining whether their practices achieve certain goals. Olympic divers have a clear sense of the very specific conventions or criteria for what constitutes an effective dive that judges apply in assessing their work. Effective assessment also involves assessing the uses of literacy practices within an event or social context relative to the conventions and criteria operating in that event or context (@ = Defining criteria).

At the same time, students need to recognize that the conventions or criteria for determining practice/goal relationships will vary across different social events or contexts. Using certain conventions or criteria for self-assessing their work in one event or context may not transfer to other events or contexts.

In defining their goals, students therefore need to consider how those goals operate within specific social events or contexts. For example, a 12th grade student, Bill, is writing a letter to the school board of his high school's district arguing that the district needs to allow the high school to experiment with offering "hybrid classes." These "hybrid classes" combine time in class with time spent working in an online space without having to physically be in the classroom. As someone who likes to work on his own in the school media center on his computer, he believes that participating in these "hybrid classes" would allow him to complete more of his work during school hours. He draws on an idea proposed by one of his English teachers, who believed that students could complete a lot of their work in the media center without having to physically attend her class every day.

In crafting his letter, Bill knows that he needs to consider the rhetorical context of his writing a letter to the school board, a context in which certain genre conventions are operating that define what's an effective letter. He knows that he has to provide relevant background information about "hybrid classes" to school board members, who may have little knowledge of how "hybrid classes" operate. He also anticipates school board members' potential skepticism about whether students would devote time outside of class to completing their schoolwork in a relatively unsupervised context. And, he knows that, in writing to an adult audience, he needs to bolster his arguments with valid reasons and supporting evidence, seek to gain his audience's sympathy with his preference for working on his own during the school day, as well as employ a relatively formal style—all characteristics of effective, argumentative writing, characteristics he learned in his 11th grade composition class. He also knows that, given his status as a student, he needs to document support from teachers and/or administrators.

Bill's knowledge of these social genre conventions derives from his participation in what James Gee (2010b) defines as an "appreciative system," an appropriate, effective practice for achieving a certain goal in a certain context or community. To achieve his goal of convincing the school board members to consider his recommendation, he selects certain literacy practices designed to convince them of the viability of providing "hybrid classes." Gee defines this "basic circuit of human action" as a probe/get a response from the world/reflect process based on an appreciative system (p. 14). This "appreciative system" is based on a set of conventions or norms constituting what is considered to be effective, acceptable, or appropriate practices for achieving certain goals or outcomes within the domains of playing a video game, engaging in chemistry experiments, designing a building, preparing a legal brief, etc.—in this case, bringing policy recommendations to a school board. For Gee, self-assessing therefore involves knowledge of conventions operating in these domains, or, in Bill's case, knowledge of the conventions of writing to a school board.

Learning Conventions Constituting Self-Assessment

All of this raises questions about how students learn the conventions operating in various "appreciative systems" in different domains, conventions constituting their self-assessment of action/goal relationships. In Bill's case, he transferred his experiences serving on the student council in which he had to pose arguments to teachers and administrators to crafting his letter to the school board. Or, students may transfer their knowledge of conventions from one discipline to another.

Students therefore acquire knowledge of conventions or criteria through active engagement in social events or contexts, as opposed to being simply assigned or told these conventions. While you may provide them with criteria for effective use of literacy practices in certain events or contexts, unless they have also had some experience in these events or contexts they may not understand how to apply these criteria. While Bill's teacher may have provided him with criteria such as "considers audience's prior knowledge and beliefs in formulating an argument," unless Bill has had some experience in the domain of writing for actual adult audiences, he may not understand the meaning of that stated criterion.

Unfortunately, students have often not acquired experiences in those domains in ways that can transfer to their work in your English classes. Students from low-income backgrounds, who have not had the opportunities to engage in the kinds of experiences afforded to middle-income students, may lack knowledge of these conventions. As someone from a middle-class background, Bill had perceived his parents engaged in formal arguments related to proposing changes in their respective workplaces, experiences that transferred to his letter writing.

However, all students from all different backgrounds and income levels bring rich experiences to your classroom. Consistent with Carol Lee's (2007) cultural modeling approach, knowing about your students' cultural background experiences can help you in planning activities that build on the different cultural experiences your students bring to the classroom. For example, if you have a large number of Latino students with family or relatives in Mexico or Central America in your classroom, you may draw on their experiences with communicating with those family members or relatives, or on their experiences in translating Spanish to English for family members or relatives. Or, as previously noted, in working with African-American students, you can draw on their experiences with language genres such as "playing the dozens" to apply to responding to symbolic uses of language in literature (Lee, 2007).

Considering Dispositions

In giving feedback, you are responding to not only students' literacy practices, but also to their dispositions related to their uses of literacy practices. For example, you may indicate to a student that you're pleased with their persistence in working to address a challenging issue or their openness and flexibility in working collaboratively with others. It's important to describe these dispositions since they shape how students use literacy practices. The fact that a student can be open and flexible in working with others has much to do with their effectiveness in *collaborating with others*.

A joint statement on assessing writing identified various dispositions or habits of mind that students should acquire in taking a first-year college writing course (Council of Writing Program Administrators, National Council of Teachers of English, National Writing Project, 2011, p.2):

- Openness—the willingness to consider new ways of being and thinking in the world.
- Engagement—a sense of investment and involvement in learning.
- Creativity—the ability to use novel approaches for generating, investigating, and representing ideas.
- Persistence—the ability to sustain interest in and attention to short- and long-term projects.
- Responsibility—the ability to take ownership of one's actions and understand the consequences of those actions for oneself and others.
- Flexibility—the ability to adapt to situations, expectations, or demands.
- Metacognition—the ability to reflect on one's own thinking as well as on the individual and cultural processes used to structure knowledge.

We perceive these dispositions as forms of actions or social practices or uses of texts and objects that are mediated by larger institutional or cultural practices. Students' emotions or dispositions, for example, their critical engagement with texts, influence their beliefs and attitudes about event tasks or texts. Lewis and Tierney (2011) cite the example of two African-American students who respond negatively to the portrayals of female sexuality in the Disney *Pocahontas* based primarily on a racist discourse of whiteness—noting that the character of Pocahontas in the film is portrayed as a relatively white character with little consideration of her Native American cultural heritage. These students' critical engagement is not simply a function of their individual traits as students who may or may not be engaged in their learning. Their engagement is a function of how this film culturally positioned these students in ways that provoke their critical engagement in resistance to discourses of whiteness.

DEFINING CRITERIA FOR ASSESSING STUDENT USE OF LITERACY PRACTICES

In devising and discussing assignments, it is useful to clarify the criteria for what it means to effectively employ literacy practices in specific contexts. In doing so, it is important to discuss and/or negotiate these criteria with students so that they understand how to apply them for self-assessing. For each of the following literacy practices described in Chapter 3, we describe some criteria you might employ in assessing students' uses of these practices, as well as some dispositions to consider in making such assessments.

Framing Events

In *framing events*, students need to know how to infer ways that goals, norms, roles, and beliefs shape people's or characters' actions in a specific event. To assess students' ability to frame events, you can develop criteria related to students' ability to identify goals, plans, norms, roles, and beliefs in events, as well as their ability to use them to explain actions—for example, to explain a character's actions in terms of their goals, plans, norms, roles, and/or beliefs, as well as entertaining alternative explanations for these actions.

You may also develop criteria having to do with the validity of these explanations—the fact that students provide supporting evidence for their explanations of actions. For example, if students explain Gatsby's actions in *The Great Gatsby* (Fitzgerald, 1991) in terms of his goals and beliefs, they need to provide information from the novel demonstrating how those goals and beliefs shaped his actions.

And, for assessing their ability to frame events in writing, communicating, or speaking in a certain context, you can consider students' ability to infer the goals, plans, norms, roles, and beliefs operating in that context, as well as their engagement and flexibility in that event, and also their responsibility to contributing to the event. For example, in assessing a student's written analysis of the lack of bike trails in her part of a city to submit to the city council, you may assess that student's ability to clearly define her purpose, persona, and beliefs about the need for more bike trails based on her framing of writing to the city council.

Students may then self-assess their ability to frame events in terms of how their framing was or was not consistent with other participants' or their audience's framing. For example, in organizing a meeting of their peers, students may note how their own framing differed from their peers' framing of the purpose for the meeting, resulting in their having the flexibility to negotiate these differences to derive a purpose agreeable to all participants.

Constructing and Enacting Identities

In assessing students constructing and enacting identities, you are evaluating students' ability to adopt roles or identities through uses of relevant certain social practices and adoption of certain dispositions. For example, you may assess students' engagement in adopting roles in a role play related to their openness or flexibility in assuming perspectives distinct from perspectives they may adopt outside the role play. And, you may assess their level of self-confidence or sense of agency in employing certain literacy practices in certain contexts. African-American students may assume that they lack the ability to do well on tests of verbal ability, a "self-fulfilling prophecy" that results in them not performing well on these tests (Steele & Aronson, 1995). If students believe that they are not good test-takers or that they lack verbal abilities measured on these tests, they do not do as well as students who are more self-confident about their abilities. Again, rather than perceiving self-confidence or agency simply as an individual trait, you may note how their self-confidence or agency is shaped by their participation in certain contexts—that, in their performance in a school play, they knew how to effectively interact with the director and other actors.

You may also note changes over time in students' use of literacy practices involved in constructing their identities (Figure 12.1). For example, you may note that, over time, a student gained a sense of confidence in her willingness to speak out in discussions. And, using portfolio reflections, students may compare their own self-assessment of changes

Figure 12.1 Identity

Armando Testa Communication Agency for San Patrignano.

in your course with your perceptions of those changes, providing reasons for those changes. For example, a student may note that she was more willing to speak out in discussions because she became more engaged with the material in a course, leading her to want to contribute to the discussions.

Relating to and Collaborating with Others

You may assess students' ability to relate to and collaborate with others in terms of their ability to empathize with their peers, share their own perspectives, negotiate differences of opinion, and assume responsibilities for collaborating with others. For example, you may note that in classroom discussions a student is consistently restating her peer's position on a topic prior to making her own contribution to the discussion.

You may also assess students' openness to entertaining alternative perspectives that may differ from perspectives they typically adopt, for example, their ability to assume characters' alternative perspectives as well as adopt different roles in a drama or role-play activity.

Synthesizing and Interpreting Texts

In assessing students' ability to synthesize and interpret texts by summarizing and paraphrasing the key points or positions in their own words in speaking, listening, or writing, you can assess students' ability to elaborate on their recounting or retelling in response to texts or in sharing narratives. For example, in retelling events in a novel, you may note that a student added information about characters' beliefs to explain their actions. Or, you may assess their ability to adopt and compare different characters' perspectives reflecting different beliefs and attitudes about events.

You can also assess students' ability to adopt a "point-driven stance" (Hunt & Vipond, 1992) based on their ability to infer a text's thematic point through noting certain consistent patterns in actions or dialogue, or inferring the ideological stance associated with a text—for example, how the novel *Catch-22* (Heller, 1961) adopts a satiric stance on the military. You can also assess students' ability to employ "rules of notice" (Rabinowitz, 1987) to infer the significance of certain cues, titles, beginnings, endings, complications in characters' plans, or conflicts to adopt a point-driven stance; for example, how they identified how conflicts between wealthy and poor characters in a novel implied a stance regarding the corrupting influence of wealth on characters.

Students can self-assess changes in their ability to synthesize and interpret texts by noting the degree to which they go beyond simply retelling to interpreting larger thematic meanings. They may note that responding to the novel *Feed* (Anderson, 2002) by adopting a point-driven stance allows them to perceive the novel in terms of the larger theme of how people are constructed through corporate consumerist branding.

Constructing Texts

In developing criteria for assessing students' construction of multimodal texts in the form of stories, poems, blog posts, videos, etc., you can draw on some basic concepts of communication norms—relevancy, sufficiency, and validity (Grice, 1975), as well as coherence and significance.

In considering *relevancy*, students need to be able to provide information, reasons, and ideas relevant to the topic and rhetorical contexts. This requires that they select information, reasons, and ideas relevant to their audience's prior knowledge, needs, and expectations. For example, in writing some directions on how to employ an online image-sharing tool such as Flickr, students need to know what and how much their audiences already know about online image-sharing tools. To assess relevancy, students need to have a clear idea about their primary purpose or point that will serve as the basis for assessing relevancy. Knowing that in their blog posts they are trying to argue for the need to provide political candidates with free advertising, they need to assess how their reasons for providing free advertising will best support their position.

In assessing *sufficiency*, you are considering whether students have enough information or evidence to adequately support their positions or contentions. In many cases, students do not have enough information simply because they did not conduct an adequate search of material or did not engage in enough research on their topics, issues, or texts. In other cases, students may have too much information, requiring that they sort through that information to find the most useful information. To assess sufficiency, students again need to have a clear sense of their positions or contentions so that they determine whether or not they have enough information.

In providing information, students also need to determine the *validity* of that information based on vetting sources and author credentials. Students may draw information from sources that are not credible or that skew the information based on their ideological orientation. To assess their ability to determine validity, you or your students could determine the degree to which students are actually testing the validity of their resources.

You are also assessing the *coherence* of a student's text, recognizing that notions of coherence or effective organization vary markedly according to genre conventions and philosophies of text meaning. While it is assumed that the traditional school essay is typically organized based on a defined, logical, thesis/support progression, the organization of a postmodern digital story with multiple, alternative pathways entails quite different notions of coherence.

One key criterion related to coherence is the degree to which students signal, cue, or provide audiences with a roadmap defining the direction and development of their ideas. In providing reader-based feedback, you can then describe how the students set up expectations for the logical direction of their ideas and how providing those expectations helped you navigate their text.

Students also need to consider the *significance* of adopting a position or their actions relative to the potential consequences. Assessing the significance of their position or actions means that they are able to recognize the value of their work based on how it contributes to a certain activity, domain, or community. For example, you may note that a student's report on problems with their school's bus service to submit to the school's administration represents a significant contribution to addressing those problems.

Students can self-assess their text production based on these different criteria by responding to their teacher's or peers' feedback, noting how changes in use of certain features improve their readers' responses. For example, if they received feedback that their supporting reasons were not relevant to their positions, in future writing (when they provide more relevant supporting reasons, and receive positive reactions), they will note how making those changes improved the quality of their writing.

Critiquing Systems

In assessing students' ability to critique systems, you are determining their ability to apply historical, institutional/civic, cultural, psychological, and economic perspectives to critique systems. For example, in applying an historical or economic perspective analyzing cause-and-effect relationship to the rise and fall of oil prices, students need to be able to know how to engage in historical analysis to identify historical incidents of changes in oil prices as well as have an understanding of economics to analyze the influence of economic forces on oil prices (Shute, Dennen, Kim, Donmez, & Wang, 2010).

You can also assess students' ability to identify tensions and contradictions in systems that reflect status quo problems that need to be addressed. For example, in studying the cultural world of the small town as portrayed in literature, students may identify the contradiction associated with the assumption that small-town people must be considered as failures because they are still living in the small town even though they enjoy the sense of community in their small town.

In self-assessing their ability to critique systems, students may note changes in the degree to which they are able to go beyond simply analyzing social practices in terms of individuals' actions and beliefs versus the ability to analyze social practices as shaped by institutional systems. For example, rather than perceive the issue of tracking in their school as due to the actions of students, teachers, or administrators, they are able to perceive tracking as a function of schooling as institutional system shaped by historical and economic forces.

VARYING CRITERIA ACCORDING TO DIFFERENCES IN GRADE LEVEL USING LEARNING PROGRESSIONS OR TRAJECTORIES

One of the features of the Common Core State Standards is their use of "learning progressions" based on assumptions about grade-level differences given students' developmental differences from grades 6 to 12. In developing your criteria, you certainly need to employ quite different criteria for assessing students at grade 6 than you would use for assessing students at grade 12. For example, the Common Core reading standard for the ability to employ evidence from texts to support inferences varies from "specific" (grade 6), "several sources" (grade 7), "a wide range" (grade 8), "that most strongly supports" (grades 9–10), and "strong and thorough" (grades 11–12) (CCSS, 2010, pp. 32–33). These criteria do reflect differences in students' ability—that 6th graders are expected to be able to cite "specific" evidence, while 11th and 12th graders are expected to cite "strong and thorough" evidence.

However, differences in these criteria are also somewhat arbitrary, in that differences in the quality of evidence cited may all depend on the social or cultural context in which students are citing that evidence to achieve certain purposes for their reading, as opposed to reading simply for the sake of reading a text. As we also noted in Chapter 2, we are critical of the assumptions in the Common Core State Standards about students' "learning progressions" based on a cognitive developmental model that does not take into account the ways in which differences in students' learning are also shaped by participation in social and cultural contexts.

This suggests that, in formulating criteria related to grade-level differences, you consider the social and cultural context in which students are working, drawing on the previously mentioned criteria of relevancy. For example, 10th grade students are reading texts about issues of teen homelessness and schooling to develop a report for their community. In citing evidence from their reading, students are not only selecting evidence that "most strongly supports" their contention about the need to address this issue, but also selecting evidence relevant to their particular community's programs for addressing homelessness.

Thinking about the contexts shaping their work involves recognizing individual students' "zone of proximal development" (ZPD) (Vygotsky, 1986)—the space or range of their actual and potential development. In estimating their zone of proximal development, you can then gear your feedback in ways that are not too sophisticated for students, but still challenge them to go beyond their current ability level, while also recognizing that a student's zone of proximal development may vary across different texts and assignments.

A student's zone of proximal development may reflect prior experiences that have limited his sense of potential growth. For example, in responding to a student's writing, you may notice that this student has difficulty in expressing his ideas in writing. In talking with the student, you discover that he had received a lot of negative feedback from previous teachers, resulting in their being apprehensive about expressing his ideas in writing, given a fear of being judged in a negative manner. Knowing that a student is apprehensive about writing means that you can then provide him with a lot of positive feedback designed to bolster his self-confidence as a writer.

Recognizing Bias in Assessing Students

In working with students, it is important to recognize that your assumptions and expectations about your students' abilities based on differences in race, class, or gender may influence your assessments of those students. Some research shows that teachers have lower expectations and unfavorable attitudes towards students of color, resulting in these students internalizing these expectations so that they are less motivated to excel (van Ewijk, 2011). This means that you need to reflect on how your assumptions about students' ability related to race, class, and gender differences influence the expectations you have for your students. If you recognize that you have low expectations—that you expect that your students won't complete their work or do well in your classroom given their race, class, or gender and/or their lack of home support—you may then want to rethink some of those expectations.

ACTIVITY: FORMULATING CRITERIA FOR ASSIGNMENTS

In giving assignments, it's important that you identify criteria based on those literacy practices students employ in completing your assignments. Because students may not be familiar with these criteria, you may also want to discuss them with the students, as well as model application of the criteria, giving some illustrative examples. Knowing these criteria will then help students self-assess their work as they are completing the assignment.

Take an assignment that you plan to use in your teaching. Identify the literacy practices involved in completing this assignment—for example, making connections between different stories to infer common themes. Then, formulate criteria that you'll use to assess students' ability to employ this literacy practice. For example, to assess students' ability to make connections between different stories to infer a common theme, you may employ the criteria of students clearly formulating a common theme and providing evidence from each story that supports their formulation of that theme. You may also include some illustrative examples to show students how to apply these criteria.

EMPLOYING RUBRICS OR SCALES FOR RATING STUDENTS' WORK

Based on your criteria, you may also develop rubrics or scales that provide students with rating scales or checklists in which you rate students' work or students rate their own work (@ = Employing rubrics or scales). There are three basic types of rubrics or scales—holistic, analytic, and primary trait. Holistic rubrics or scales rate the text or work based on an overall score. For example, in scoring a student's essay, you may rate that essay on a scale of "1" to "6" in terms of your overall subjective assessment of an essay's quality, drawing on specific criteria for what constitutes a "1," "2," etc. Analytic rubrics or scales break out specific, defined criteria for assessing student performance on their text production or performance on a task. For example, the frequently used "six-trait" rubric provides specific criteria for rating students' writing on a scale of "1" to "6" for "ideas," "organization," "voice," "word choice," "sentence fluency," and "conventions" (http://educationnorthwest.org/resource/464). Primary-trait rubrics or scales identify those traits and specific criteria for those traits, unique to a particular assignment or writing.

There is considerable debate about the value and use of rubrics or scales for rating students' work (Wilson, 2006; Kohn, 2006; Mabry, 1999). Rubrics or scales are often used in assessments to achieve high reliability, defined as high levels of agreement between judges or scorers. However, to achieve high agreement, rubrics are often framed in terms of formalist or quantitative criteria—for example, the fact that in writing an essay a student employs a thesis statement and provides supporting reasons, or that a student uses a certain number of reasons to support their thesis. They do so because judges or scorers are often more likely to agree on more formalist or quantitative criteria than with more subjective criteria such as use of voice or clarity of their stance (Kohn, 2006; Mabry, 1999).

As a result, rubrics may often employ these formalist or quantitative criteria, resulting in an emphasis on these criteria in assignments or instruction related to the assignment. This can then result in evaluation of writing that focuses more on employing the desired organizational structure, for example, use of the five-paragraph theme structure. Students then focus more on simply conforming to the organizational structure than on the development or expression of ideas (Mabry, 1999).

While providing students with rubrics can certainly be helpful for students in clarifying the criteria by which their work will be evaluated, it can also serve to limit their focus to conforming to these criteria. As a result, you or your students may find that the rubrics may not capture the unique qualities of students' particular work. In her critique of rubrics, Maja Wilson (2006) cites the example of assessing what she perceived to be one of her students' narratives describing her experiences with her family, thunderstorms, and visiting Texas. She notes that "I then attempted to apply the Michigan Educational Assessment Program (MEAP) six-point rubrics to assess her writing, rubrics based on whether the writing was engaging, clear, and focused" (p. 109). She might have assigned a failing "2" score, to quote the criteria, in that there was "limited control over writing conventions [that] may make the writing difficult"; "the writing was a bit of a mess: inconsistent paragraphing, full of unintended fragments, unclear transitions, and rife with spelling, punctuation, and sentence structure errors" (p. 109). However, she was personally moved by the writing, noting that "*this* paper was what made being a writing teacher the best job in the world" (p. 110). Maja noted that she:

Stumbled onto some rather large insights as she wrote. While her description of thunderstorms was interesting in itself, she surprised herself and me as she began to connect the sound of the rain to her search for an answer and reliance on herself in the midst of uncertainty and rejection. Her writing brought both of us somewhere new. (p. 111)

Maja was also concerned that making revisions to her writing, according to the rubrics' emphasis on coherent organization, "would have changed the loose, poetic structure of what she had begun to do" (p. 112).

Another issue with rubrics is the degree to which they serve to focus primarily on performance itself—on *how well* students are doing, as opposed to *what* they are doing. As Alfie Kohn (2006) noted, "There's a big difference between thinking about the content of a story one is reading (for example, trying to puzzle out why a character made a certain decision), and thinking about one's own proficiency at reading" (p. xiv). It is also the case that focusing on the how can lead to "more superficial thinking, less interest in whatever one is doing, less perseverance in the face of failure, and a tendency to attribute results to innate ability and other factors thought to be beyond one's control" (p. xiv).

In summary, rubrics can certainly be useful in providing feedback to students based on rating their effectiveness in addressing certain criteria. However, because the criteria employed in rubrics are often formalist or quantitative, rubrics may be less useful in terms of assessing students in their engagement in critical inquiry and literacy practices. While rubrics may appear to help teachers justify the grades they assign, rubrics may significantly detract from your most important task as a teacher: listening well to your students and understanding their work.

CASE STUDY: SARAH PANCOST'S HALLWAY (ASSESSING WRITING)

In this chapter, we've discussed some of the pros and cons of using rubrics to assess students' writing in terms of providing students with useful feedback that will improve their writing.

In this case study, you will watch and listen to Sarah Pancost, practicing high school English teacher, as she discusses her beliefs about assessment and her methods of assessment. You will also hear about contrasting beliefs and practices within her English department. After discussing her comments, you'll step into her classroom, where you'll have the opportunity to read two students' essays in response to a specific prompt. You will then assess these students' essays with a rubric that you will design with your peers. After doing so, you will discuss the difficulties, limitations, and strengths of both creating a rubric and assessing students' work with it. You will also brainstorm alternate methods of assessing student writing with your peers. Ultimately, you will have a glimpse into the demanding challenge that faces all English teachers: assessing student work in an effective and realistic manner.

Please find two to three peers and go to the LiteraryWorlds.org site, and the *Teaching to Succeed* link, to find this case study for Chapter 12.

SUMMATIVE ASSESSMENTS

In contrast to ongoing, formative assessments, summative assessments provide information about students' long-term learning and abilities. They serve to assess students' performances as groups, to judge the effectiveness of the instruction students are receiving (@ and Summative assessments).

There are a number of different types of summative assessments— your own tests or exams; portfolio assessments; or district, state, or national standardized assessments. Some of these assessments are "performance-based" in that they require students to demonstrate their use of certain literacy practices as a means of demonstrating their abilities or knowledge.

Assessments as Incentive for Performance

Most of the district or state-wide summative assessments employed since the 2001 No Child Left Behind mandate have been standardized reading, writing, and math tests used to determine if schools demonstrate "annual yearly progress" (AYP) in all students' test scores. The assumption underlying the uses of these tests is that, because schools would face sanctions if the test scores did not improve, such tests will serve as incentives for teachers to provide more and better instruction in reading, writing, and math, and lead students to be more motivated to learn.

However, a research review by the National Research Council (Hout & Elliott, 2011) on whether these tests provide a positive incentive for learning found that they provide little incentive and, in some cases, negative incentives. One study found that use of high-stakes state exit tests has led to no improvements in National Assessment of Educational Progress (NAEP) scores from 1971 to 2007 (Grodsky, Warren, & Kalogrides, 2009). And, over a period of 1975–2002, these tests had negative effects on graduation rates (Warren, Kulick, & Jenkins, 2006), with more difficult tests leading to lower graduation rates than less difficult exams (Dee & Jacob, 2007).

There is also evidence that building instruction around preparing students for these tests limits teachers to correct-answer reading comprehension tasks related to multiple-choice test items, as well as single draft writing. Eighth grade students taking the NAEP exam reported a decline in revising their drafts from 2002 and 2007. One reason for this decline is that their teachers discouraged the use of computers for their writing, due to the fact that the 9th and 10th grade state writing assessments required handwriting skills (Applebee & Langer, 2006). The report recommends that new forms of assessment need to be developed that are more consistent with positive forms of incentives.

The Common Core State Standards Assessments

As of summer 2011, assessments based on the Common Core were being developed by two consortia projects: SMARTER Balanced Assessment Consortium (SBAC; http://k12.wa.us/smarter/default.aspx), which includes 25 states; and Partnership for the Assessment of Readiness for College and Careers (PARCC; http://www.achieve.org/PARCC), which includes 26 states, projects funded by the U.S. Department of Education Race to the Top funding. It is anticipated that these assessments will be implemented in 2014 (@ = CCSS assessment consortium groups [PARCC and SBAC]).

These assessments will include both optional, formative, perform-ance tests to determine students' growth during the year, and end-of-the-year summative tests. As of summer 2011, under the PARCC system the exams generate a summative score for each student. That score would be based on two summative tests to be taken near the end of the school year: a computer-based test and a test consisting of essays and perform-ance tasks. Students would also take speaking and listening tests, to be administered at times more convenient for schools.

The computer tests will be "computer adaptive" in that when students move through the test on a computer the tasks will change depending on the students' performance, as well as including accommo-dations based on learning disabilities or limited English proficiency. The fact that these assessments will be completed on computers represents an important shift in test administration, as reflected in the fact that the 2012 NAEP writing assessment will be also completed on computers.

Ideally, these assessments will focus on performance tasks that involve students in active demonstrations of their uses of literacy prac-tices—for example, their ability to synthesize disparate texts related to a particular issue to formulate a position on that issue. In August 2011, PARCC released some curriculum frameworks describing their interpretations of and possible ways in which the Common Core State Standards could be assessed (http://www.parcconline.org/parcc-content-frameworks). Similarly, Smarter Balance developed its own frameworks identifying specific types of evidence for learning associated with addressing the standards (http://www.k12.wa.us/SMARTER/Resources.aspx).

At the same time, there may be a number of limitations to these assessments. They may continue to emphasize the importance of high-stakes summative assessments as more important than formative assess-ments, an emphasis that may only perpetuate the teaching-to-the-test phenomenon of the No Child Left Behind testing mandates.

And, even the use of performance-based tasks may involve content or experiences that disadvantage low-income students who lack the test-taking skills or cultural capital associated with topics addressed in these tasks. For example, if students are asked to write about their experiences and attitudes towards social networking—the topic of the 2010 SAT written essay prompt—students who may not have had experiences with social networking are at a disadvantage.

A larger challenge for low-income students is that they may not see reasons to be engaged in what they perceive to be decontextualized reading or writing tasks—tasks with no actual, authentic purpose other than doing well on a test. While their peers may simply perceive these tasks as just one more familiar instance of decontextualized test-taking, if low-income (or any other) students do not perceive any tangible reason for reading or writing, they may not be motivated to do well on the test.

Uses of E-Portfolios

One alternative type of summative assessment involves the use of e-portfolios (@ = E-portfolios). Rather than using commercial portfolio templates, students can create their own portfolios using free website tools such as Google Sites or Weebly, blogs, or wikis. E-portfolios allow students to include links to all of their writing and image/video productions completed in a course or school year, as well as reflections on what they have learned in completing this work or how they have changed in their work over time. Students may also create separate showcase portfolios that include particular illustrative examples of their work, along with reflections on why they selected certain samples of their work.

To encourage reflection, you may ask students to describe what represents their best work and why they perceive it as their best work; what specific literacy practices or dispositions they have acquired; how they have changed in their uses of these practices, reading interests, or in their dispositions; what work gave them the most versus least satisfaction; ways in which they plan to continue to change; how they will access relevant resources to build their "personal learning network"; and how they think their work made a difference in their lives and in the lives of others. To assess students' portfolios, you can provide feedback on the quality and depth of their reflections, as well as your own perceptions on the quality of their work and their growth over time in uses of critical inquiry and literacy practices.

CHAPTER 13

Teacher Reflection and Professional Development

CHAPTER OVERVIEW

Reflecting on Your Knowledge, Beliefs, Abilities, and Dispositions

Ongoing Professional Development

Conducting Action Research to Foster Focused Reflection

Staying Abreast of New Developments and Improving Your Teaching

Case Study: Your Reflect-to-Develop Hallway

In this final chapter, we discuss ways to foster your reflection on your teaching, as well as provide you with resources to enhance your professional development as a teacher.

REFLECTING ON YOUR KNOWLEDGE, BELIEFS, ABILITIES, AND DISPOSITIONS

Your process of professional reflection begins before you even enter the classroom. A quality teacher preparation program should foster your self-critical thinking about becoming a teacher. Some of the reflection activities we describe may be, or may have been, a part of your methods courses or program. You may also be required to develop portfolio materials to meet your program and state certification requirements as well as for use in seeking employment.

Meeting the NCATE Standards

Many university-based teacher education programs are reviewed by external accreditation groups such as the NCATE (National Council for Accreditation of Teacher Education, 2008). These programs need to provide evidence that their graduates are meeting certain NCATE standards, including knowledge of English language arts and teaching methods (@ = NCATE standards).

Creating E-Portfolios

To meet NCATE standards, a teacher education program needs to provide evidence of its graduates' ability to formulate and adopt beliefs, abilities, and dispositions towards teaching and students, evidence that they can provide through sample student portfolios. During a certification program candidates may be required to create an e-portfolio so that your program has access to this evidence. It is also important to create e-portfolios for use in seeking employment. Some employers will want access to your e-portfolio as evidence of your preparation and work.

While your program may have its own e-portfolio template, as noted in the last chapter, you can create e-portfolios using a website (Google Sites, Weebly), blog, or wiki (Beach, Anson, Kastman-Breuch, & Swiss, 2008) (for examples of portfolios: @ = Teaching portfolios). In creating your e-portfolio, it's important to create clearly defined categories on the front page for organizing your materials: lesson plans/units, papers, and evidence of your student work, as well as your teaching philosophy, ability to address certain of the Common Core State Standards, and information about yourself. You can also employ links between materials to define connections between, for example, your philosophy of teaching English and the units you've developed.

In formulating your reflections in an e-portfolio, you are not only using your reflections to identify ways to improve your teaching, but you are also demonstrating to your instructors and future employers that you have the ability to critically self-reflect on your teaching. For the purposes of the job market you may want to create a more selective, "showcase" portfolio designed to highlight your work.

As noted in the last chapter, the quality of your self-reflection is critical for the success of e-portfolios. As you begin your e-portfolio, this self-reflection may seem awkward and artificial, but over time you may become more adept at reflecting on your work. One study found that, as preservice teachers began their portfolios, their writing was often descriptive, with little critical self-reflection (Çimer, 2011). However, due to instructor feedback and guidance, over time, their reflections became more self-critical.

Creating Teaching Websites

Another way you can demonstrate your preparedness for teaching is to create the first draft of a website that you might actually use with your future classes (Figure 13.1). You can create that site on free resources such as Weebly, Wikispaces, or Wordpress, and you should design it with several audiences in mind—above all, your future students, but also their parents and your colleagues. Each audience may have separate pages in your site. This site should express your interests and passions, and at the same time be sufficiently appealing to students and professionals to impress colleagues and administrators. Search online for websites currently in use by secondary English teachers and draw on outstanding examples as your inspiration. Demonstrate your mastery of technology,

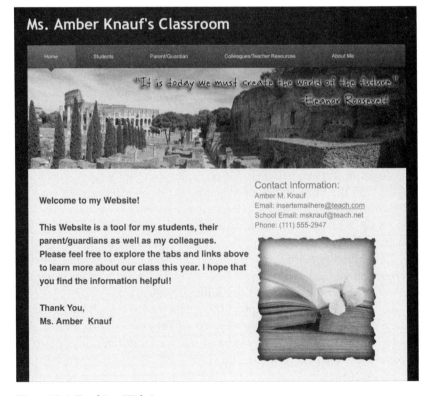

Figure 13.1 Teaching Website

and develop a diversity of links to valuable resources for secondary English teaching. You might also include recommended reading lists, resources for parents, an "about me" page, along with content-relevant resources and activities. Such a site can include some of the same material as in your e-portfolio, clearly addressed to real audiences. You can buy your own URL inexpensively. This kind of working site, ready to go in the classroom, is typically more impressive to a future employer than a standard academic portfolio.

Reflecting on Your Beliefs and Abilities

In your e-portfolio and/or on your teaching website, you can reflect on your beliefs—as described in Chapter 2—setting forward your own philosophy of teaching English and how that philosophy shapes your planning and justifications for using certain teaching methods. For example, you may posit the importance of students *creating multimodal texts* through combining print, images, video, and sound, a focus you justify in terms of the fact that, in a digital world, people are more likely to employ multimodal texts to convey their ideas. Using the professional language of English language arts instruction shows employers that you have been well prepared in your field.

You are also reflecting on your abilities or strengths as a teacher, particularly in terms of demonstrating to future employers what you can offer to their schools. To do so, you can cite examples of your lesson plans or units, along with sample student work to demonstrate your effectiveness in planning and executing instruction, that result in exemplary teaching.

Reflecting on Your Dispositions towards Teaching and Students

In addition to reflecting on your beliefs and abilities, you are also reflecting on your dispositions. The NCATE (2008) standards state that:

Candidates work with students, families, colleagues, and communities in ways that reflect the professional dispositions expected of professional educators as delineated in professional, state, and institutional standards. Candidates demonstrate classroom behaviors that create caring and supportive learning environments and encourage self-directed learning by all students. Candidates recognize when their own professional dispositions may need to be adjusted and are able to develop plans to do so.

You can reflect on your dispositions towards teaching and students by describing how you demonstrate engagement and enthusiasm towards your teaching as well as your ability to empathize with your students. You can provide evidence of these dispositions through descriptions of how you organize your classrooms or ways you communicate with students and parents—for example, by including letters or online posts you use to explain your teaching activities to parents.

ONGOING PROFESSIONAL DEVELOPMENT

Ongoing professional reflection and development should be a crucial part of your experience as a teacher from your first year to your last. Some measure of professional development is likely required by the state in which you teach. Drawing on the National Board for Professional Teaching Standards requirements for veteran teachers' board certification—a rigorous program that includes intensive study, expert evaluation, self-assessment, and peer review—an increasing number of states are changing their certification requirements to go beyond simply completing your degree program and mandated tests (such as a Praxis Preprofessional Preparation Skills Test [PPST], which measures reading, writing, and mathematics and is often used to gain admission to teacher education programs). For example, the Performance Assessment for California Teachers (PACT) requires development of portfolios containing teaching units, reflections on a unit and a video of one's teaching, evidence of student learning, and reflections on one's teaching abilities and future development. In their portfolios, candidates demonstrate to reviewers their ability to consider student experiences and prior knowledge, as well as accommodations for ELL and special-needs learners (@ = State certification requirements). In addition to—and regardless of—your state's certification requirements, significant responsibility is on you to find ways to continue to learn and grow as a teacher.

CONDUCTING ACTION RESEARCH TO FOSTER FOCUSED REFLECTION

You can also engage in self-reflection through conducting action-research projects in your own classroom. Classroom action research allows you to investigate the needs, interests, and learning of your students and to thoughtfully make changes in your instruction. Many graduate programs in English education offer courses in conducting classroom research, and the results are frequently the basis of presentations at professional conferences and publications in professional journals. However, it is not necessary to take a course to engage in classroom research. As we discussed in the previous chapter on assessment, you should always be monitoring your teaching based on how students are learning. Working with other teachers and creating teacher research support groups is an important part of professional development. There are a number of resources and books to help you develop your skills as a reflective practitioner and a researcher in your own classroom.

Throughout this book, we've asked you to respond to virtual cases based on some actual teachers' challenges in teaching English. There are also some other online cases on the website (@ = Online teacher cases). By doing so, you are learning how to think systematically about the relationships between teaching and learning, a process you then apply to your daily teaching. You're also learning to go beyond just focusing on yourself as teacher to "learning to notice" how students are reacting to teaching by addressing questions such as:

1. What is important about what is going on here?
2. How can I come to understand what is happening here?
    What is this a case of? (Sherin & van Es, 2008, p. 480)

You can also engage in this reflection about your own or another teacher's teaching through conducting action research on certain aspects of the relationship between teaching and learning (for examples on the website, @ = Teacher action research). Rather than engaging in random reflections, action research formalizes reflection through focusing your attention on certain issues of teaching and learning in some systematic manner.

To engage in action research, you can identify certain difficulties, challenges, or issues in your own or another teacher's classroom—if your students aren't engaged with a certain activity, you can then step back and reflect on possible reasons for the lack of engagement. Once you've identified those reasons, the next time you employ this activity, you can make changes in how you conduct this activity. Or, you may be intrigued with how certain new methods or approaches might contribute to certain kinds of learning. In doing so, you may examine not only what and whether students learned what you or the teacher hoped students would learn, but also how students perceived their learning experience in terms of the engagement and interest.

Posing Questions

Based on perceived difficulties, challenges, or issues, or on some anticipated new approaches, you may pose questions that serve to organize your research. Rather than focus on *yourself*—asking questions such as "How am *I* experiencing my teaching? How do *I* think my teaching is going? What classroom approaches make sense to *me*?"—it's important to reflect on *how your students are experiencing* your instruction through asking questions such as "How are *you* experiencing the learning? How do *you* view your own work? What is the potential impact of classroom practices on *you*?" (Shadiow, 2010, p. 103).

Focusing on your students' experiences, then, involves considering individual differences in how students experience an activity in terms of differences in their interests, knowledge, beliefs, and goals, information you can obtain by having them provide written descriptions of themselves in their e-portfolio, classroom blog site or social networking, a video, or through a survey or introductory letter. You can interview students about their experiences with a certain activity or their perceptions of your classroom or school. It is often helpful to focus students' attention on their writing or e-portfolio. You can also have them create maps to depict their spatial perceptions of their classroom or school and then ask them to elaborate on those perceptions.

One key focus for action-research projects has to do with students' experiences in, and perceptions of, schools. It is also the case that students are often stressed out with the pressures of "doing school" in which students who were attending high school with a 95 percent college attendance record perceive school as simply playing a game of following the rules, getting good grades, pleasing teachers, frequently cheating, and being sleep-deprived all for the need to be accepted in college, but without any sense of engagement or authentic learning (Pope, 2003). You may study students' perceptions of their school experience related to the larger purpose of schooling and learning, as well as their attitudes about grades, college admissions, and work pressures. You can also shadow a student as she moves through her school day and ask her how her engagement varied during that day, and reasons for that variation.

To determine student learning resulting from your own or another teacher's instruction, you can track changes in students' use of literacy practices by comparing their writing or recorded talk over time. For example, two teachers addressed the question "What happens when kids are trained to ask the questions?" (Wilhelm, 2009). They tracked changes in the types of questions students would write in the beginning of class to determine changes in these question types. By the end of the year, students were employing both inferential and critical questions, questions connecting to their lived experiences and focusing on issues portrayed in texts.

Studying Your School's and Community's Culture

It's important that you have a strong understanding of the culture of your school, as well as the community influencing that school, so that you can gear your teaching according to the norms and attitudes operating in that culture. In studying the school and community culture, you may address questions such as:

- What are the prevailing norms, beliefs, attitudes, and goals underlying the school's and/or community's culture?
- Who defines these norms, beliefs, attitudes, and goals, and how are they manifested in students' and teachers' social practices?
- How do teachers or students differ in their perceptions of these norms, beliefs, attitudes, and goals?
- What, if any, are the expressions of deviation from these norms, beliefs, attitudes, and goals, and what do these expressions represent?
- What are the different groups or cliques operating in the school and/ or community, and how and why do they differ in terms of their own norms, beliefs, attitudes, and goals?
- What are the different spaces in the school and/or community, and who defines these spaces and in what ways?

To study your school culture, you can conduct some ethnographic analysis of the culture by observing certain events and practices to discern norms and attitudes constituting the school culture. For example, you can observe school assemblies, pep rallies, sports events, or dances/ social gatherings, to discern the social norms reflecting different degrees of student involvement in, and/or administrative control of, these events.

You can also observe the lunchroom and map out who sits with whom in terms of race, class, gender, and/or grade level/age differences, as seating patterns reflect variations in the degree of segregation within the school, reflecting larger school demographics. To determine these demographics you can conduct what Susan Groenke (2010) defines as an "equity audit" to collect data about student demographics in the school district in terms of race, class, and gender for both students and teachers, as well as information about differences in these groups within and across courses, and how these demographic differences reflect differences within and across the community served by a school. For example, in Groenke's methods course, preservice teachers noted that there were no advanced placement classes in the more rural, low-income schools in a district. They also found that all English language learning students (ELLs) in a district were sent to one of the poorer, understaffed schools in the district. And, they noted that there were no teachers of color in a largely white, middle-class school, and that the honors students believed that they were superior to the other students.

Tools for Conducting Action Research

There are a number of different tools you can use to capture specific data as part of conducting action research (these are similar to the ethnography writing tools described in Chapter 8):

- *Field notes* of your perceptions and reflections on specific events, interactions, or spaces.
- *Short narratives* about your own or participants' experiences, and reflections on those experiences—for example, describing your first visit to the school.
- *Interviews* with teachers and/or students, asking them to reflect on experiences or react to your own perceptions, and determine their agreement with those perceptions.
- *Artifacts or documents*—school policy statements, curriculum guides, student writing, sports trophies, etc. Interview students about those artifacts or documents.
- *Digital images or video* to create a record of student work and interactions. For example, if you created a video of you leading a discussion, you could create a transcript of that video and reflect on the percentage of your talk versus student talk, your use of closed versus open questions, the amount of interaction between students, the depth and development of students' talk, and the degree to which they adopt critical stances.
- *Annotations to your videos* using YouTube annotations, VideoANT (http://ant.umn.edu), VoiceThread (http://voicethread.com), or Viddler (http://www.viddler.com) (@ = Tools for annotations of videos). For example, in a video of a preservice teacher leading a discussion of a poem, Richard provides annotated feedback to specific instances in the discussion about the teacher's effective uses of open-ended questions and facilitation of the discussion (http://mediamill.cla.umn.edu/mediamill/display/44436).

Analyzing Data

Based on the data you collect, you can then begin to reflect on certain consistent patterns to address your research questions, patterns that may provide explanations for the phenomena you are observing. For example, in examining the feedback you provided students in recorded writing conferences, you may have wondered whether and how that feedback would lead to students' self-assessing in the conference and/or revisions of their drafts. You can then review recordings of the conferences to identify instances of student self-assessments and revisions of the writing to identify whether and how your feedback fostered self-assessment and/or revisions.

You can then use these results to assess the effectiveness of your own or another teacher's instruction, along with changes you or the teacher may need to make to address problems in instruction. If, for example, you find that your students are not engaging in any substantive self-assessing in your writing conferences, you may then want to focus more on modeling ways of self-assessing for them. You may also find a wide variation in students' learning, suggesting the need to consider individual differences in your instruction.

STAYING ABREAST OF NEW DEVELOPMENTS AND IMPROVING YOUR TEACHING

As a future member of the teaching profession, it is also important that you engage in ongoing professional development to improve your teaching. As in any profession, it is essential that you keep abreast of new developments, resources, and research associated with effective English instruction. And, you can enhance your resume for seeking employment by demonstrating to future employers your involvement in and commitment to professional development. The following are some activities and resources you can use to engage in professional development.

Participation in Professional Organizations and Training

As a professional, it is also important that you join a professional organization as a student member, such as NCTE (the National Council of Teachers of English) (http://www.ncte.org), the International Reading Association (IRA) (http://www.reading.org), or the Modern Language Association (http://www.mla.org), which entitles you to receive journals such as *Voices from the Middle* for middle school language arts teachers; *English Journal* for secondary teachers; and IRA's *Journal of Adolescent and Adult Literacy* for educators of all adolescents and adults. These national organizations, as well as state affiliates, hold conferences and workshops that provide sharing of teaching ideas and resources. Another important resource and publication for teachers, created by a consortium of progressive educators, is *Rethinking Schools* (http://rethinkingschools.org).

Building Personal Learning Networks (PLNs)

One challenge as a teacher is that you may have only limited access to professional development in your school. To keep up with and obtain information about teaching English, you can build personal learning networks (PLNs) that provide you with online access to other English teachers' work. To create PLNs, you can subscribe to and comment on teachers' blogs, wikis, podcasts, or social networking sites such as the English Companion Ning (http://englishcompanion.ning.com) (@ = Online professional development sites).

ACTIVITY: CREATING A DIGITAL PERSONAL LEARNING NETWORK (PLN)

Create a digital personal learning network using a blog, wiki, or website to store links to resources, databases, peers/mentors, professional organizations, podcasts, and social networks (Twitter, Diigo, Ning, Facebook, educational groups). You could organize your network according to your course topics or teaching methods. You can then share this information with your students on your course blogs, wikis, or websites, as well as invite your colleagues—for example, members of your middle school planning team—to share their links to your PLN.

Finding and Working with Mentors

As you probably know, a significant number of new teachers leave the profession in their first three years of teaching. An analysis of factors leading English teachers wanting to quit teaching found that with more experience teachers were less likely to leave (for every five years of teaching, English teachers being classified as likely to quit decreased by 23 percent) (Hancock & Scherff, 2010). Other major factors related to teacher attrition include: teacher apathy associated with stress, burnout, and dissatisfaction; degree of peer support; and degree of administrative support. All of these factors reflect the importance of finding personal and professional support during your initial years of teaching.

While preservice teachers in one study perceived themselves as initially ready to meet the challenges of teaching, as they began teaching they perceived themselves as being more in survival mode, suggesting that new teachers are struggling to develop a professional identity (Thomas & Beauchamp, 2011).

Given these challenges, it is useful to identify and work with mentors who can provide guidance and support in what can often be a difficult initial period in your career. While schools may have assigned mentors who meet with you on a regular basis, you may also seek out other veteran teachers, who can serve as mentors on a more informal basis. Mentors can share their teaching ideas/lessons, ways to access resources and people in the school, inform you about the school culture and unstated rules, and help you engage in problem-solving.

CASE STUDY: YOUR REFLECT-TO-DEVELOP HALLWAY

In this chapter, we've described a range of different ways to develop as a professional over time.

In this final case study, you will identify ways that you'll stay connected to English Education scholarship and professional development opportunities, employ personal learning networks (PLNs), participate in professional organizations such as the National Council of Teachers of English (NCTE), the International Reading Association, and Modern Language Association (MLA), and how you can use your e-portfolio to showcase your teaching abilities and experiences. This discussion will capitalize on all you've learned about various literacy frameworks and your beliefs as an English teacher, preparing you further to be a positive influence in the lives of your future students, colleagues, and community members.

Please find two or three peers and go to the LiteraryWorlds.org site and the *Teaching to Succeed* link to find this case study for Chapter 13.

In Conclusion

As we conclude this book, we hope that you have benefited from the ideas we've presented on teaching English and your participation with the virtual cases. We also hope that you recognize the need not only to address the Common Core State Standards, but to go beyond these standards through adopting a critically engaged literacy practices perspective on teaching and learning that values student engagement in authentic classroom spaces. We leave it up to you to create these spaces and hope to hear about them as you present at conferences and write about your and your students' accomplishments.

References

Abouzeid, L. (2009). *Year of the elephant.* Austin, TX: Center for Middle Eastern Studies.

Achebe, C. (2009). *Things fall apart.* New York: Norton.

Al-Qa'id, Y. (1997). *War in the land of Egypt.* Northampton, MA: Interlink Publishers.

Alexie, S. (2009). *The absolutely true diary of a part-time Indian.* New York: Little, Brown.

Alvarez, L., & Kolker, A. (Directors). (1988). *American tongues* [motion picture]. United States: Center for New American Media.

Alvermann, D. E. (2001). *Effective literacy instruction for adolescents.* The National Reading Conference. Retrieved February 16, 2011 from http://dev.nrconline.org

American Psychological Association. (2009). *Publication manual of the American Psychological Association*, 6th ed. Washington, DC: American Psychological Association.

Anderson, M. T. (2002). *Feed.* Boston: Candlewick Press.

Andriessen, J. (2006). Arguing to learn. In K. Sawyer (Ed.), *Handbook of the learning sciences* (pp. 443–460). Cambridge: Cambridge University Press.

Angelou, M. (1969). *I know why the caged bird sings.* New York: Bantam Books.

Applebee, A. (1996). *Curriculum as conversation: Transforming traditions of teaching and learning.* Chicago: University of Chicago Press.

Applebee, A. N., & Langer, J. A. (2006). *The state of writing instruction in America's schools: What existing data tell us.* Albany, NY: Center on English Learning and Achievement. Retrieved February 25, 2010 from http://www.albany.edu/aire/news/news_literacy.html

Applebee, A., Langer, J., Nystrand, M., & Gamoran, A. (2003). Discussion-based approaches to developing understanding: Classroom instruction and student performance in middle and high school English. *American Educational Research Journal, 40*, 685–731.

Arver, C. (2011). A virtual world for *Lord of the Flies*: Engaging students and meeting Common Core Standards. In A. Webb (Ed.), *Teaching literature in virtual worlds: Immersive learning in English studies* (pp. 14–25). New York: Routledge.

Atwell, N. (1987). *In the middle: New understandings about writing, reading, and learning.* Portsmouth, NH: Heinemann.

Aufderheide, P., & Jaszi, P. (2011). *Reclaiming fair use: How to put balance back in copyright.* Washington, DC: Center for Social Media.

Austen, J. (2009). *Pride and prejudice.* Bronx, NY: Middleton Classics.

Austin, J. L. (1962). *How to do things with words.* Oxford: Oxford University Press.

Bakhtin, M. M. (1981). *The dialogic imagination: Four essays* (Ed. M. Holquist, trans. C. Emerson & M. Holquist). Austin: University of Texas Press.

Bambara, T. (1992). The lesson. In T. Bambara, *Gorilla my love*. New York: Vintage.

Barniskis, E. (2011). Huck or Chuck: Using online role-play and Ning to negotiate race in the high school English classroom. *Minnesota English Journal, 46*. Retrieved April 10, 2011 from http://www.mcte.org

Barton, D. (2006). *Literacy: An introduction to the ecology of written language*. Oxford, UK: Blackwell.

Barton, D., & Hamilton, M. (2000). Literacy practices. In D. Barton, M. Hamilton, & R. Ivanic (Eds.), *Situated literacies: Reading and writing in context* (pp. 7–15). New York: Routledge.

Bawarshi, A. (2003). *Genre and the invention of the writer*. Logan: Utah State University Press.

Baynham, M., & Prinsloo, M. (Eds.). (2010). *The future of literacy studies*. New York: Palgrave Macmillan.

Bazerman, C. (1994). Systems of genres and the enactment of social intentions. In A. Freedman & P. Medway (Eds.), *Genre and the new rhetoric* (pp. 79–101). London: Taylor & Francis.

Beach, R. (2007). *Teachingmedialiteracy.com: A guide to links and activities*. New York: Teacher College Press.

Beach, R. (2009). Using VideoAnt annotations to provide "audience-based" assessment to students' video productions. 2009 K–12 Online Conference. Retrieved April 12, 2011 from http://tinyurl.com/y9srmcn

Beach, R., Anson, C., Kastman-Breuch, L., & Swiss, T. (2008). *Teaching writing using blogs, wikis, and other digital tools*. Norwood, MA: Christopher-Gordon Publishers.

Beach, R., Campano, G., Edmiston, B., & Borgmann, M. (2010). *Literacy tools in the classroom: Teaching through critical inquiry, grades 5–12*. New York: Teachers College Press.

Beach, R., & Dockter, J. (2010). Students' critical engagement in writing about and responding to portrayals of urban neighborhoods. Paper presented at the Annual Meeting of the Literacy Research Association, Fort Worth, TX.

Beach, R., & Doerr-Stevens, C. (2009). Learning argument practices through online role-play: Toward a rhetoric of significance and transformation. *Journal of Adolescent & Adult Literacy, 52*(6). Retrieved March 20, 2011 from http://tinyurl.com/4afhv83

Beach, R., Hull, G., & O'Brien, D. (2011). Transforming English language arts in a Web 2.0 world. In D. Lapp & D. Fisher (Eds.), *Handbook of research on teaching the English language arts* (pp. 161–167). New York: Routledge.

Beach, R., & Myers, J. (2001). *Inquiry-based English instruction: Engaging students in literature and life*. New York: Teachers College Press.

Beach, R., & O'Brien, D. (2003). Preservice teachers' participation in a co-inquiry practicum experience in an urban neighborhood. Paper presented at the annual meeting of the National Reading Conference, Scottsdale, AZ.

Beach, R., & Swiss, T. (2010). Digital literacies, aesthetics, and pedagogies involved in digital video production. In P. Albers & J. Sanders (Eds.), *Perspectives on research and practice in integrating arts, multimodality, and new literacies into English language arts classes* (pp. 300–320). Urbana, IL: National Council of Teachers of English.

Beach, R., & Yussen, S. (2011). Practices of productive adult book clubs. *Journal of Adolescent & Adult Literacy, 55*(2), 121–131.

Beckelhimer, L. (2010). From Hitler to hurricanes, Vietnam to Virginia Tech: Using historical nonfiction to teach rhetorical context. *English Journal, 99*(4), 55–60.

Ben-Chaim, M. (2010). Reading is a cultural activity. *Learning Diversity*. Retrieved June 10, 2011 from http://www.learningdiversity.org/2010/11/reading-is-a-cultural-activity-2/

Bernier, N. (2010, March 16). Texas textbook tussle could have national impact. National Public Radio. Retrieved June 25, 2011 from http://www.npr.org/templates/story/story.php?storyId=124737756

Bitz, M. (2010). *When commas meet Kryptonite: Lessons from the comic book project*. New York: Teachers College Press. *Adolescent & Adult Literacy, 55*.

Blake, R., & Cutler, C. (2003). AAE and variation in teachers' attitudes: A question of school philosophy? *Linguistics and Education, 14*, 163–194.

Blau, S. (2003). *The literature workshop: Teaching texts and their readers*. Portsmouth, NH: Heinemann.

Bleich, D. (1978). *Subjective criticism*. Baltimore, MD: Johns Hopkins University Press.

Bloome, D., Carter, S. P., Christian, B. M., Otto, S., & Shuart-Faris, N. (2005). *Discourse analysis and the study of classroom language and literacy events: A microethnographic perspective*. Mahwah, NJ: Erlbaum.

Boal, A. (1993). *Theater of the oppressed*. New York: Theater Communications Group.

Boal, A. (2002). *Games for actors and non-actors*, 2nd ed. London: Routledge.

Bochner, A., & Ellis, C. (2006). Communication as autoethnography. In G. Shepherd, J. St. John, & T. Striptha (Eds.), *Communication as . . .: Stances on theory* (pp. 110–122). Los Angeles: Sage Publications.

Bourdieu, P. (1974). The school as a conservative force: Scholastic and cultural inequalities. In J. Eggleston (Ed.), *Contemporary research in the sociology of education* (pp. 32–46). London: Methuen.

Bowers-Campbell, J. (2011). Take it out of class: Exploring virtual literature circles. *Journal of Adolescent & Adult Literacy, 54*(8), 557–567.

boyd, d. (2009). Living and learning with social media. *Penn State Symposium for Teaching and Learning with Technology*. State College: Pennsylvania State University. Retrieved July 20, 2011 from http://www.danah.org/papers/talks/PennState2009.html

Brooks, K. (2011). Resistance is futile: "Reaccenting" the present to create classroom dialogues. *Pedagogies: An International Journal, 6*(1), 66–80.

Brooks, S. L. (2010). Two way conversation: The interplay of cultural models and teachers' practices in the high school literature class. Unpublished doctoral dissertation. University of Minnesota, Twin Cities.

Brown, A. L., & Palincsar, A. S. (1989). Guided cooperative learning and individual knowledge acquisition. In L. B. Resnick (Ed.), *Cognition and instruction: Issues and agendas* (pp. 393–451). Hillsdale, NJ: Erlbaum.

Bruce, B. C., & Bishop, A. P. (2008). New literacies and community inquiry. In J. Coiro, M. Knobel, C. Lankshear, & D. Leu, (Eds.), *The handbook of research in new literacies* (pp. 699–742). New York: Routledge.

Bruner, J. (1990). *Acts of meaning*. Cambridge, MA: Harvard University Press.

Bruner, J. (2002). *Making stories: Law, literature, life*. New York: Farrar, Straus, and Giroux.

Burke, K. (1969). *Language as symbolic action*. Berkeley: University of California Press.

Campbell, R. (2011). The power of the listening ear. *English Journal, 100*(5), 66–70.

Carbone, P. M., & Orellana, M. F. (2010). Developing academic identities: Persuasive writing as a tool to strengthen emergent academic identities. *Research in the Teaching of English, 44*(3), 292–316.

Carlson, J., & Gjevre, B. (2010). Car junkies. Unpublished ethnography report.

Carter, J. B. (Ed.). (2007). *Building literacy connections with graphic novels: Page by page, panel by panel.* Urbana, IL: National Council of Teachers of English.

Carter, S. (2006). Redefining literacy as a social practice. *Journal of Basic Writing, 25*(2), 94–125.

Carter, S. (2008). *The way literacy lives: Rhetorical dexterity and basic writing instruction.* Albany, NY: SUNY Press.

Cazden, C. B. (2001). *Classroom discourse: The language of teaching and learning,* 2nd ed. Portsmouth, NH: Heinemann.

Chambliss, M. J., & Murphy, P. K. (2002). Fourth and fifth graders representing the argument structure in written texts. *Discourse Processes, 34*(1), 91–115.

Chizhik, A. W. (2009). Literacy for playwriting or playwriting for literacy. *Education and Urban Society, 41*(3), 387–409.

Christensen, L. (2009). *Teaching for joy and justice.* Milwaukee: Rethinking Schools.

Çimer, S. O. (2011). The effect of portfolios on students' learning: Student teachers' views. *European Journal of Teacher Education, 34*(2), 161–176.

Cisneros, S. (1991). *The house on Mango Street.* New York: Vintage.

Clooney, G. (Director). (2005). *Good night, and good luck* [motion picture]. United States: Warner Pictures.

Coiro, J. (2003). Reading comprehension on the Internet: Expanding our understanding of reading comprehension to encompass new literacies. *The Reading Teacher, 56*(5), 458–464.

Coiro, J., & Dobler, B. (2007). Exploring the online reading comprehension strategies used by sixth-grade skilled readers to search for and locate information on the Internet. *Reading Research Quarterly, 42,* 214–257.

Coiro, J., & Fogleman, J. (2011). Using websites wisely. *Educational Leadership, 68*(5), 34–38.

Common Core State Standards. (2010). *Common Core State Standards for English Language Arts.* Retrieved July 1, 2011 from http://www.corestandards.org/

Cooper, M. M. (2010). Being linked to the matrix: Biology, technology, and writing. In S. A. Selber (Ed.), *Rhetorics and technologies: New directions in writing and communication* (pp. 1–30). Columbia, SC: University of South Carolina Press.

Council of Writing Program Administrators, National Council of Teachers of English, National Writing Project (2011). *Framework for success in postsecondary writing.* Urbana, IL: National Council of Teachers of English.

Cran, W. (Director). (1997). *The story of English* [motion picture]. United States: Home Vision Entertainment.

Cran, W. (Director). (2005). *Do you speak American?* [television series]. New York: WNET.

Cummins, J., Chow, P., & Schecter, S. (2006). Community as curriculum. *Language Arts, 83,* 297–307.

Daniels, H. (1994). *Literature circles: Voice and choice in the student-centered classroom.* Portland, ME: Stenhouse.

Daniels, H., & Steineke, N. (2004). *Mini-lessons for literature circles.* Portsmouth, NH: Heinemann.

Darling-Hammond, L. (2011, May 21). The service of democratic education. *The Nation.* Retrieved July 31, 2011 from http://www.thenation.com/article/160850/service-democratic-education

Davidson, C. (2010, December 19). Collective IQ. HASTAC. Retrieved December 20, 2010 from http://www.hastac.org/blogs/cathy-davidson/collective-iq

Dee, T. S., & Jacob, B. A. (2007). Do high school exit exams influence educational attainment or labor market performance? In A. Gamoran, (Ed.), *Will No Child Left Behind help close the poverty gap?* Washington, DC: Brookings University Press.

Delpit, L. (2006). *Other people's children: Cultural conflict in the classroom.* New York: New Press.

Digital Media Program. (2011). Roosevelt High School Website. Retrieved June 25, 2011 from http://roosevelt.mpls.k12.mn.us/Digital_Media.html

Dockter, J., Haug, D., & Lewis, C. (2010). Redefining rigor: Critical engagement, digital media, and the new English/language arts. *Journal of Adolescent & Adult Literacy, 53*(5), 418–420.

Doerr-Stevens, C., Beach, R., & Boeser, E. (2011). Using online role-play to promote collaborative argument and collective action. *English Journal, 100*(5), 33–39.

Douglass, F. (2005). *Narrative of the life of Frederick Douglass: An American slave.* New York: Barnes and Noble Classics.

Duncan-Andrade, J., & Morrell, E. (2008). *The art of critical pedagogy: Possibilities for moving from theory to practice in urban schools.* New York: Peter Lang.

Dyson, A. H. (2010). Writing childhoods under construction: Re-visioning "copying" in early childhood. *Journal of Early Childhood Literacy, 10*(1), 7–31.

Edmiston, B. (2000). Drama as ethical education. *Research in Drama Education, 5*(1), 63–85.

Edmiston, B. (2003). What's my position? Role, frame, and positioning when using process drama. *Research in Drama Education, 8*(2), 221–229.

Egan, K. (2011). *Learning in depth: A simple innovation that can transform schooling.* Chicago: University of Chicago Press.

Elbow, P. (1973). *Writing without teachers.* New York: Oxford University Press.

Elbow, P. (1998). *Writing with power.* New York: Oxford University Press.

Eleveld, M. (2007). *The spoken word revolution redux.* New York: Sourcebooks MediaFusion.

Emig, J. (1972). *The composing processes of twelfth graders.* Urbana, IL: National Council of Teachers of English.

Engestrom, Y. (2009). From learning environments and implementation to activity systems and expansive learning. *Actio: An International Journal of Human Activity Theory, 2*, 17–33.

Ennis, R. H. (1995). *Critical thinking.* Upper Saddle River, NJ: Prentice Hall.

Erstad, O., Gile, O., Sefton-Green, J., & Vasbo, K. (2009). Exploring "learning lives": Community, identity, literacy and meaning. *Literacy, 43*(2), 100–106.

Eurodata TV. (2011). *The kids report.* Paris: Médiamétrie.

Eva-Wood, A. L. (2008). Does feeling come first? How poetry can help readers broaden their understanding of metacognition. *Journal of Adolescent & Adult Literacy, 51*(7), 564–576.

Fanetti, S., Bushrow, K. M., & DeWeese, D. L. (2010). Closing the gap between high school writing instruction and college writing expectations. *English Journal, 99*(4), 77–83.

Fairbanks, E. (1990). *Days of Rondo*. St. Paul, MN: Minnesota Historical Society.

Farley, T. (2011, January 25). Points to ponder about the Common Core Standards. *Huff Post Education*. Retrieved September 28, 2011 from http://www.huffingtonpost.com/todd-farley/points-to-ponder-about-th_b_811769.html

Faulkner, W. (2000). *As I lay dying*. New York: Modern Novel.

Ferguson, R. F. (1998). Teachers' perceptions and expectations and the Black-White test score gap. In C. Jencks & M. Phillips (Eds.), *The Black-White test score gap* (pp. 273–317). Washington, DC: Brookings Institute Press.

Filkins, S. (2010). Supporting student comprehension in content area reading. National Council of Teachers of English. Retrieved February 19, 2011 from http://www.readwritethink.org/professional-development/strategy-guides/supporting-student-comprehension-content-30517.html

Fisher, M. T. (2007). *Writing in rhythm: Spoken word poetry in urban classrooms*. New York: Teachers College Press.

Fitzgerald, F. S. (1991). *The great Gatsby*. New York: Cambridge University Press.

Flower, L. (2008). *Community literacy and the rhetoric of public engagement*. Carbondale: Southern Illinois University Press.

Flower, L., & Hayes, J. R. (1981). A cognitive process theory of writing. *College Composition and Communication, 32*, 365–387.

Flynn, J. E. (2011). The language of power: Beyond the grammar workbook. *English Journal, 100*, 27–30.

Freadman, A. (2002). Uptake. In R. Coe, L. Lingard, & T. Teslenko (Eds.), *The rhetoric and ideology of genre: Strategies for stability and change* (pp. 39–53). Cresskill, NJ: Hampton Press.

Freire, P. (1968). *Pedagogy of the oppressed*. New York: Seabury Press.

Frey, K. S., Hischstein, M. K., & Guzzo, B. A. (2000). Second step: Preventing aggression by promoting social competence. *Journal of Emotional & Behavioral Disorders, 8*(2), 102–112.

Frey, N., & Fisher, D. (Eds.). (2008). *Teaching visual literacy: Using comic books, graphic novels, anime, cartoons, and more to develop comprehension and thinking skills*. Los Angeles: Corwin Press.

Frey, N., & Fisher, D. (2011). *Formative assessment action plan: Practical steps to more successful teaching and learning*. Alexandria, VA: American Society for Curriculum and Development.

Friedman, T. (2005). *The world is flat: A brief history of the 21st century*. New York: Farrar, Straus, and Giroux.

Fry, E. (1977). *Elementary reading instruction*. New York: McGraw Hill.

Gabriel, T. (2011, May 13). Speaking up in class, silently, Using social media. *New York Times Learning Lesson*. New York Times.

Gaines, E. (1993). *A lesson before dying*. New York: Random House.

Gee, J. P. (1996). *Social linguistics and literacies: Ideology in discourses*. 2nd ed. London: Taylor & Francis.

Gee, J. P. (2004). *Situated language and learning: A critique of traditional schooling*. New York: Routledge.

Gee, J. P. (2007). *What video games have to teach us about learning and literacy*, 2nd ed. New York: Palgrave Macmillan.

Gee, J. P. (2008). *Social linguistics and literacies: Ideology in discourses*. New York: Routledge.

Gee, J. P. (2010a). Digital media and learning as an emerging field, Part I: How we got here. *International Journal of Learning and Media, 1*(2), 13–23.

Gee, J. P. (2010b). The "natural home" of assessment: Human action and social conventions. In V. J. Shute & B. J. Becker (Eds.), *Innovative Assessment for the 21st Century* (pp. 13–39). New York: Springer.

Gee, J. P. (2011). Digital natives, digital brains? *Huffington Post*. Retrieved June 21, 2011 from http://www.huffingtonpost.com/james-gee/digital-natives-digital-b_b_865263.html

Gee, J. P., & Hayes, E. R. (2011). *Language and learning in the digital age*. New York: Routledge.

Gervais, M. (2006). Exploring moral values with young adolescents through process drama. *International Journal of Education & the Arts, 7*(2), 1–34.

Giannetti, L. (2007). *Understanding movies*. Upper Saddle River, NJ: Prentice Hall.

Godley, A., & Minnici, A. (2008). Critical language pedagogy in an urban high school English class. *Urban Education, 43*(3), 319–346.

Godley, A., Sweetland, J., Wheeler, R., Minnici, A., & Carpenter, B. (2006). Preparing teachers for dialectically diverse classrooms. *Educational Researcher, 35*, 30–37.

Goffman, I. (1986). *Frame analysis: An essay on the organization of experience*. Boston: Northeastern University Press.

Golding, W. (1999). *Lord of the flies*. London: Faber & Faber.

Goodman, B. (2011). Linguistic audacity: Shakespeare's language and student writing. *English Journal, 100*, 39–43.

Gorman, J. (2010). Where girls become women and friends become family. Unpublished ethnography report.

Grice, H. P. (1975). Logic and conversation. In A. Jaworski & N. Coupland (Eds.), *The discourse reader* (pp. 76–87). New York: Routledge.

Grodsky, E., Warren, J. R., & Kalogrides, D. (2009). State high school exit examinations and NAEP long-term trends in reading and mathematics, 1971–2004. *Educational Policy, 23*(4), 589–614.

Groenke, S. L. (2010). Seeing, inquiring, witnessing: Using the equity audit in practitioner inquiry to rethink inequity in public schools. *English Education, 43*(1), 83–96.

Gubrium, J. F., & Holstein, J. A. (Eds.). (2003). *Postmodern interviewing*. Los Angeles: Sage Publishers.

Guthrie, J., Taboada, A., & Wigfield, A. (2011). Alignment of cognitive processes in reading with motivations for reading. In D. Lapp & F. Fisher (Eds.), *Handbook of research on teaching the English language arts*, 3rd ed. (pp. 125–131). New York: Routledge.

Hagemann, J. (2001). A bridge from home to school: Helping working class students acquire school literacy. *English Journal, 90*, 74–81.

Hammer, R., & Kellner, D. (Eds.). (2009). *Media/cultural studies: Critical approaches*. New York: Peter Lang.

Hancock, C. B., & Scherff, L. (2010). Who will stay and who will leave? Predicting secondary English teacher attrition risk. *Journal of Teacher Education, 61*(4), 328–338.

Hansberry, L. (1994). *A raisin in the sun*. New York: Vintage.

Hattie, J., & Timperley, H. (2007). The power of feedback. *Review of Educational Research, 77*, 81–112.

Haughey, J., & Barns, J. (2011). Midsummer madness and virtual *Tempest*: Shakespeare as foolish role-play game. In A. Webb (Ed.), *Teaching literature in virtual worlds: Immersive learning in English studies* (pp. 26–39). New York: Routledge.

Heath, S. B., & Street, B. (2008). *On ethnography: Approaches to language and literacy research*. New York: Teachers College Press/Urbana, IL: National Council of Teachers of English.

Heathcote, D., & Bolton, G. (1995). *Drama for learning: Dorothy Heathcote's Mantle of the Expert approach for teaching drama.* Portsmouth, NH: Heinemann.

Heintz, A., Borsheim, C., Caughlan, S., Juzwik, M. M., & Sherry, M. B. (2010). Video-based response & revision: Dialogic instruction using video and web 2.0 technologies. *Contemporary Issues in Technology and Teacher Education, 10*(2), 175–196.

Heller, J. (1961). *Catch-22.* New York: Simon and Schuster.

Heller, J. R. (2003). Toni Cade Bambara's use of African American Vernacular English in "The Lesson." *Style.* Retrieved July 12, 2011 from http://findarticles.com/p/articles/mi_m2342/is_3_37/ai_n6006606/

Hillocks, G. (1984). What works in teaching composition: A meta-analysis of experimental treatment studies. *American Journal of Education, 93*(1), 133–170.

Hillocks, G. (1987). A synthesis of research on writing. *Educational Leadership, 45,* 71–82.

Hillocks, G. (1995). *Teaching writing as reflective practice.* New York: Teachers College Press.

Hillocks, G. (2002). *The testing trap: How state writing assessments control learning.* New York: Teachers College Press.

Hirsch, E. D., Jr. (1987). *Cultural literacy: What every American needs to know.* Boston, MA: Houghton Mifflin Company.

Hobbs, R. (2010). *Digital and media literacy: A plan of action.* Washington, DC: The Aspen Institute/Knight Foundation. Retrieved April 9, 2011 from http://www.knightcomm.org/digital-and-media-literacy

Holland, D., Lachicotte, W., Skinner, D., & Cain, C. (1998). *Identity and agency in cultural worlds.* Cambridge, MA: Harvard University Press.

Holland, D., & Lave, J. (Eds.). (2001). *History in person: Enduring struggles, contentious practice, intimate identities.* Santa Fe, NM: School of American Research Press.

Holland, N. N. (1975). *5 readers reading.* New Haven, CT: Yale University Press.

Hollie, S. (2001). Acknowledging the language of African American students: Instructional strategies. *English Journal, 90,* 54–59.

Holzchuch, P., & Loosbrock, S. (2010). Not all knots. Unpublished ethnography report.

Hosseini, K. (2004). *The kite runner.* New York: Riverhead.

Hosseini, K. (2008). *A thousand splendid suns.* New York: Riverhead.

Housen, A. (2007). Art viewing and aesthetic development: Designing for the views. In P. Villeneuve (Ed.), *From periphery to center: Art museum education in the 21st century* (pp. 102–134). Reston, VA: The National Art Education Association.

Hout, M., & Elliott, S. W. (Eds.). (2011). *Incentives and test-based accountability in education.* National Research Council. Retrieved June 7, 2011 from http://www.nap.edu/catalog/12521.html

Hulan, N. (2010). What the students will say while the teacher is away: An investigation into student-led and teacher-led discussion within guided reading groups. *Literacy Teaching and Learning, 14*(1–2), 41–64.

Hunt, R., & Vipond, D. (1992). First, catch the rabbit: The methodological imperative and the dramatization of dialogic reading. In R. Beach, R. J. Green, M. Kamil, & T. Shanahan (Eds.), *Multidisciplinary Perspectives on Literacy Research* (pp. 69–89). Urbana, IL: National Conference on Research in English.

Jacobs, H. (2006). *Incidents in the life of a slave girl.* Clayton, DE: Prestwick House.

Jacobs, H. H. (2010). *Curriculum 21: Essential education for a changing world.* Alexandria, VA: American Society for Curriculum and Development.

James, M. (2008). Assessment and learning. In S. Swaffield (Ed.), *Unlocking assessment: Understanding for reflection and application* (pp. 20–35). New York: Routledge.

Janks, H. (2010). *Literacy and power.* New York: Routledge.

Jenkins, J., Clinton, K., Purushotma, R., Robison, A., & Weigel, M. (2006). *Confronting the challenges of participatory culture: Media education for the 21st century.* Cambridge, MA: MIT Press.

Jocson, K. (2007). *Urban youth as poets: Empowering literacies in/outside of schools.* New York: Peter Lang.

Johannessen, L. R., Kahn, E., & Walter, C. C. (2009). *Writing about literature,* 2nd ed. Urbana, IL: National Council of Teachers of English.

Johnson, D. W., & Johnson, R. T. (2009). Energizing learning: The instructional power of conflict. *Educational Researcher, 38*(1), 37–51.

Jones, S. (2006). Language with an attitude: White girls performing class. *Language Arts, 84,* 114–124.

Juzwik, M. (2009). *The rhetoric of teaching: Understanding the dynamics of Holocaust narratives.* Cresskill, NJ: Hampton Press, Inc.

Karakelle, S. (2009). Enhancing fluent and flexible thinking through the creative drama process. *Thinking Skills and Creativity, 4*(2), 124–129.

Kelly, S., & Caughlan, S. (2011). The Hollywood teachers' perspective on authority. *Pedagogies: An International Journal, 6*(1), 46–65.

Kent, T. (1993). *Paralogic rhetoric.* London: Associated University Press.

Kincheloe, J. L. (2001). Introduction. In J. L. Kincheloe & D. Weil (Eds.), *Standards and schooling in the United States*, vol. 1 (pp. 1–89). Santa Barbara, CA: ABC/CLIO.

Kinloch, V. (2009). *Harlem on our minds: Place, race, and the literacies of urban youth.* New York: Teachers College Press.

Kirkland, D. (2010). English(es) in urban contexts: Politics, pluralism, and possibilities. *English Education, 42,* 293–306.

Kiuhara, S. A., Graham, S., & Hawken, L. S. (2009). Teaching writing to high school students: A national survey. *Journal of Educational Psychology, 101*(1), 136–160.

Kochhar, R., Fry, R., & Taylor, P. (2011, July 26). *Wealth gaps rise to record highs between Whites, Blacks, Hispanics: Twenty-to-one.* Washington, DC: Pew Research Center.

Kohn, A. (2006). Foreword. In M. Wilson, *Rethinking rubrics in writing assessment.* Portsmouth, NH: Heinemann.

Kohn, A. (2010). How to create nonreaders: Reflections on motivation, learning, and sharing power. *English Journal, 100*(1), 16–22.

Kopple, B. (Director). (1976). *Harlan County, USA* [motion picture]. United States: Cabin Creek Productions.

Krajcik, J. S., & Sutherland, L. M. (2010). Supporting students in developing literacy in science. *Science, 328,* 456–459.

Kress, G. (2003). *Literacy in a new media age.* New York: Routledge.

Kurnaz, M. (2009). *Five years of my life: An immigrant in Guatemala.* New York: Palgrave Macmillan.

Labov, W. (1972). *The language of the inner city.* Philadelphia: University of Pennsylvania Press.

Lakoff, G. (2002). *Moral politics: How liberals and conservatives think.* Chicago: University of Chicago Press.

Lamb, M. R. (2010). Teaching nonfiction through rhetorical reading. *English Journal, 99*(4), 43–49.

Langer, J. A. (1995). *Envisioning literature: Literary understanding and literature instruction.* New York: Teachers College Press.

Lankshear, C., & Knobel, M. (2003). *New literacies: Changing knowledge and classroom learning.* Philadelphia: Open University Press.

Lattimer, H. (2010). *Reading for learning: Using discipline-based texts to build content knowledge.* Urbana, IL: National Council of Teachers of English.

Leander, K. (2009). Composing with old and new media: Toward a parallel pedagogy. In V. Carrington & M. Robinson (Eds.), *Digital literacies: Social learning and classroom practices* (pp. 147–164). New York: Peter Lang.

Leander, K., & Sheehy, M. (Eds.). (2004). *Spatializing literacy research and practice.* New York: Peter Lang.

Lee, C. G. (2007). *Culture, literacy, and learning: Taking bloom in the midst of the whirlwind.* New York: Teachers College Press.

Lee, H. (1960). *To kill a mockingbird.* Philadelphia: HarperCollins.

Lefstein, A., & Snell, J. (2011). Promises and problems of teaching with popular culture: A linguistic ethnographic analysis of discourse genre-mixing in a literacy lesson. *Reading Research Quarterly, 46*(1), 40–69.

LeMoine, N. (1998). *English for your success.* Maywood: People's Publishing.

L'Engle, M. (1962). *A wrinkle in time.* New York: Farrar, Straus and Giroux.

Lenhart, A., Kahne, J., Middaugh, E., Macgill, A., Evans, C., & Vitak, J. (2008). Report: Teens: Video games and civics. *Pew Internet and American Life Project.* Retrieved April 11, 2011 from http://www.pewinternet.org/Reports/2008/Teens-Video-Games-and-Civics.aspx

Leu, D. J., Jr., Coiro, J., Castek, J., Hartman, D. K., Henry, L. A., & Reinking, D. (2008). Research on instruction and assessment of the new literacies of online reading comprehension. In C. C. Block, S. Parris, & P. Afflerbach (Eds.), *Comprehension instruction: Research-based best practices* (pp. 321–346). New York: Guilford Press.

Leu, D. J., O'Byrne, W. I., Zawilinski, L., McVerry, J. G., & Everett-Cacopardo, H. (2009). Expanding the new literacies conversation. *Educational Researcher, 38,* 264–269.

Lewis, C., & Dockter, J. (2011). Reading literature in secondary schools: Disciplinary discourses in global times. In S. Wolf, K. Coats, P. Enciso, & C. A. Jenkins (Eds.), *Handbook of research on children's and young adult literature.* (pp. 76–91). New York: Routledge.

Lewis, C., & Tierney, J. D. (2011). Mobilizing emotion in an urban English classroom. *Changing English.*

Lewison, M., Leland, C., & Harste, J. C (2008). *Creating critical classrooms: K–8 reading and writing with an edge.* Mahwah, NJ: Erlbaum.

Lippi-Green, R. (1997). *English with an accent: Language, ideology, and discrimination in the United States.* New York: Routledge.

Loertscher, D. (2011). The power of technology to enhance learning. *Teacher Librarian, 38*(3), 40–41.

Loertscher, D., Koechlin, C., & Zwaan, S. (2008). *The new school learning commons where learners win.* Castle Rock, CO: Hi Willow Research and Publishing.

Loertscher, D., & Marcoux, E. B. (2010). *Learning commons treasury.* Castle Rock, CO: Hi Willow Research and Publishing.

Mabry, L. (1999). *Portfolios plus: A critical guide to alternative assessment.* Los Angeles: Corwin Press.

Maltese, D., & Naughter, K. (2010). Taking down walls: An international wiki creates a community of thinkers. *Voices from the Middle, 18*(1), 17–25.

Marshall, J. (1987). The effects of writing on students' understanding of literary texts. *Research in the Teaching of English, 21*, 30–63.

Mathis, W. (2010). *The "Common Core" standards initiative: An effective reform tool?* Boulder, CO: Education and the Interest Center/Phoenix, AZ: Arizona State University/Education Policy Research Unit. Retrieved January 2, 2010 from http://www.scribd.com/doc/36149332/PB-NatStans-Mathis#open_download

McCann, T. M., Johannessen, L. R., Kahn, E., & Flanagan, J. M. (2006). *Talking in class: Using discussion to enhance teaching and learning.* Urbana, IL: National Council of Teachers of English.

McGonigal, J. (2011). *Reality is broken: Why games make us better and how they can change the world.* New York: Penguin Press.

McHenry, D. (2011). What video games can teach us about the educational process. HechingerEd blog. Retrieved April 11, 2011 from http://hechingered.org/content/what-video-games-can-teach-us-about-the-educational-process_3686/?utm_source=feedburner&utm_medium=feed&utm_campaign=Feed%3A+Hechingered+%28HechingerEd%29

McIntosh, P. (1988). *White privilege: Unpacking the invisible knapsack.* Wellesley, MA: Wellesley College Center for Research on Women.

McKibben, B. (2010). *Eaarth: Making a life on a rough new planet.* New York: Times Books.

Medina, C., & Campano, G. (2006). Performing identities through drama and teatro practices in multilingual classrooms. *Language Arts, 83*, 332–341.

Medina, T., & Rivera, L. R. (Eds.). (2001). *Bum rush the page: A def poetry jam.* New York: Three Rivers Press.

Miller, A. (1996). *Death of a salesman.* New York: Penguin.

Miller, A. (2003). *The crucible.* New York: Penguin.

Miller, A. (2000, June 17). Are you now or were you ever? *Guardian/Observer.* Retrieved June 10, 2011 from http://writing.upenn.edu/~afilreis/50s/miller-mccarthyism.html

Milner, R. (2005). Developing a multicultural curriculum in a predominantly white teaching context. *Curriculum Inquiry, 35*(4), 391–427.

Modern Language Association. (2009). *MLA handbook for writers of research papers*, 7th ed. New York: Modern Language Association.

Moore, M. (Director). (2004). *Fahrenheit 9/11* [motion picture]. United States: Dog Eat Dog Films.

Morrell, E. (2008). *Critical literacy and urban youth: Pedagogies of access, dissent, and liberation.* New York: Routledge.

Morrison, T. (2004). *Beloved.* New York: Vintage.

Mullis, I.V. S., Kennedy A. M., Martin, M. O., & Sainsbury, M. (2006). *PIRLS 2006 Assessment Framework and Specifications.* Chestnut Hill, MA: TIMSS and PIRLS International Study Center, Boston College.

Myers, J., & Eberfors, F. (2010). Globalizing English through intercultural critical literacy. *English Education, 42*(2), 148–170.

Myers, W. D. (2009). *Sunrise over Fallujah.* New York: Scholastic.

National Council for Accreditation of Teacher Education. (2008). *Professional standards accreditation of teacher preparation institutions.* Washington, DC: Author.

National Council of Teachers of English. (2008). *The definition of 21st century literacies.* Urbana, IL: Author. Retrieved June 15, 2011 from http://www.ncte.org/governance/literacies

National Council of Teachers of English. (2010). *Resolution on the Common Core State Standards, Orlando, Florida.* Urbana, IL: National Council of Teachers of English.

Newell, G., Beach, R., Smith, J., & VanDerHeide, J. (2011). Teaching and learning argumentative reading and writing in educational contexts: A review of research. *Reading Research Quarterly, 46*(3), 273–304.

Newkirk, T. (2010). Standards and the art of magical thinking. *Education Week, 29*(33), 29.

Nye, N. S. (1999). *Habibi.* New York: Simon Pulse.

Ohler, J. (2007). *Digital storytelling in the classroom.* Los Angeles: Corwin Press.

Oldaker, A. (2010). Creating video games in a middle school language arts classroom: A narrative account. *Voices from the Middle, 17*(3), 19–26.

O'Leary, M. E. (2007). A license to lie: Writing through the facts to the truth. *Teaching English in the Two-Year College, 35*(2), 159–168.

Partnership for 21st Century Skills. (2011). *P21 curriculum framework.* Washington, DC: Author.

Patall, E. A., Cooper, H., & Robinson, J. C. (2008). The effects of choice on intrinsic motivation and related outcomes: A meta-analysis of research findings. *Psychological Bulletin, 134,* 270–300.

Pennycook, A. (2010). *Language as local practice.* New York: Routledge.

Perry, T. & Delpit, L. (Eds.). (1998). *The real Ebonics debate: Power, language and the education of African-American children.* Boston: Beacon Press.

Perry, W. G. (1970). *Forms of intellectual and ethical development in the college years: A scheme.* New York: Holt, Rinehart and Winston.

Persky, H. R., Daane, M. C., & Jin, Y. (2003). *The nation's report card: Writing 2002* (NCES 2003-529). Washington, DC: National Center for Education Statistics, Institute of Education Sciences, U.S. Department of Education.

Pink, D. H., & Pas, R. T. (2008). *The adventures of Johnny Bunko: The last career guide you'll ever need.* New York: Riverhead Trade.

Pope, D. C. (2003). *Doing school: How we are creating a generation of stressed-out, materialistic, and miseducated students.* New Haven: Yale University Press.

Pope, R. (2006). *Textual intervention: Critical and creative strategies for literacy studies.* New York: Routledge.

Pough, G. D., Richardson, E., Raimist, R., & Durham, A. S. (Eds.). (2007). *Home girls make some noise!: Hip-hop feminism anthology.* Mira Loma, CA: Parker Publishing.

Pressley, M. (1985). *Cognitive learning and memory in children: Progress in cognitive development research.* New York: Springer.

Pullen, D. L., & Cole, D. R. (Eds.). (2010). *Multiliteracies and technology enhanced education: Social practices and the global classroom.* Hershey, NY: Information Science.

Rabinowitz, P. (1987). *Beyond reading: Narrative conventions and the politics of interpretation.* Ithaca, NY: Cornell University Press.

Ravitch, D. (2010, July). Standards are good but not good enough. National Journal blog. Retrieved January 18, 2011 from http://education.nationaljournal.com/2010/07/conflicting-research-on-core-s.php#1608291

Rex, L. A., Thomas, E. E., & Engel, S. (2010). Applying Toulmin: Teaching logical reasoning and argumentative writing. *English Journal, 99*(6), 56–61.

Reyes, G. T. (2006). *Finding the poetic high: Building a spoken word poetry community and culture of creative, caring, and critical intellectuals.* Multicultural Education (Winter), 10–15.

Richardson, A. E. (2010). Exploring text through student discussions: Accountable talk in the middle school classroom. *English Journal, 100*(1), 83–88.

Riddile, M. (2010). PISA: It's poverty not stupid. Nasspblog. Retrieved January 2, 2010 from http://nasspblogs.org/principaldifference/2010/12/pisa_its_poverty_not_stupid_1.html

Riefenstahl, L. (Director). (1935). *Triumph of the will* [motion picture]. Germany: Leni Riefenstahl Productions.

Rivera, T. (2007). *And the earth did not devour him*. New York: Hampton Brown.

Riverbend. (2005). *Baghdad burning: Girl blog from Iraq*. New York: The Feminist Press at CUNY.

Rosenblatt, L. (1978). *The reader, the text, the poem*. Carbondale, IL: Southern Illinois University Press.

Rosenblatt, L. (1995). *Literature as exploration*. New York: Modern Language Association.

Rozema, R., & Webb, A. (2008). *Literature and the Web: Reading and responding with new technologies*. Portsmouth: Heinemann.

Ruiz, R. (1998). Orientations in language planning. In S. McKay & S. L. Wong (Eds.), *Language diversity: Problem or resource?* (pp. 3–25). New York: Newbury House.

Russell, D. R. (1995). Activity theory and its implications for writing instruction. In J. Petraglia (Ed.), *Reconceiving writing, rethinking writing instruction* (pp. 51–78). Hillsdale, NJ: Erlbaum.

Russell, D. R. (2009). Uses of activity theory in written communication research. In A. Sannino, H. Daniels, & K. D. Gutiérrez (Eds.), *Learning and expanding with activity theory* (pp. 40–52). New York: Cambridge University Press.

Ruzich, C., & Canan, J. (2010). Computers, coffee shops, and classrooms: Promoting partnerships and fostering authentic discussion. *English Journal, 99*(5), 61–66.

Rymes, B. (2001). *Conversational borderlands: Language and identity in an alternative suburban high school*. New York: Teachers College Press.

Sacco, J. (2002). *Palestine*. Seattle: Fantagraphics Books.

Saifer, S., Edwards, K., Ellis, D., Ko, L., & Stuczynski, A. (2011). *Culturally responsive standards-based teaching: Classroom to community and back*. Los Angeles: Corwin Press.

Sardone, N. B., & Devlin-Scherer, R. (2011). Digital games for English classrooms. *Teaching English with Technology, 10*(1), 35–50. Retrieved April 11, 2011 http://www.iatefl.org.pl/call/callnl.htm

Satrapi, M. (2004). *Persepolis: The story of a childhood*. New York: Pantheon.

Sayles, J. (Director). (1987). *Matewan* [motion picture]. United States: Cinecom Entertainment.

Schillinger, T. (2011). Blurring boundaries: Two groups of girls collaborate on a wiki. *Journal of Adolescent & Adult Literacy, 54*(6), 403–413.

Schlosser, E. (2001). *Fast food nation: The dark side of the all-American meal*. New York: Harper.

Schmitt, N., Keeney, J., Oswald, F. L., Pleskac, T. J., Billington, A. Q., Sinha, R., et al. (2009). Prediction of four-year college student performance using cognitive and noncognitive predictors and the impact on demographic status of admitted students. *Journal of Applied Psychology, 94*(6), 1479–1497.

Seraji, M. (2009). *Rooftops of Tehran: A novel*. New York: New American Library.

Siegel, J. (1999). Stigmatized and standardized varieties in the classroom: Interference or separation? *TESOL Quarterly, 33*, 701–728.

Shadiow, L. (2010). Teaching English education and lurching forward. *English Education, 43*(1), 97–106.

Sheehy, M. (2003). The social life of an essay: Standardizing forces in writing. *Written Communication, 20*(3), 333–385.

Sherin, M. G., & van Es, E. A. (2005). Using video to support teachers' ability to notice classroom interactions. *Journal of Technology and Teacher Education, 13*(3), 475–491.

Shipka, J. (2009). Negotiating rhetorical, material, methodological, and technological difference: Evaluating multimodal designs. *College Composition and Communication, 61*(1), W343–W366.

Shirky, C. (2009). *Here comes everybody: The power of organizing without organizations.* New York: Penguin.

Shute, V. J., Dennen, V. P., Kim, Y.-J., Donmez, O., & Wang, C.-Y. (2010). *21st century assessment to promote 21st century learning: The benefits of blinking.* Digital Media Learning Central. Retrieved June 6, 2011 from http://dmlcentral.net/resources/4031

Siemons, G. (2010, March 10). Collapsing to connections. Connectivism. Retrieved March 11, 2010 from http://www.connectivism.ca/?p=234

Siemons, G. (2008). The unique ideas in connectivism. Retrieved April 12, 2011 from http://connectivism.ca/blog/2008/08/what_is_the_unique_idea_in_con.html

Simon, D. (Director). (2002–2008). *The wire* [television series]. United States: Home Box Office.

Sinclair, U. (2004). *The jungle.* New York: Simon & Schuster.

Sipe, R. B. (2009). *Adolescent literacy at risk? The impact of standards.* Urbana, IL: National Council of Teachers of English.

Smagorinsky, P., Gibson, N., Bickmore, S., Moore, C., & Cook, L. (2004). Praxis shock: Making the transition from a student-centered university program to the corporate climate of schools. *English Education, 36*, 214–245.

Smith, M. W., & Wilhelm, J. (2010). *Fresh takes on teaching literary elements: How to teach what really matters about character, setting, point of view, and theme.* New York: Scholastic.

Soja, E. W. (1998). *Thirdspace: Journeys to Los Angeles and other real-and-imagined places.* Malden, MA: Blackwell.

Soto, G. (1997). *Novio boy: A play.* New York: Graphia.

Sperling, M., & DiPardo, A. (2008). English education research and classroom practice: New directions for new times. *Review of Research in Education, 32*, 62–108.

Speth, J. G. (2008). Progressive fusion. *The Nation, 287*(10), 27–30.

Spiegelman, A. (1986). *Maus I. A survivor's tale.* New York: Pantheon.

Spiegelman, A. (1991). *Maus II. A survivor's tale.* New York: Pantheon.

Staples, S. F. (2008). *Under the persimmon tree.* New York: Square Fish.

Steele, C. M., & Aronson, J. (1995). Stereotype threat and the intellectual test performance of African-Americans. *Journal of Personality and Social Psychology, 69*, 797–811.

Steinbeck, J. (1982). *Of mice and men.* New York: Bantam.

Steinbeck, J. (2002). *The pearl.* New York: Penguin.

Steinbeck, J. (2006a). *The grapes of wrath.* New York: Penguin.

Steinbeck, J. (2006b). *In dubious battle.* New York: Penguin.

Stevens, L. P., & Dugan, M. (2010). The dynamic design of learning with text: The grammar of multiliteracies. In D. L. Pullen & D. R. Cole (Eds.), *Multiliteracies and technology enhanced education: Social practice and the global classrooms* (pp. 53–60). Hershey, PA: Information Science.

Stone, J. C., & Schowen, R. A. (2010). Convergence: A framework for a "new" critical literacy. In D. L. Pullen & D. R. Cole (Eds.), *Multiliteracies and technology enhanced education: Social practice and the global classroom* (pp. 35–51). Hershey, PA: Information Science.

Stornaiuolo, A., Hull, G., & Nelson, M. (2009). Mobile texts and migrant audiences: Rethinking literacy and assessment in a new media age. *Language Arts, 86*(5), 382–392.

Street, B. V. (1995). *Social literacies: Critical approaches to literacy in development, ethnography, and education.* New York: Longman.

Street, B. V., & Lefstein, A. (Eds.). (2007). *Literacy: An advanced resource book.* New York: Routledge.

Street, B.V., & Street, J. (1991). The schooling of literacy. In D. Barton & R. Ivanic (Eds.), *Writing in the community* (pp. 143–166). Los Angeles: Sage.

Sunstein, B. S., & Chiseri-Strater, E. (2007). *FieldWorking: Reading and writing research.* Boston: Bedford/St. Martin's.

Swaffield, S. (Ed.). (2008). *Unlocking assessment: Understanding for reflection and application.* New York: Routledge Press.

Thein, A. H., Beach, R., & Parks, D. (2007). What does change *really* look like when white students read multicultural literature? A "perspective-taking" approach to transformative practice. *English Journal, 97*(2), 54–60.

Thein, A. H., Guise, M., & Sloan, D. L. (2011). Problematizing literature circles as forums for discussion of multicultural and political texts. *Journal of Adolescent & Adult Literacy, 55*, 15–24.

Thein, A. H., Oldakowski, T., & Sloan, D. L. (2010). Using blogs to teach strategies for inquiry into the construction of lived and text worlds. *Journal of Media Literacy Education, 2*(1), 23–36.

Thoman, E. (2006). *Literacy for the 21st century: An overview & orientation guide.* Los Angeles: Center for Media Literacy. Retrieved July 28, 2011 from http://www.medialit.org/literacy-21st-century

Thomas, L., & Beauchamp, C. (2011). Understanding new teachers' professional identities through metaphor. *Teaching and Teacher Education, 27*(4), 762–769.

Thomas, D., & Brown, J. S. (2011). *A new culture of learning: Cultivating the imagination for a world of constant change.* Authors.

Tienken, C. H. (2008). Rankings of international achievement test performance and economic strength: Correlations or conjecture? *International Journal of Education Policy and Leadership, 3*(4), 1–15.

Tobar, H. (2011). Learning the power of art to uplift, inspire. *Los Angeles Times.* Retrieved March 8, 2011 from http://www.latimes.com/news/local/la-me-0304-tobar-20110304,0,119294.column

United States Department of Education. (2010). *National education technology plan 2010: Learning powered by technology.* Washington, DC: Author. Retrieved July 28, 2011 from http://www.ed.gov/technology/netp-2010

Valenza, J. K. (2005). *Super searchers go to school.* Medford, NJ: Information Today.

van Ewijk, R. (2011). Same work, lower grade? Student ethnicity and teachers' subjective assessments. *Economics of Education Review, 30*, (5), 1045–1058.

Vasudevan, L., Schultz, K., & Bateman, J. (2010). Through multimodal storytelling rethinking composing in a digital age: Authoring literate identities. *Written Communication, 27*, 442–465.

Viswanathan, G. (1989). *Masks of conquest: Literary study and British rule in India.* New York: Columbia University Press.

Voskuil, G., & Dykema, M. (2011). From migrant labor to high society: *Of mice and men* and *The great Gatsby* in virtual worlds. In A. Webb (Ed.), *Teaching literature in virtual worlds: Immersive learning in English studies* (pp. 40–50). New York: Routledge.

Vygotsky, L. (1986). *Thought and language*. Cambridge, MA: MIT Press.

Walker, A. (1994). *Everyday use*. New Brunswick, NJ: Rutgers University Press.

Warren, J. R., Kulick, R. B., & Jenkins, K. N. (2006). High school exit examinations and state-level completion and GED rates, 1975 through 2002. *Education Evaluation and Policy Analysis, 28*(2), 131–152.

Webb, A. (2001). *Literature and lives: A response-based, cultural studies approach to teaching English*. Urbana: NCTE Press.

Webb, A. (2011a). *Teaching literature in virtual worlds: Immersive learning in English studies*. New York: Routledge.

Webb, A. (2011b). *Teaching the literature from today's Middle East*. New York: Routledge.

Webb, A. (2011c). Content learning in literary virtual worlds: The village of Umuofia. In A. Webb (Ed.), *Teaching literature in virtual worlds: Immersive Learning in English Studies* (pp. 64–81). New York: Routledge.

Wells, G. (2011). Integrating CHAT and action research. *Mind, Culture, and Activity, 18*(2), 161–180.

Wenger, E. (1999). *Communities of practice*. New York: Cambridge University Press.

Whaley, L. & Dodge, L. (1993). *Weaving in the women: Transforming the high school curriculum*. Portsmouth: Boynton/Cook.

Wheeler, R., & Swords, R. (2006). *Code-switching: Teaching Standard English in urban classrooms*. Urbana, IL: National Council of Teachers of English.

White, J. (2011). De-centering English: Highlighting the dynamic nature of the English language to promote the teaching of code-switching. *English Journal, 100*, 44–49.

Wilhelm, J. D. (2001). *Improving comprehension with think aloud strategies*. New York: Scholastic.

Wilhelm, J. D. (2004). *Reading is seeing*. New York: Scholastic.

Wilhelm, J. D. (2009). The power of teacher inquiry: Developing a critical literacy for teachers. *Voices from the Middle, 17*(2), 36–39.

Wilhelm, J. D., Boas, E., & Wilhelm, P. J. (2009). *Inquiring minds learn to read and write: 50 problem-based literacy & learning strategies*. New York: Scholastic.

Wilson, C., & Schlosser, E. (2006). *Chew on this: Everything you don't want to know about fast food*. New York: Houghton Mifflin.

Wilson, M. (2001). The changing discourse of language study. *English Journal, 90*, 31–36.

Wilson, M. (2006). *Rethinking rubrics in writing assessment*. Portsmouth, NH: Heinemann.

Winn, M. T. (2010a). "Betwixt and between": Literacy, liminality, and the celling of Black girls. *Race Ethnicity and Education, 13*(4), 425–447.

Winn, M. T. (2010b). "Our side of the story": Moving incarcerated youth voices from margins to center. *Race Ethnicity and Education, 13*(3), 313–325.

Wohlwend, K. E., & Lewis, C. (2011). Critical literacy, critical engagement, and digital technology: Convergence and embodiment in glocal spheres. In D. Lapp & D. Fisher (Eds.), *The handbook of research on teaching the English language arts* (pp. 188–194). New York: Routledge.

Wolfe, P. (2010). Student microtransformation in English classrooms. *Research in the Teaching of English, 44*(3), 317–337.

Wolfram, W., Adger, C. T., & Christian, D. (1999). *Dialects in schools and communities*. Mahwah, NJ: Erlbaum.

Worth, S. E. (2008). Storytelling and narrative knowing: An examination of the epistemic benefits of well-told stories. *Journal of Aesthetic Education, 42*(3), 42–56.

Wortham, S. (2001). *Narratives in action: A strategy for research and analysis.* New York: Teachers College Press.

Wright, R. (2005). *Native son.* New York: Harper.

Yang, G. L. (2008). *American born Chinese.* New York: Square Fish.

Zemliansky, P. (2008). Methods of discovery: A guide to research writing. Retrieved September 28, 2011 from http://methodsofdiscovery.net/

Zuidema, L. (2005). Myth education: Rationale and strategies for teaching against linguistic prejudice. *Journal of Adolescent & Adult Literacy, 48,* 666–675.

Zunshine, L. (2006). *Why we read fiction: Theory of mind and the novel.* Columbus: Ohio State University Press.

Index

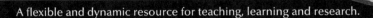